Survey of the
New Testament

by
Paul N. Benware

MOODY PRESS
CHICAGO

All Scripture quotations, unless noted otherwise, are from the *New American Standard Bible,* © 1960, 1962, 1963, 1968, 1971, 1972, 1973, 1975, and 1977 by The Lockman Foundation, and are used by permission.

Library of Congress Cataloging in Publication Data

Benware, Paul N., 1942-
    Survey of the New Testament / by Paul N. Benware.
      p.   cm. — (Everyman's Bible commentary)
    Includes bibliographical references.
    ISBN 0-8024-2092-3
    1. Bible. N.T.—Commentaries. I. Title. II. Series.
BS2315.B46   1990
225.6'1—dc20   89-29056
                                         CIP

10

Printed in the United States of America

Survey of the
New Testament

To Anne, David, Laurie,
Matthew, and Timothy—
a new covenant family

CONTENTS

THE PAULINE EPISTLES

THE GENERAL EPISTLES

Part 5: The Revelation:
The New Covenant Fulfilled

Notes on Special Topics

INDEX OF GRAPHICS

Part 1

Introduction, Overview, Background:
The New Covenant Anticipated

1

INTRODUCTION
TO THE NEW TESTAMENT

THE IMPORTANCE OF THIS SURVEY BOOK

The New Testament continues the story begun in the Old Testament. It is the marvelous climax of God's inspired revelation to mankind. In the Old Testament, God had promised to bring blessing and redemption to man through the Messiah, and the New Testament is the record of God's doing just that. Without the twenty-seven books of the New Testament, there would be great uncertainty regarding the promises and purposes of God. And many significant questions would remain unanswered.

The New Testament is much smaller than the Old Testament and it covers a period of time far shorter than that of the Old. But the New Testament covers that most significant era in the history

COMPARISONS OF THE TWO TESTAMENTS

OLD TESTAMENT	NEW TESTAMENT
39 books	27 books
929 chapters	260 chapters
Covers over 4,000 years	Covers about 100 years
About 31 authors	About 9 authors

of man—those years when God became man and brought salvation to a lost mankind.

The New Testament is worthy of a lifetime of study, as it answers the most significant questions people have asked—What is the purpose of life? Is there any real hope? What is God like? Can I be freed from guilt and sin? Am I loved? Jesus Christ, the Word of God, is the profound answer.

THE PURPOSE OF THIS SURVEY BOOK

The purpose of this study is to assist the Bible student in seeing the content, unity, and progression of the New Testament Scriptures. In order to understand the content of the New Testament, each of the twenty-seven books will be studied, noting the themes and emphases found in them. Although a verse-by-verse study of each book will not be possible, there will be adequate time spent to discover the main ideas and unique features of each book.

In order to see something of the existing unity of the New Testament, some emphasis will be given to the New Covenant. The New Covenant is the great unifying theme of the New Testament (see chart on page 19). It should be noted that the term *new testament* really means ''new covenant.''

It is also a purpose of this survey book to help the student see something of the logical progression of the New Testament. For many, the New Testament simply contains a large number of stories, sermons, and doctrinal letters that have no clear logical connection to them. Hopefully, this study will reveal something of the logical flow of the New Testament.

THE APPROACH OF THIS SURVEY BOOK

The New Testament is made up of twenty-seven books. Four of these books (the gospels) record the life and ministry of Jesus Christ. About one third of the total volume of the New Testament is found in these four gospels. It is important, not only to understand the emphasis of each individual gospel, but also to combine the four gospels and see the pattern and progression of the life of

Christ. Therefore, this survey will include a chronological study of the life of Christ, harmonizing the four gospels.

The book of Acts follows the four gospels in the New Testament. Acts is the one book of church history in the New Testament. Many of the New Testament letters find their historical roots in the book of Acts, and so this study will link these letters to the historical record of Acts. By linking the letters to the historical base whenever possible, the order and pattern of the New Testament will be seen more clearly.

The study of the New Testament books will be preceded by necessary background material. In order to have a better understanding of the gospels and the New Testament letters, there needs to be some familiarity with the political forces, institutions, movements, and ideas that were part of the Roman world of the first century. It is also important to reach back into the intertestamental period and view some of the events that took place there that influenced life in New Testament times.

This study of the New Testament will conclude with the examination of the book of Revelation and additional topics in appendixes.

The outline of the New Testament used in this survey is structured as follows.

I. The Gospels:
   The New Covenant Instituted

   A. Matthew
   B. Mark
   C. Luke
   D. John

II. The Acts:
    The New Covenant Proclaimed

III. The Epistles:
     The New Covenant Explained

2

OVERVIEW OF THE NEW TESTAMENT

The New Testament is the story of God's efforts to redeem the lost, sinful human race. It is the record of the establishing of the New Covenant, which was God's way of saving lost mankind. In the Old Testament (e.g., Jer. 31:31-34), God had promised that He would make a "new covenant" with His people Israel. Israel's Messiah would be the One who would bring this covenant into existence. The New Covenant would focus on the spiritual life and redemption of Israel. However, as the New Testament unfolded, it became clear that the New Covenant would reach beyond Israel and include the rest of mankind (Gen. 12:3; Luke 22:20; Heb. 8:6-13). The New Covenant was God's provision of salvation for lost people who could not save themselves. Jesus Christ, Israel's Messiah, inaugurated the New Covenant with His sacrificial death on the cross.

THE GOSPELS

The story of the New Testament begins with the four gospels, which tell of the coming of Jesus Christ into the world. The gospels record His life and His ministry. His sinless life, authoritative teaching, and authenticating miracles proved that He was the Messiah, the Son of God. His life ended when He voluntarily gave up His life on the cross of Calvary. It was His sacrificial death on the cross that instituted God's "new covenant," making it possible for people to be free of their sin and to live in a right relationship with God.

THE BOOK OF ACTS

After Christ's resurrection from the dead, He informed His followers of their mission to go throughout the world and tell of the New Covenant. They had the joyful task of announcing to both Jews and Gentiles that anyone could be redeemed and reconciled to God because of Jesus Christ's substitutionary death on the cross. The book of Acts records the spread of that good news during the first thirty years that followed Christ's resurrection.

THE EPISTLES

The epistles (letters) of the New Testament record the doctrinal truth related to the New Covenant. These twenty-one letters give all the information needed for Christians to live as ''new covenant'' people. Christians living in the new age of the church would not be living under the requirements of the ''old covenant'' (the law code given by Moses). Rather, their rule of life would be found in the new revelation given by God in the New Testament letters. These letters record the commands, principles, and standards that are to govern the lives of those who claim to have entered into this ''new covenant'' relationship with God based on Christ's work on the cross.

THE BOOK OF REVELATION

The New Testament concludes with the book of Revelation, which tells of the final, glorious application of the New Covenant. Revelation assures us that God is indeed sovereign and that He will completely fulfill His many promises to believing Israelites and to believing Gentiles. Those people who have received eternal life through the New Covenant will live forever with the Lord in the marvelous new heavens and new earth. However, those who have refused to enter into the New Covenant by faith in the Savior Jesus Christ will face Him as the sovereign judge and will be banished forever to the lake of fire.

THE NEW COVENANT

The New Covenant is an enlargement of the great Abrahamic Covenant. The New Covenant is one of three "sub-covenants" which further define the provisions originally given to Abraham (Gen. 12:1-3; 13:14-17; 15:1-21; 17:1-22; 22:15-18). The New Covenant is largely occupied with the matter of salvation. After the Fall of man and the entrance of sin into the world, it was God's declared purpose to bring salvation to people. The New Testament Scriptures are clear that the animal sacrifices of the Old Testament could only cover ("atone") sin, but could never take away sin (e.g., Heb. 9:11-15, 24-28; 10:4-14). It is only the blood of Christ that is capable of removing sin and setting men free from the penalty and the power of sin. It is only the blood of Christ that can remove sin and make it possible for sinful people (Israelite or Gentile) to have fellowship with a holy God. Jesus spoke of His death as the basis of the New Covenant (Luke 22:20). Originally, in the Old Testament, Israel and Judah were the subjects of the New Covenant (Jer. 31:31-34). However, in this present church age, the New Covenant is primarily applied to Gentiles (2 Cor. 3:1-18; Heb. 8:8-13). But in the future, because of God's promises to Abraham and his descendants, Israel will become the focus of the New Covenant (cf. Dan. 9:24; Rom. 11:25-27). During the days of the Great Tribulation, Israel's eyes will be opened, and many will come to faith in the Messiah, thus becoming partakers of the New Covenant.

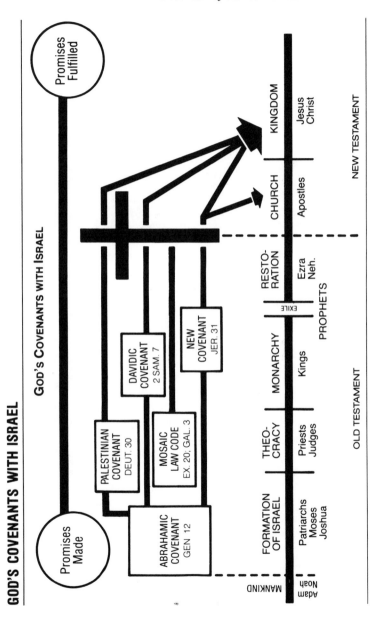

GOD'S COVENANTS WITH ISRAEL

God's Covenants with Israel

Promises Made

Promises Fulfilled

ABRAHAMIC COVENANT
GEN. 12

PALESTINIAN COVENANT
DEUT. 30

MOSAIC LAW CODE
EX. 20, GAL. 3

DAVIDIC COVENANT
2 SAM. 7

NEW COVENANT
JER. 31

MANKIND
Adam
Noah

FORMATION OF ISRAEL
Patriarchs
Moses
Joshua

THEO-CRACY
Priests
Judges

MONARCHY
Kings

EXILE

RESTO-RATION
Ezra
Neh.

CHURCH
Apostles

KINGDOM
Jesus Christ

PROPHETS

OLD TESTAMENT

NEW TESTAMENT

3

BACKGROUND
TO THE NEW TESTAMENT

As the pages of the New Testament are opened, it soon becomes apparent that many things have changed since the close of the Old Testament. It would be a mistake to assume that the world in which Jesus and the apostles lived was the same one that Ezra, Nehemiah, and Malachi lived in. Things were quite different. It is important, therefore, to note some of these changes before entering into a study of the text of the New Testament.

THE END OF THE OLD TESTAMENT

The Old Testament recorded the spiritual failures of the nation of Israel. Israel repeatedly violated the commands of God until God disciplined His people by sending them into Babylonian captivity. After seventy years in captivity, God allowed His people to return to their land and to function as a nation again. Men like Ezra, Nehemiah, Haggai, and Malachi were instrumental in this return and restoration. However, as the Old Testament came to a close with the historical book of Nehemiah and the prophetic book of Malachi, once again the spiritual life of Israel began to deteriorate. God's final word, through the prophet Malachi, was primarily a rebuke for Israel's sinfulness. But included in that message was the promise that the Lord and His messenger would someday come (Mal. 3:1; 4:5-6). That promise would not be fulfilled for about four hundred years until John the Baptist (the messenger) would announce the coming of the Lord Jesus Christ.

FOUR HUNDRED YEARS OF PROPHETIC SILENCE

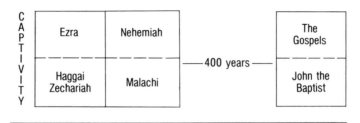

C A P T I V I T Y	Ezra	Nehemiah	— 400 years —	The Gospels
	Haggai Zechariah	Malachi		John the Baptist

THE INTERTESTAMENTAL PERIOD

The time between the Old and New Testaments is often called the ''Four Hundred Silent Years.'' This designation is true only with regard to the voice of God being heard; that is, no Scripture was written and no direct revelation came through prophets. Those four hundred years were not silent in the sense that we have no information about that period. Many things took place during those centuries that are well documented. And those events affected life in the times of the New Testament. It is necessary, therefore, to investigate briefly the intertestamental period.

A.   THE HISTORICAL BACKGROUND TO THE NEW TESTAMENT

1. The Persian period (539-331 B.C.)

An independent Jewish state came to an end when the armies of Nebuchadnezzar of Babylon overran Judah in 605 B.C. For about twenty years after that the Jews did have a king, but he was clearly under the authority of the Babylonians. In 586 B.C. the Jews attempted to revolt against Babylon, but failed in that attempt. That resulted in the destruction of the city of Jerusalem, the plundering and burning of the Temple, and the deportation of many to Babylon. And for the next fifty years the Jews remained under the domination of the Babylonians (cf. 2 Kings 24:1–25:30; Jer. 39:1-18).

The Jews came under Persian control when the Persians and their allies wrestled world domination away from the Babylonians in 539 B.C. Under the Persians the Jews were treated fairly well. They seemed to have enjoyed the favor of the Persians, possibly because both peoples were monotheistic. Cyrus, the Persian king, allowed the Jews to return to their own land and gave them permission to rebuild the Temple in Jerusalem (Ezra 1:1-4). With the encouragement of the prophets, Haggai and Zechariah, opposition and problems were overcome and the Temple was completed in 516 B.C. (Ezra 1:5–6:22). Later, under the leadership of Ezra (458 B.C.) and Nehemiah (444 B.C.), others returned and built the walls of Jerusalem. Those leaders, aided by the prophet Malachi, attempted to bring about moral and spiritual reformation. Although they were not totally successful in their efforts, they did impact the nation of Israel for the intertestamental period. They elevated the Word of God to new heights of importance and strictly applied the principles of the law to everyday life. So while most of the Jews fell away from the law of God during those centuries, some held firmly to the Word of God, refusing to compromise with pagan influences.

2. The Greek period (331-143 B.C.)

a. Alexander the Great (331-323 B.C.). Alexander the Great rose to power and led his Greek army to a swift and complete defeat of the Persians. After he had defeated the Persians in Asia Minor, he swept into Palestine and the Jews had a new master. The Jews did not resist Alexander when he came and he, in turn, treated them well.

Alexander's conquests caused the rapid and thorough spread of *Hellenism* (Greek culture). This culture permeated life everywhere, including Palestine. The Greek language became the common trade and diplomatic language and by New Testament times it was the language of the common man. This factor of a nearly universal language would come to have a significant impact on the rapid spread of the gospel of Jesus Christ in New Testament times.

With the early death of Alexander at the age of thirty-three (323 B.C.), his vast empire was divided into four parts. Because

Alexander had no heir old enough to take his throne, four of his generals eventually partitioned up the empire. Of the four, only two (Ptolemy and Seleucus) are important for our study of New Testament backgrounds. The empire of Ptolemy was centered in Egypt while Seleucus's empire was centered in Syria.

b. The Ptolemies (321-198 B.C.). The land of the Jews became part of Ptolemy's empire at the division of Alexander's empire. The Ptolemies controlled the Jews for more than a century. The Jews generally lived quiet and prosperous lives during this period, though periodic wars between the Ptolemies and the Seleucids turned Palestine into a war zone, resulting in damage to Jewish life and to the economy. But even in this situation the Jews were often treated favorably because both sides were desirous of Jewish support.

An important event occurred in the reign of Ptolemy Philadelphus (285-247 B.C.). He had the Hebrew Old Testament translated by Jewish scholars into the Greek language in order to meet the needs of Jews who had been reared in Greek culture. Many Jews, such as those who were born and reared in Alexandria, Egypt, understood Greek far better than Hebrew. This version, which is called the Septuagint, became a significant document to the Jewish community living outside of Palestine. And later, it was the Bible of the early church.

c. The Seleucids (198-143 B.C.). Warfare and intrigue characterized much of the relationship that existed between the Ptolemies and the Seleucids. In 198 B.C. Antiochus III of Syria, with the help of a strong Jewish faction, defeated the Ptolemies and drove them back into Egypt. With the victory of Antiochus III, Hellenism swept the land of Palestine. The advancement of Hellenism continued under Antiochus IV (Epiphanes). Antiochus IV not only promoted Hellenism among the Jews, but also attacked Jewish religion and culture.

> The Syrian king Antiochus IV or Epiphanes (175-163 B.C.) replaced the Jewish high priest Onias III with Onias's brother Jason, a Hellenizer who started making Jerusalem into a Greek city. A gymnasium with an adjoining race track was

built. There Jewish lads exercised nude in Greek fashion, to the outrage of pious Jews. The track races opened with invocations to pagan deities, and even Jewish priests attended such events. Hellenization also included attendance at Greek theaters, adoption of Greek dress, surgery to remove the marks of circumcision, and exchange of Hebrew for Greek names.[1]

The Temple was plundered of its treasures and was converted into a shrine of Olympian Zeus. On December 15, 168 B.C., an image of the god was set up on its altar, and ten days later a sow was sacrificed in the god's honor. Heathen altars were erected everywhere throughout the country, and the observance of heathen festivals was made compulsory. Judaism was proscribed completely. The death penalty was inflicted upon those who possessed or read the Torah. Sabbath observance and circumcision were forbidden.[2]

So wicked was Antiochus IV that he is used in the Bible as a picture of the Antichrist who will appear in the end times.

This situation was, of course, intolerable to those pious Jews who were devoted to God's law. A rebellion against the Seleucids of Syria was inevitable. The revolt started when a prominent priest, named Mattathias, from the town of Modein, defied a Syrian official who came to Modein to enforce a pagan sacrifice. The courageous Mattathias not only refused to obey the king's representative, but opposed such a sacrifice by killing a Jew who willingly stepped forward to carry out the sacrifice.

When he had finished speaking these words, a Jew came forward in the sight of all to offer sacrifice upon the altar in Modein, according to the king's command. When Mattathias saw it, he burned with zeal and his heart was stirred. He gave vent to righteous anger; he ran and killed him upon the altar. At the same time he killed the king's officer who was forcing them

1. Robert H. Gundry, *A Survey of the New Testament*, rev. ed. (Grand Rapids: Zondervan, 1981), p. 5.
2. Merrill C. Tenney, *New Testament Survey* (Grand Rapids: Eerdmans, 1961), p. 28.

to sacrifice, and tore down the altar. Thus he burned with zeal for the law.[3]

Mattathias realized the seriousness of his actions and fled to the hills with his five sons and other pious Jews. Mattathias soon died, but the movement was taken over by his son Judas (known as "Maccabeus," which means "the hammer"). The rebels achieved great success under Judas's leadership. Initially the Jews engaged in a guerilla warfare, making it nearly impossible for the armies of Antiochus IV to subdue them. "These victories were gained by Judas with greatly inferior forces, due to his strategy and his religious enthusiasm."[4] Three years after Antiochus IV had desecrated the Temple in Jerusalem, Judas and his forces soundly defeated the Syrians and were able to recapture Jerusalem and cleanse and rededicate the Temple (December, 165 B.C.). Finally in 143 B.C., peace with the Syrians was achieved and the Jews had become independent of them.

    3. The Hasmonean period (143-63 B.C.)

Simon, a brother of Judas, was the first ruler of the independent Jewish state. (Note that the term *Hasmonean* is derived from the family name of Mattathias, "Hashmon.") Simon was declared to be the high priest and the civil leader of the Jews for as long as he lived. This act brought a new power to the office of the high priest, as both the religious and civil authority resided in it. (The increased power in the office of high priest is evidenced in the days of Christ and the apostles.) Simon's reign was short but beneficial to the Jews. "A treaty was negotiated with Rome which was confirmed in 139 B.C., recognizing the independence of the Jewish state and commending it to the friendship of Rome's subjects and allies. Economic conditions improved, justice was ably administered in the courts, and Jewish religious life was revived."[5] Unfortunately, however, much of the Hasmonean period was characterized by power struggles and strife. Various factions

3. First Maccabees 2:23-26, *Revised Standard Version*.

4. J. Dwight Pentecost, *The Words and Works of Jesus Christ* (Grand Rapids: Zondervan, 1981), p. 531.

5. Tenney, *New Testament Survey*, p. 30.

within the Jewish state had very different views and the tendency to divide was constantly present.

Simon and two of his sons were murdered, but another son, John Hyrcanus, became the political-religious ruler. John Hyrcanus did much to further the strength and position of the new Jewish state. He was a capable military leader and regained territory that had once belonged to the Jews. He was able to defeat the Syrians, Samaritans, Edomites, and Idumeans. In many ways, those were great days for the Jews. But not all that John Hyrcanus did was applauded by the people and those differences led to strife and civil war later on. For example, John Hyrcanus made an alliance with Rome. That alliance was seen by the separatists (such as the emerging party of the Pharisees) as a compromise of their faith and religious convictions. Also, Hyrcanus forced Judaism on the Idumeans, which was seen as a defilement of the Jews' special covenant relationship with God. Furthermore, many of the Jews refused to accept the priestly claims of the Hasmoneans, knowing that they were not descendants of Aaron. It is also probable that John Hyrcanus wanted to be viewed as ''king'' even though he was not of the Davidic line.[6] Those issues did not disappear at the death of John Hyrcanus in 106 B.C. Internal strife became a part of life in the new Jewish state until it reached its climax in 63 B.C. In that year the Roman army intervened in a civil war being fought by two members of the Hasmonean dynasty. The Roman army brought peace into that situation. But with the coming of the Roman army there came Roman domination.

4. The Roman period (63 B.C.—New Testament)

Roman rule began when Rome intervened in the Jewish civil strife in 63 B.C. At that time Rome set up John Hyrcanus II as king, but he was subject to Rome. It was clear that real power belonged to Rome. Even while Hyrcanus II ruled, an Idumean, named Antipater, rose to favor with the Romans. Antipater was able to get his sons placed into positions of power in Palestine. One of his sons was Herod. Herod (the Great) would eventually be declared king and be the dominant force in Palestine. He would rule from 37-4 B.C. Herod the Great was a man of great ability, but he was also a man of great wickedness.

---

6. W. O. Oesterley and T. H. Robinson, *A History of Israel* (London: Oxford, 1932), p. 282.

The history of the rise of Herod's Kingdom is a drama of extra-ordinary moves of political chicanery accompanied by a succession of atrocious crimes arising from jealousy mostly within Herod's own heart, and against his own family. With rare ability he gained and kept the favor of succeeding Roman Emperors, sacrificing all scruples in order to do so. . . . His reign was one succession of monstrous crimes until his death.[7]

The life and rule of Herod the Great brings us into the days of the New Testament as one of his last "monstrous crimes" (the killing of the babies of Bethlehem) is recorded in the gospel of Matthew. The family of Herod continued to play an important role in the days of Christ and the early church. Given below is a chart listing those of Herod's family found in the New Testament.

THE HERODIAN RULERS IN THE BIBLE

PERSON	YEARS RULED	TERRITORY	RELATION TO HEROD	SCRIPTURE
Herod the Great	37-4 B.C.	King of Palestine	—	Matthew 2:1 Luke 1:5
Herod Antipas	4 B.C.-A.D. 39	Tetrarch of Galilee, Perea	Son	Luke 3:1; 13:31; 23:7
Archelaus	4 B.C.-A.D. 6	Ethnarch of Judea, Samaria, Idumea	Son	Matthew 2:22
Herod Philip II	4 B.C.-A.D. 34	Tetrarch of Iturea, Trachonitis	Son	Luke 3:1
Herod Agrippa I	A.D. 37-44	King of Palestine	Grandson	Acts 12:1-23
Herod Agrippa II	A.D. 48-70	Tetrach of Chalcis, other territories	Great-grandson	Acts 25, 26

Other Herodian relatives mentioned in the New Testament: Herod Philip I (Mark 6); Herodius (Mark 6); Drusilla (Acts 24); Bernice (Acts 25). None were rulers.

7. Pentecost, *Words and Works*, p. 532.

B.   THE RELIGIOUS BACKGROUND TO THE NEW TESTAMENT

Just as there are a great many religious systems and ideas in modern society, so there were in the days of the Roman Empire. Christ, the apostles, and the early church confronted a wide range of religions and philosophies. A brief word about these is needed in order to sense something of the spiritual context that the Lord Jesus and the apostles lived and ministered in.

1. Religions and philosophies in the Roman world

a. The Graeco-Roman pantheon. As the Roman Empire spread, there was increasing contact and assimilation of Greek culture and religion. The many gods and goddesses of Rome were soon identified with the gods and goddesses of the Greek pantheon. For example, Venus, the Roman goddess of love was also identified as the Greek goddess of love, Aphrodite; Mars was Ares; Diana was Artemis; Jupiter was Zeus, and so on.

By the time of the New Testament, the worship of that host of gods and goddesses was on the decline. The power struggles, the intrigue, and the immorality of those gods, along with their apparent inability to help their worshipers, caused this decline in faith among the people of the Empire. The whole system of deities was challenged and scorned by many philosophers and teachers. Yet, there were some who still adhered to the old gods and worshiped them. But the vitality and the number of worshipers was clearly declining by the time the church entered the Roman world.

In the New Testament there are several places where the Graeco-Roman pantheon is seen. In Acts 14, Paul and Barnabas healed a lame man and were immediately identified by the local priests as the gods Hermes (Mercury) and Zeus (Jupiter). Acts 19 records the unrestrained, emotional demonstration of the followers of the goddess Diana (Artemis). And one of Paul's famous sermons was given on Mars Hill (Ares), which was named after a notable god of the pantheon.

b. Emperor worship. Long before Rome emerged as the ruler of the world, nations had exalted their rulers to the place of deity. Because those ancient nations were polytheistic, it was not a great issue to have one more added to the group of existing deities. So the imperial cult of Rome was not unique.

At first Roman emperors were deified after their death by the Roman senate. But in the first century A.D., there were some, like Nero, who claimed that status before death. Needless to say, Christians would not worship emperors (dead or alive) and that refusal to participate brought about persecution of the church. To the Romans, the issue was not simply a religious matter, but also a patriotic one. The apparent lack of allegiance to Rome by the Christians brought the wrath of Rome on many of them.

c. The mystery religions. There were in the Roman Empire a great variety of experience-oriented religions that fall under the heading of "mystery religions." Those "mystery religions" were so named because they promised a mystical union with some deity for those initiates who learned the secrets of that religion. As compared to emperor worship or the traditional religion of the pantheon, these religions offered a more personal, experiential faith to people, and appealed to the emotions rather than to the will or the intellect. Ecstatic experience rather than teaching was emphasized. (What teachings there were often were vague and highly symbolic.) Although there were a variety of mystery religions, there was a common emphasis. The adherents entered into a union with their god by means of secret rites which only the membership knew. This union with deity guaranteed immortality for the worshipers.[8] "The mysteries also featured secret initiatory and other rites involving ceremonial washing, blood sprinkling, sacramental means, intoxication, emotional frenzy, and impressive pageantry by which devotees came into union with deity. Social equality within the mysteries helped make them attractive."[9]

There is a continuing discussion among New Testament scholars as to the influence of the mystery religions on the church. Although there is no direct reference to them in the New Testament, some believe the apostle Paul may have used some of their terminology in order to communicate more effectively to the peo-

8. D. M. Edwards, "Mystery," in *International Standard Bible Encyclopedia* (Grand Rapids: Eerdmans, 1939), 3:2104.
9. Gundry, *A Survey of the New Testament*, p. 35.

ple of the Roman Empire. It is likely that some of the teachings of the mystery religions may have been borrowed from Christianity.[10]

d. Gnosticism. The name *gnosticism* comes from the Greek word *gnosis*, which means "knowledge." Salvation could be achieved by obtaining certain knowledge. This philosophy was based on Plato's dualism, which taught that matter was evil and spirit was good.

> God, said the Gnostics, was too great and too holy to have created the material world with all of its baseness and corruption. The Gnostics held that from the supreme deity had proceeded a series of successive emanations, each one a little inferior to the one from which it sprang, until finally the last of these emanations, or "aeons," as they were called, created the world. Matter was thus equated with evil. If man wished to obtain salvation, he could do so by renouncing the material world and by seeking the invisible world.[11]

This seeking was greatly aided by the Gnostic teachers.

Gnosticism spawned two divergent applications in the practical, everyday lives of people. First, there was asceticism, or the severe suppression of the appetites and desires of the body. Some lived their lives attempting to restrict and control the desires of the "evil" material body. A second application of this philosophy was libertinism. Others, believing the material body to be evil and not subject to salvation, lived indulging the desires and appetites of the body. They reasoned that because only the spirit could be saved, what one did with the material body was fundamentally irrelevant to ultimate reality—so indulge.

Although a fully developed Gnosticism did not appear until the second century A.D., the early forms of it were present in the first century. Many scholars believe that the New Testament books of Colossians and 1 John were written in part to refute that emerging philosophy.

e. Other philosophies. Besides Gnosticism, many other philosophies were found in the New Testament times. Acts 17:21 reveals that philosophy was a passion of many and that something

10. Ibid., pp. 35-36.
11. Tenney, *New Testament Survey*, p. 74.

"new" was always of great interest. One can only imagine all the "new" ideas that wandering teachers and philosophers concocted to satisfy this appetite for "new" understandings of life.

Alongside the so-called new ideas there were basic philosophic views present during New Testament times. These are nicely summarized by Robert Gundry.

> The intelligentsia were turning to purer forms of philosophy. *Epicureanism* taught pleasure (not necessarily sensual) as the chief good in life. *Stoicism* taught dutiful acceptance of one's fate as determined by an impersonal Reason which rules the universe and of which all men are a part. The *Cynics*, who have many counterparts, regarded the supreme virtue as a simple and unconventional life in rejection of the popular pursuits of comfort, affluence, and social prestige. The *Sceptics* were relativists who abandoned belief in anything absolute and succumbed to doubt and conformity to prevailing custom. These and other philosophies, however, did not determine the lives of very many people. Generally, superstition and syncretism characterized the masses. Thus, Christianity entered a religiously and philosophically confused world. . . . Gloom and despair prevailed.[12]

Those philosophies failed because they really did not understand the true nature of man (in the image of God, but fallen), nor the nature of the one and only Creator God.

2. Religion in Israel

The religions and philosophies found in the Roman Empire did affect the church as it took the gospel of Jesus Christ into the Empire. But the life of Christ and the early years of the church were affected far more by the religious and political climate in Israel. Certain institutions, religious sects, and political groups were very much a part of that climate.

a. The Pharisees. The name *Pharisee* comes from a Hebrew word that means "to separate," and so the Pharisees were referred to as the separated ones.[13] From the time of the Jews' re-

12. Gundry, *A Survey of the New Testament*, p. 37.
13. Norval Geldenhuys, *Commentary on the Gospel of Luke* (Grand Rapids: Eerdmans, 1966), p. 189.

turn from the Babylonian captivity through the intertestamental period, a movement for purity for the things of the Lord Jehovah grew. During the intertestamental period, there came into existence in Judaism a movement that was determined to free Israel from pagan influences. These "Hassidim," or "pious ones," were zealous for religious reform and known for their resistance to Hellenism. They were probably the foundation of the sect of the Pharisees. The separatist movement was given great momentum when the Syrian king Antiochus Epiphanes (175 B.C.) tried to force heathen practices on the Jewish people. From about 125 B.C. the distinct party of the Pharisees can be found in the Jewish society.

The Pharisees believed strongly in a separation from the ways and the practices of the Gentiles. And they taught, in great detail, what was involved in that separation. For example,

> Three days before a heathen festival all transactions with Gentiles were forbidden, so as to afford them neither direct nor indirect help towards their rites; and this prohibition extended even to private festivities. . . . It was unlawful for Jewish workmen to assist in anything that might be subservient either to heathen worship or heathen rule, including in the latter the erection of courthouses and similar buildings. . . . Milk drawn from a cow by heathen hands, bread and oil prepared by them, might indeed be sold to strangers, but not used by Israelites. If a heathen were invited to a Jewish house, he might not be left alone in the room, else every article of food or drink on the table was henceforth to be regarded as unclean. If cooking utensils were bought of them, they had to be purified by fire or by water; knives to be ground anew, spits to be made red-hot before use.[14]

This quotation reveals much about the prevailing attitude of the Pharisees in Christ's day.

The Pharisees had an unbending loyalty to the Scriptures and desired to live strictly by the law. But in their desire to make the

14. Alfred Edersheim, *Sketches of Jewish Social Life in the Days of Christ* (Grand Rapids: Eerdmans, 1967), pp. 26-28.

law workable in everyday life, they developed a system of regulations and traditions, which by the time of Christ had become a terrible burden on the people. The Pharisees promoted those traditions to a place of equal or (practically speaking) greater importance than the written law of Moses. They became proud of their separation and knowledge and viewed themselves as superior to the rest of society. It was their pride, self-righteousness, and their violation of the spirit of the law that brought about the harsh condemnation of them by the Lord Jesus. It should be added, however, that their zeal for the Scriptures was an important factor in keeping the messianic hope burning brightly in Israel in those days of Roman rule.

The actual number of Pharisees in the days of Christ was around six thousand.[15] They were not a very large group, but still they wielded tremendous power in Israel because they had the support of the people. Even the Roman rulers in Palestine, who had no regard for the Pharisees' religious teachings, were aware that they posed a real threat to the stability of the land.

> We see, therefore, that doubtless the Pharisees were the people's party; they represented the common people as opposed to the aristocracy on both religious and social matters. Their much respected piety and their social leanings towards supressing differences of class, gained them the people's support and assured them, step by step, of the victory. There is something very impressive about the way in which the people unreservedly followed the Pharisees. . . . As a whole the people looked to the Pharisees, in their voluntary commitment to works of supererogation, as models of piety, and as embodiments of the ideal life which the scribes, these men of divine and secret knowledge, had set before them. It was an act of unparalleled risk which Jesus performed when, from the full power of his consciousness of sovereignty, he openly and fearlessly called these men to repentance, and this act brought him to the cross.[16]

15. Joachim Jeremias, *Jerusalem in the Time of Jesus* (Philadelphia: Fortress, 1969), p. 252.
16. Ibid., pp. 266-67.

The Pharisees were mainly composed of members of the middle class, though there were a few priests and Levites in their ranks as well. Most of them were merchants and tradesmen.

There were several different groups within the pharisaic community, and they did differ among themselves on various points of the law. Entrance into the ranks of the Pharisees was preceded by a period of probation, from one month to a year. During this time the personal piety and zeal of the candidate was observed. Tithing, fasting, and separation from uncleanness were basic matters to be observed. Once within the ranks of pharisaism, increasingly strict vows could be taken.

The Pharisees met not only in the synagogues with the rest of the populace, but also met together in communities. Each of those communities was headed by a scribe who served as a professional authority in the matter of interpreting the law. They met in their communities to study the law, and to worship together (usually on the evening before the Sabbath day). But it was in the synagogues that they exercised their greatest influence over the people of Israel.[17]

b. The scribes. The scribes were not a party as were the Pharisees but were rather a class of Israelites. They were well-educated persons whose job it was to teach and interpret the law. They are also referred to in the gospels as the ''doctors of the law'' and the ''Lawyers.'' They not only taught the law but were responsible to prosecute those who broke the law. (This is what Saul of Tarsus was doing when he was headed toward Damascus to prosecute Christians.) Evidence indicates that the great majority of the scribes belonged to the party of the Pharisees, and thus the close association in the gospel record between the scribes and the Pharisees. It must be noted that whereas most scribes were Pharisees, most Pharisees were not scribes. It would be correct to say that in the days of Christ, the most influential members of the pharisaic party were the scribes.[18]

It was the scribes who formulated the oral law, which covered every conceivable matter in Jewish life. ''The Scribes cov-

17. Pentecost, *Words and Works*, p. 546.
18. Jeremias, *Jerusalem*, p. 254.

ered up the Scriptures with their Oral Law and multiplied rules until they crushed out the spirit.''[19]

c. The Sadducees. The sect of the Sadducees originated during the intertestamental period. The name *Sadducee* may have been derived from the name ''Zadok,'' who was the high priest in the days of David and Solomon. Another possibility is that the name might have come from the word *zedekah,* which means ''righteousness.'' The exact meaning of the name is probably not too important because it is not their name but their activities that influence events in the New Testament.

The Sadducees were less numerous than the Pharisees, but they were men who were generally wealthy and in places of political authority. The party of the Sadducees included high-ranking priests and the wealthy lay nobility. The close association between the priests and the Sadducees can easily be traced back to the intertestamental rule of John Hyrcanus. The Sadducees possessed a great deal of political power in the days of Rome. Because they had so much prestige, power, and wealth to lose, they were far more cooperative with Rome than were the Pharisees. As a sect, however, they ceased to exist after the destruction of the city of Jerusalem in A.D. 70.

Because most of our information about the Sadducees comes from their enemies, some uncertainty exists about some of the statement made concerning them. However, it is clear that they refused to accept the oral law developed by the Pharisees. They seem to have limited the full authority of Scripture to just the five books of Moses (Genesis-Deuteronomy). They evidently did not believe in angels, demons, resurrection, or a coming Messiah.

d. The Essenes. Apparently the Essenes originated during the intertestamental period in the days of the Maccabees. Many scholars believe their roots (like those of the Pharisees) are to be traced back to the Hassidim. They lived in isolated communities in Judea, especially west of the Dead Sea in places like Qumran. It is believed there were about four thousand of them.[20]

---

19. Pentecost, *Words and Works*, p. 542.
20. H. Wayne House, *Chronological and Background Charts of the New Testament* (Grand Rapids: Zondervan, 1981), p. 75.

They were even more separated than the Pharisees, choosing not to live in Jewish society. They were known for their strict, rigid life-style; a life-style far more burdensome than the one created by the Pharisees. They are not mentioned by name in the New Testament, but some believe that John the Baptist may have had some contact with them.

e. The Herodians. The Herodians were more of a political party than a religious sect. They originated during the time of the Herodian dynasty and were supporters of that dynasty. They accepted Hellenization and were desirous of the political power and worldly benefits that came to loyal supporters of Herod's family. It could be that many of the Jews who collected taxes for Rome were Herodians. Normally the Herodians and the Pharisees were archenemies. But in the case of Christ they temporarily set aside their antagonism in order to unite against a common enemy. They are mentioned in Mark 3:6 and 12:13.

f. The Zealots. Probably one of the most difficult groups to identify with great accuracy is the Zealots. Scholars vary greatly in their opinions regarding the Zealots of the first century A.D. It is clear, however, that there existed in first-century Palestine groups who advocated the violent overthrow of Rome. They were absolutely intolerant of Roman presence (or anything Gentile) in Palestine. Some believe the Zealots began when Judas the Galilean led a revolt against Rome in A.D. 6.[21] Others put the origin of the group much later, around A.D. 66. In either case, they had Rome as their primary target. The term *zealot* may have been a term used for a specific group, but it may also have been used more generally to include several groups or individuals who believed that God alone was their ruler and no lordship of man would be tolerated.

The term *sicarii* appears in Jewish literature. The word is of Latin origin and has the idea of "assassins." It was applied to a group of Jewish radicals who used a *sica* (a short sword) in their hit-and-run assassinations of Romans and Roman sympathizers. Whether or not they were a part of the Zealot party is uncertain.

---

21. F. F. Bruce, *New Testament History*, (Garden City, N. J.: Doubleday, 1969), p. 97.

But the basic ideals of the Zealots and the Sicarii were the same— the removal of Rome from Palestine.

The Zealots were responsible for a number of revolts in the first century. It was their activity that brought about the terrible Roman wars of A.D. 66-72 in which Jerusalem was destroyed and tens of thousands of Jews were killed.

g. The Sanhedrin. The word *sanhedrin* was derived from Greek and given a Hebraic form. It literally means "sit together" but is rather broad in its usage. Fundamentally it has the idea of a council or a governing body and can also include the idea of a court.[22] The Great Sanhedrin was the national council of the Jews (something like a Jewish "supreme court"). It was made up of seventy-one members, the high priest being the president. The Sanhedrin met in Jerusalem in the confines of the Temple. Although the idea of a representative council can be found in the time of Ezra, the Sanhedrin of the New Testament era traces its organization to about the time of John Hyrcanus (135 B.C.), the days of Jewish independence in the intertestamental period.

There were numerous small sanhedrins, or councils, in the towns throughout Judea and Galilee, but these were limited in power and influence as they dealt strictly with local matters. The Great Sanhedrin, however, had great power and involved itself in both religious and civil matters. This power, of course, was limited because of the domination of Rome. (The Sanhedrin was stripped of a great deal of power, including that of capital punishment, in the days of Herod the Great.)[23] But the Romans did allow the Sanhedrin extensive authority in Jewish internal affairs.

It was the Great Sanhedrin that found itself in conflict with the Lord Jesus (John 9). Members attempted to arrest Him on several occasions (e.g. John 7:32); they desired to kill Him (Luke 22:2); they participated in His arrest (Mark 14:43); they broke their own laws and code of ethics in their trial of Him (e.g. Matt. 26:59; 27:41); and they are held accountable by Scripture for their actions (Acts 2:23, 36; 3:13).

22. Ibid., p. 77.
23. Emil Schurer, *A History of the Jewish People in the Time of Jesus* (New York: Schocken, 1961), pp. 109-10.

The Great Sanhedrin is identified by a variety of designations in the gospels and the book of Acts. It is sometimes referred to as the "council" (Matt. 26:59; Acts 4:15), the "council of elders" (Acts 22:5), and the "senate" (Acts 5:21). But it is mainly identified in the New Testament by its component elements, such as "chief priests and pharisees," "chief priests, elders and scribes," or the "rulers, elders and scribes."[24] The "elders" were men from the leading families in Judaism, many of whom would trace their roots back to the key families of Ezra's day. The "chief priests" were actually priests of higher rank and authority than the ordinary priest.[25] And the Pharisees were sometimes referred to as the scribes, showing the close association between these two. The Sanhedrin, therefore, was a body made up of men with greatly differing religious and political views.

      h. The synagogue. The word *synagogue* means a "gathering of people" or a "congregation." It was a place where the Jews gathered to study the Scriptures and to worship God.

With the destruction of the Jerusalem Temple in 586 B.C. at the hands of the Babylonians, the Jews no longer had a place to worship. They were taken to Babylon away from their homeland. The synagogue can be traced back to this Babylonian captivity, when Jews, encouraged and led by Ezekiel, met for study and worship (Ezek. 8:1; 20:1-3). The synagogue was an important factor in keeping the displaced Jews from lapsing into heathenism. Gradually it became customary, after the Jews returned from exile, for local meeting places to be established for study and worship. During the intertestamental period, synagogues multiplied both in and out of Palestine.[26]

At the time of Christ, synagogues could be found everywhere throughout the land. It was said by some rabbis that, when Jerusalem was destroyed by the Romans in A.D. 70, there were more than 450 synagogues in Jerusalem alone. And although that may

24. Werner Forster, *Palestinian Judaism in New Testament Times* (London: Oliver and Boyd, 1964), p. 124.
25. Jeremias, *Jerusalem*, pp. 178-79.
26. Alfred Edersheim, *The Life and Times of Jesus the Messiah* (New York: Longmans and Green, 1900), 1:432-34.

be an exaggeration, it does indicate that they were very numerous in Christ's day. It took ten pious men to start one, so even the smaller towns could have a synagogue. It would not be difficult to find the synagogue upon entering a town. It was located on the highest point of ground in the town, or if not, it had a spire on top, which would make it the highest building around. This was done to symbolize that the functions of the synagogue were the most important thing possible for the people to engage in. Also, this supposedly fulfilled Isaiah 2:2 where the house of the Lord would be established on the chief of the mountains and raised above the high hills. (If the synagogue was lower than other buildings it was thought to be in danger of destruction.)[27]

The services of the synagogue enjoyed great freedom, and any competent Israelite could participate even if he was just visiting (such as Jesus or Paul). There was order to the service and portions of the Law and the Prophets were read systematically during the year. Each synagogue had a ruler whose duty it was to oversee the services and ensure order. The scrolls were central to the synagogue and were handled with great care. When used in a service, the scrolls were handled by an ''attendant'' and were immediately put back into their proper place when the reading of them concluded (Luke 4:20). In the synagogue services men and women were separate from one another, and only the men participated in the services.

The synagogue also became an important place for the training of Jewish boys in the faith of Judaism (girls were taught at home). All boys had the opportunity of synagogue training until about the age of twelve.

The synagogue played a significant part in the life of the average Jew in the days of Christ. Although the Temple existed then, the synagogue remained the central place in the life of the average Jew as he studied the Scriptures and worshiped God.

i. The Temple. The Temple in Jerusalem had originally been built by King Solomon, but between Solomon's reign and the time of Christ it suffered burning, looting, and varying degrees

27. Edersheim, *Sketches*, pp. 250-64.

of destruction. The Temple of Christ's day was rebuilt by Herod the Great. Herod began an extensive rebuilding project about 19 B.C. and the task (using as many as 18,000 workers) was not completed until about A.D. 64, just a few years before the Romans destroyed it in A.D. 70.[28]

The Temple complex had three courts: the large outer "court of the Gentiles," the "court of women;" and the "court of Israel." Gentiles were permitted in the court of the Gentiles, but faced death if they dared to enter the two inner courts. A four and a half foot fence surrounded the inner courts with warning signs posted on it. Israelite women could enter the inner court area, but could not proceed past the court of women and go into the court of Israel. Only Israelite men could enter the court of Israel and only the priests could enter the Temple proper. The sanctuary of the Temple was reached by climbing twelve steps.

Inside the Temple itself the arrangement was like that of the Old Testament Tabernacle. The "holy place" in this Temple was about 60 feet long and the "holy of holies" was about 30 feet square. The Temple house itself gleamed with gold. The 150-square foot front of the Temple was all gold plated. Gold and marble were used everywhere (gold spikes were even put on the roof to keep the birds off the Temple). This magnificent Temple was indeed a wonder in the ancient world.

The Romans allowed the Jews to have their own police force to guard the Temple area. The Levites, who formed this police force, stood guard at the gates and constantly patrolled the courts. They were to ensure that no unauthorized person should go where they were prohibited.[29] This would be quite a task on feast days when tens of thousands would crowd into the Temple area. (It is estimated that the Temple complex could contain more than two hundred thousand people at one time.)[30]

The Temple was the focal point of Jewish religion and worship. It was here that the blood sacrifices were made and the feasts of the Jews were celebrated. (See below for a list of those feasts.)

28. Jeremias, *Jerusalem*, pp. 21-24.
29. Ibid., p. 209.
30. Alfred Edersheim, *The Temple* (Grand Rapids: Eerdmans, 1975), p. 69.

THE JEWISH SACRED YEAR

FEAST	DATE	PURPOSE
The Passover	Nisan 14 (March/April)	To remember the deliverance of Israel from Egyptian bondage.
The Feast of Unleavened Bread	Nisan 15-21	Part of the Passover celebration. Ate unleavened bread and celebrated the beginning of the wheat harvest.
Pentecost (Feast of Weeks)	Sivan 6 (May/June)	Marked the end of the wheat harvest.
The Feast of Trumpets	Tishri 1 (September/ October)	Known as Rosh Hashanah, it was the celebration of the new year (civil year).
The Day of Atonement	Tishri 10	A day of fast set apart for national repentance and atonement for sin.
The Feast of Tabernacles	Tishri 15-22	Also known as "Booths", it commemorated Israel's wilderness experience.
The Feast of Lights	Kislev 25 (November/ December)	Not found in the Mosaic law. It was a celebration of the Maccabean cleansing and rededicating of the Temple.
The Feast of Purim	Adar 14-15 (February/ March)	Not found in the Mosaic law. Purim ("lots") remembered God's deliverance of Israel in the days of Esther.

The porches that ringed the Temple area were places where daily the rabbis would sit and teach their followers. (Jesus, and later the apostles, taught in the porch areas of the Temple.) The Temple was crucial to Jewish religious life and its destruction in A.D. 70 by the Romans was a national disaster.

THE HERODIAN TEMPLE

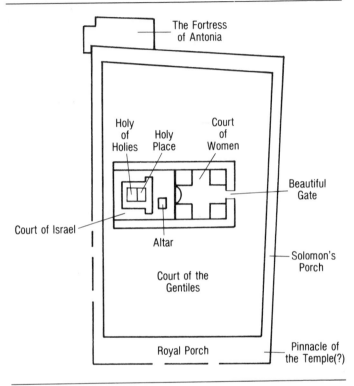

The Fortress of Antonia

Holy of Holies

Holy Place

Court of Women

Beautiful Gate

Court of Israel

Altar

Court of the Gentiles

Solomon's Porch

Royal Porch

Pinnacle of the Temple(?)

Part 2

The Gospels:
The New Covenant Instituted

4

PERSPECTIVES ON THE GOSPELS

The term *gospel* means "good news." Very early in the church age this general word for good news took on the technical idea of the good news about Jesus Christ and His marvelous salvation. These first four books of the New Testament tell this story of Jesus Christ's salvation for lost man and, therefore, are referred to as the gospels.

The Relationships of the Gospels

It is impossible to say with any certainty why there are four gospels in the New Testament and not two, three, or five. We know that numerous written accounts of Christ's life existed in the first century (Luke 1:1-2), but that only four were recognized as Holy Spirit inspired.

Several possible reasons have been advanced for the existence of four gospels. Some hold that there were four primary views of the Messiah in the Old Testament and that the gospels reflect those views: Matthew views Jesus as the King; Mark sees Him as the Servant of the Lord; Luke presents Jesus as Man; and John views Christ as God.

Others feel that there were four gospels because of the need to reach four basic groups of people in the first century. Matthew was writing to the Jew; Mark's audience was the Roman; Luke addressed the Greek; and John was writing to Christians in the church.

A.   A COMPARISON OF THE FOUR GOSPELS

The four gospels are not biographies of the life of Christ for the simple reason that almost thirty years of His life are really not dealt with. Moreover, there are numerous omissions in each of the four gospels and many of these are of important events (e.g., the ascension of Christ and the raising of Lazarus from the dead are not found in three of the four gospels).

The gospels are four different views of Jesus Christ. They are thematic presentations. Each of the authors approached Christ's life from his own viewpoint and developed that viewpoint, selecting certain teachings and miracles.

COMPARISONS OF THE FOUR GOSPELS

Comparisons	Matthew	Mark	Luke	John
Christ Viewed as	King	Servant	Man	God
Written to	Jews	Romans	Greeks	Church
Number of Chapters	28	16	24	21
Unique Material	42%	7%	59%	92%
Old Testament Quotes	53	36	25	20

B.   A DISCUSSION OF THE SYNOPTIC GOSPELS

1. The synoptic viewpoint

Matthew, Mark, and Luke are commonly referred to as the "synoptic gospels." *Synoptic* is a Greek word that means a "seeing together" or "having a common view." This term emphasizes that Matthew, Mark, and Luke basically have a common viewpoint of the life and ministry of Christ. They, therefore, carry the title of the synoptic gospels. It is reasonable to assume that John (written much later than Matthew, Mark, and Luke) intended for his gospel to complement the synoptics. It is clear that he avoided using a great deal of material found in the synoptics.

2. The synoptic problem

The *synoptic problem* is the phrase used to describe the difficulty scholars have in dealing with the apparent interrelationship of Matthew, Mark, and Luke. Scholars have pointed out that not only do the synoptic gospels have the same general historical structure, but they often have certain clear verbal agreements. The similarities are so numerous and with such obvious verbal agreement that it cannot be coincidental. Many conclude that there was literary dependence among Matthew, Mark, and Luke. But the question is "Exactly which writer depended on which other writers?" And how does one account for the striking differences in their accounts? The answering of these and other related questions have occupied the attention of New Testament scholars for some time. Several basic solutions have been set forth.[1]

One theory suggests that *oral tradition* is the key in solving this issue. This view postulates that as the apostles and leaders of the early church preached about the works and the teachings of Christ, their preaching tended toward a fixed form. (For example, when telling about the feeding of the five thousand, the same basic facts were always given.) The miracles and the teachings of Christ were passed on relatively unchanged from person to person. Thus by the time they were written down a basic, fixed form had been achieved, and that accounts for the similarities.[2] Although there may be some validity to the idea of oral tradition, it does not account for the differences in the gospel narratives, and it does not adequately deal with the difficulty of the church's spreading out into various parts of the world and thus beyond the apostles' influence.

A second theory, the *two-document hypothesis*, has been received favorably. This theory states that Mark was the first gospel written and that Matthew and Luke based their gospels on Mark. Furthermore, the theory contends, Matthew and Luke also used a second document called "Q" (from the German word *quelle*,

1. Everett F. Harrison, *Introduction to the New Testament* (Grand Rapids: Eerdmans, 1968), pp. 136-53.
2. Merrill C. Tenney, *New Testament Survey* (Grand Rapids: Eerdmans, 1961), pp. 134-35.

meaning "source"). This source document "Q" is alleged to account for the numerous similarities between Matthew and Luke in places where the two differ from Mark. The arguments surrounding this theory are many and complex. However, there are certain significant problems with this view. First, there is such a heavy emphasis on the use of written documents in this theory (and other similar ones) that the personal relationships and contacts of the gospel writers are not properly emphasized. Matthew was an eyewitness to those things that he wrote about (which raises the question as to why Matthew should depend on Mark, who was not present when these events occurred). Mark was not an eyewitness, but was closely associated with the apostles. Luke, during the two years of Paul's Caesarean imprisonment, stayed in Palestine and probably had a great deal of contact with the apostles and others who were eyewitnesses. The three writers could even have had contact with one another. They did pen their gospels in close association with those people who had surrounded Christ in His earthly life and ministry.

Another problem with the two-document hypothesis is its basis on the hypothetical document "Q." There is no copy of such a document and great question as to whether or not such a document ever existed.[3] Yet another difficulty with the theory is the priority of Mark. The tradition of the church from very ancient times has been the priority of Matthew. This ancient tradition clearly has Matthew writing the earliest gospel. The more recent documentary theory of the nineteenth century has no evidence that the ancient view is in error.[4]

Perhaps Luke himself has the key to the solution of the synoptic problem. In the prologue to his gospel (Luke 1:1-4), he explains how his gospel came into existence. It is quite clear that he did not simply copy someone else's work, editing here and there. Luke did use some written records, which he carefully checked for accuracy. (Maybe Mark was one of them, or maybe Mark bor-

3. Robert H. Gundry, *A Survey of the New Testament*, rev. ed. (Grand Rapids: Zondervan, 1981), pp. 65-67.
4. Robert L. Thomas and Stanley N. Gundry, *A Harmony of the Gospels* (Chicago: Moody, 1978), pp. 276-77.

rowed one of Luke's resource books!) Unlike Matthew, and to some degree Mark, Luke was not an eyewitness of the events pertaining to Christ's life. But he did speak with those who were eyewitnesses.

Luke also mentions the "ministers of the word." These may have been individuals in the early church who had a special function as tradition-bearers, passing on in a fairly set form truths about Christ, Evidently there were sayings of Jesus that were passed on from person to person in a fixed form, as is illustrated in Acts 20:35. Luke used many sources and spoke with many people in writing his gospel. And much the same was probably true of Matthew and Mark. In all of this discussion, the foundational role of the Holy Spirit must be remembered. One of the Spirit's ministries was to guide men into the truth and enable them (especially the apostles) to recall, without distortion or error, the truth about Christ (John 14:26; 16:14-15; 1 Cor. 2:12). And this the Spirit did. Nineteen centuries have gone by since the gospels were written, with the result that many of the facts about how the authors wrote is not clear. It is quite clear, however, that what they wrote is accurate, without error, directed by the Holy Spirit, and is therefore authoritative in our lives.[5]

THE SETTING OF THE GOSPELS

A.   THE GEOGRAPHY OF PALESTINE

The Lord Jesus lived and ministered in the land of Palestine, an area of about 12,000 square miles. Palestine proper is about 175 miles from north to south (from Mount Hermon to the southern end of the Dead Sea) and is about 50 miles wide (from the Mediterranean Sea to the Jordan River).

Palestine is divided into four clearly defined topographical features that run north and south between the Mediterranean Sea and the great eastern desert region. The first of these is the *coastal plain*, which runs along the entire western coast of Palestine. The second major topographical feature is the *central range* (also known as "the hill country"). It is actually an extension of

5. Ibid., pp. 278-79.

the Lebanon Mountains in the north. The range extends southward as far as the desert that begins near Hebron.[6] The third section is the *Jordan valley*, which is part of a 4,000 mile rift extending from southeastern Turkey to Mozambique, Africa.

> The Jordan depression is one of the most remarkable geological phenomena on the earth's surface. The sources of the Jordan at Banias . . . near Caesarea Philippi are 1,200 feet above the Mediterranean. The river drops to 1,292 feet below sea level at the delta where it enters the Dead Sea. . . . From the point where the Jordan leaves the Sea of Galilee to the place where it enters the Dead Sea is sixty-five miles. The Jordan has a barrier of cliffs on either side from two to fifteen miles apart. The plain of Jericho, immediately north of the Dead Sea, is fourteen miles wide.[7]

The fourth topographical feature is the *eastern range* (the Transjordan Plateau). This high tableland is between 30 and 80 miles in width, and in places rises to more than 5,000 feet above sea level. It is a fertile area, receiving significant rainfall.[8]

When the Lord Jesus and His disciples went from place to place, it often involved traversing rugged terrain. Even going a relatively few miles could involve climbs and descents of thousands of feet. For example, to go the approximately twenty miles from the Jordan River to Jerusalem would involve a climb of almost 4,000 feet. Travel in Palestine was very much affected by the location of plains, rivers, and mountains.

The climate of Palestine is directly related to the radical differences in topography. Basically the climate of Palestine resembles the southwestern part of the United States, but there is more to it than that.

> The face of the Holy Land is most varied, mainly because of sharp climatic differences from region to region. . . . These

6. Charles F. Pfeiffer, *Baker's Bible Atlas* (Grand Rapids: Baker, 1966), pp. 25-26.
7. Ibid.
8. Barry J. Beitzel, *The Moody Atlas of Bible Lands* (Chicago: Moody, 1985), pp. 20-25.

contrasts form the dry Arabah at the edge of the Judean Desert, with its rugged scarps, and opposite are the fertile and watered plateaus of Transjordan. These variations of land and climate brought about extremely different patterns of settlement within Palestine, which resulted in corresponding political divisions in most periods. . . . The Holy Land lies between the sea and the desert, and both influence its nature. The westerly wind brings life-giving rains, whereas the easterly brings only the dryness of the desert. The higher a place, or the closer to the sea, the more wet the climate. The southern part of Palestine lies within an arid zone that runs around the globe; the extensive desert regions enclose the Holy Land on the south and east. . . . The influence of the desert is extreme in the history of the Holy Land, and an awareness of this wilderness is echoed throughout the pages of the Bible.[9]

And to the north, in contrast to the southern desert, rising more than 9,000 feet is Mount Hermon, which is snow-covered throughout the entire year.

The climate and topography of the land is reflected in the gospel narratives. For example, with all the arid regions in Palestine, John the Baptist centered his ministry in the Jordan River valley because "there was much water there" for his baptizing ministry (John 3:23). Jesus' temptation was all the more significant because it took place in the barren, desolate Judean wilderness away from pleasant surroundings (Mark 1:12-13). When it came time for Jesus and His disciples to retreat for times of rest, they went to such refreshing places as those near Caesarea Philippi where the headwaters of the Jordan River were located (Matt. 16:13).

B.   THE PEOPLE OF PALESTINE

The Lord Jesus was a Jew, born into the line of David and Abraham (Matt. 1:1-17). His ministry primarily took place in Galilee and Judea, where the Jews lived. He Himself declared that His ministry at that time was to the "lost sheep of the house of Is-

9. Yohanan Aharoni and Michael Avi-Yonah, *The Macmillan Bible Atlas* (New York: Macmillan, 1968), p. 14.

rael'' (Matt. 15:24). Therefore, it is not surprising that His contact with non-Jews was infrequent.

1. The Gentiles

On certain occasions the earthly ministry of Christ did involve Gentiles, since they too inhabited Palestine. For example, Jesus did heal the daughter of a believing Gentile woman who was

POLITICAL MAP OF ISRAEL

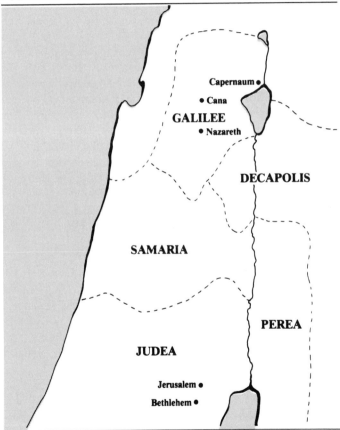

from the Tyre and Sidon region (Matt. 15:21-28). He did heal the
slave of a Roman army officer (Luke 7:1-10). And on several occasions He was in Gentile territory when He performed miracles,
suggesting that Gentiles could well have been the beneficiaries of
the miracles (such as, the feeding of the 4,000 in Mark 8:1-9, and
the healings in Decapolis, recorded in Mark 7:31-37). But Gentiles were not the focus of Christ's ministry and they were not the
majority of the population.

2. The Samaritans

The Samaritans, like the Gentiles, were also occasional recipients of Christ's ministry (such as the Samaritan woman at the
well in John 4). The Samaritans were evidently the descendants of
the colonists placed in Israel by the Assyrians. In the year 721
B.C. the Assyrians defeated the northern kingdom of Israel, de-
porting many Israelites to other lands. But the remaining Israelites
intermarried with the colonists imported by the Assyrians. Their
descendants (the Samaritans) were racially different from the
Jews, which caused them to be looked upon with great disfavor by
the Jews. The separation was deepened when the Samaritans built
their own temple on Mount Gerazim during the intertestamental
period. It is for these reasons that the Jews hated the Samaritans
and regarded them as defiled fools. When the Jewish leaders
called Jesus a "Samaritan" (John 8:48), they were expressing
their strong contempt for the Lord Jesus.

3. The Jews

The Jews, the people of the Abrahamic Covenant, were the
primary focus of Christ's earthly ministry. To them Jesus targeted
His teachings and His miracles. But even among the Jews there
was a distinction. The distinction was between the Jews who resided in Judea and those who lived in the region of Galilee.

Jesus centered His ministry in the region of Galilee, with the
town of Capernaum as the base of operations. He did not, as one
might have thought, establish the center of His ministry in Jerusalem. The Jews of Galilee in some respects were quite different
from the Jews of Judea. And noting a few of these differences
helps to explain some of the divergent attitudes toward Jesus, as

well as the variation of ministry that Jesus had in those two regions.

The Galileans were viewed as "country cousins" by those from Jerusalem and Judea. Jerusalem was the center of Jewish learning, religious life, and political power. Undisguised contempt for the Galileans is reflected in the wellknown saying, "If anyone wishes to be rich let him go north; if he wants to be wise, let him come south."[10]

> Indeed, what we know of the Galileans would quite prepare us for expecting that the gospel should have received at least a ready hearing among many of them. . . . they seem to have been a warm-hearted, impulsive, generous race—intensely national in the best sense, active, not given to idle speculations. . . . They show more earnest practical piety and strictness of life, and less adherence to those Pharisaical distinctions which so often made void the law.[11]

The Galileans strictly kept the law but were generally indifferent to the traditionalism of the Judeans. This traditionalism, of course, was a key point of conflict between Jesus and the religious leaders from Judea. His violation of their rules and regulations was one of the basic reasons for their rejection of Him.

It is also true that the Galileans were more open to the miracles that He performed. "Furthermore, the Galileans were more prone to accept miracles and faith healings than were the Jews of Judea. Even among the Rabbis this was known."[12] And, it is interesting to note, the great majority of the recorded miracles of the Lord Jesus took place in the regions of Galilee. Of the thirty-three specific miracles recorded in the four gospels, twenty-three were performed in the region of Galilee and only six took place in Judea.[13]

10. Alfred Edersheim, *Sketches of Jewish Social Life in the Days of Christ* (Grand Rapids: Eerdmans, 1967), p. 30.
11. Ibid., p. 39.
12. Harold Hoehner, *Herod Antipas* (Grand Rapids: Zondervan, 1980), p. 60.
13. Ibid.

Even by noting these few, brief generalities about the Galilean and Judean Jews, it is clearer why the greatest outpouring of Jesus' miracles took place in Galilee and why Jesus' denunciation of traditionalism was accepted there. It also becomes more understandable why the Jewish establishment of Judea was immediately suspicious and fairly non-receptive to this Jesus from Nazareth in Galilee and that they tended to reject both His message and His miracles. The greater receptivity of the Galileans may also explain why eleven of the twelve apostles selected by Christ were Galileans. (Only Judas Iscariot was apparently not from Galilee.)

THE SUBJECT OF THE GOSPELS

Our understanding of the life and the ministry of the Lord Jesus Christ is greatly enhanced when we grasp something of the pattern and sequence of events that are found in the gospels. By putting the events of Christ's life in the order that they occurred our awareness of what happened two thousand years ago is greatly increased. A brief harmony of the four gospel records will follow some important chronological notations regarding the life of Christ.

A.   A CHRONOLOGY OF CHRIST'S LIFE

Chronology is important to any historical study. It is necessary to note the time frame in which events took place. In approaching the life of Jesus Christ there are several chronological matters that need to be mentioned. These chronological points give a framework for understanding and developing our study of the life and ministry of the Lord Jesus.

1. The year of Jesus Christ's birth

The calendar we use today is based on the idea that Jesus Christ was born in the year A.D. 1 (A.D. = *anno Domini* = "in the year of the Lord"). But evidence both in the Bible and outside of it points to the birth of Christ as being several years earlier, probably in 5 or 4 B.C. According to the gospels (Matt. 2:1 and Luke 1:5), Herod the Great was still alive when Jesus Christ was born.

Historical evidence indicates that Herod died in April of 4 B.C.[14] This means, of course, that Jesus was born before April of 4 B.C. But it is most likely that Jesus was born at least one year before the date of Herod's death. This is based on the fact that when Herod was informed by the Magi of the birth of the Jewish king, he decreed that all the male babies of Bethlehem who were under two years of age were to be killed (Matt. 2:16). This decree reflected his perception that Jesus had been born sometime within the preceding two years. Therefore, a date of 5/4 B.C. for the birth of Christ is reasonable.

2. The year Jesus Christ began His ministry

The text of all four of the gospels clearly state that John the Baptist began his public ministry before the Lord Jesus began His. John the Baptist began his ministry in the fifteenth year of the Roman emperor Tiberius Caesar (Luke 3:1). Establishing the exact date of John's ministry based on the "fifteenth year" of Tiberius is no simple matter. There are a number of complex issues involved.[15] But when all of the evidence is evaluated, a good case can be built for the date of A.D. 28/29 for the beginning of John the Baptist's ministry. Since Christ began His public ministry a few months later, a date of A.D. 29 would be the likely date for His ministry to begin.

If the above date is correct, this would make Jesus about 32 or 33 years old at the start of His ministry. The only specific statement in the gospels about the age of Jesus is Luke 3:23, where Luke declares that Jesus was "about" thirty years of age when He began to minister. Luke does not say He *was* thirty, but only that He was *about* thirty. Even though the word "about" does not have unlimited flexibility, it is within reason to include several years.

3. The year of Jesus Christ's crucifixion

The Lord Jesus was put to death on the Jewish feast of Passover (John 12:1; 13:1; 18:28). The date of the Passover each year

14. Merrill Unger, *Archaeology and the New Testament* (Grand Rapids: Zondervan, 1962), pp. 56-60.
15. Harold Hoehner, *Chronological Aspects of the Life of Christ* (Grand Rapids: Zondervan, 1977), pp. 29-37.

was the fourteenth of the month Nisan. Nisan 14 fell on a Friday the year the Lord was crucified.[16] With a Friday crucifixion, only two years are options as the year of the crucifixion. "Jesus was crucified sometime between A.D. 26 and 36 because this was the period of Pontius Pilate's governorship (cf. John 19:15-16). Complex astronomical calculations reveal that during this period Nisan 14 fell on Friday twice, in A.D. 30 and in A.D. 33."[17] Of these two possibilities, A.D. 33 is the most likely because it allows for a three-year ministry for Christ.

4. The length of Jesus Christ's ministry

The ministry of Christ evidently lasted for a little over three years, from sometime in A.D. 29 to the Passover of A.D. 33. The gospel of John is particularly helpful in establishing the length of Jesus' ministry. John specifically mentions three Passover feasts that took place during the ministry of Christ (John 2:13; 6:4; 11:55). Furthermore, there is, in all probability, another Passover located between John 2:13 and 6:4, based on evidence in John 5:1 and the synoptic gospels.[18] With four Passovers recorded, Christ's ministry would be at least three years in length.

THE PASSOVERS OF JESUS' MINISTRY

Ministry begins		1		2		3	
	1st Passover John 2:13		2nd Passover John 5:1		3rd Passover John 6:4		4th Passover John 11:55

With the information given above, a general timeline for the life and ministry of the Lord can be constructed.

16. Ibid., pp. 65-74.
17. Thomas and Gundry, *Harmony,* p. 322.
18. Hoehner, *Chronological Aspects,* pp. 55-63.

CHRONOLOGY OF CHRIST'S LIFE

5/4 B.C.		A.D. 9		A.D. 29 30 31 32 33
Birth	(Years in Bethlehem, Egypt, and Nazareth)	Temple Visit	(Years in Nazareth)	Ministry

B.   AN OUTLINE OF CHRIST'S LIFE

An overview of Christ's life and ministry is needed before there can be an appreciation of the details of the gospels. Familiar to most Christians are the accounts of Christ's birth, death, and resurrection; stories such as the feeding of the 5,000; parables such as the Good Samaritan; and numerous other portions. But all too often there is little understanding of the relationships that exist between these events, miracles, and teachings. There is a pattern to the life and the ministry of Jesus Christ. When the pattern is seen, the specific accounts in the gospels become clearer. This brief harmony of the life of Christ is given to help the reader see something of the pattern of Christ's life.

The life of Christ can be outlined under eight main divisions. Although the gospel accounts themselves are not divided in such a way, this nevertheless is one way to organize the great mass of material given in the gospel records. While every single verse out of the four gospels is not included in this summary, the major passages are included and, hopefully, will make the storyline of the gospels clear and understandable. The following chart and outline give parallel overviews of the life of Christ.

A SYNTHESIS OF THE LIFE OF CHRIST

	1	2	3	4	5	6	7	8
Period in the Life of Christ	Birth and childhood of Christ	Preparation for Christ's ministry	Early ministry of Christ	Great Galilean ministry of Christ	Special training of the Twelve	Later Judean ministry of Christ	Later Perean ministry of Christ	The last days in Jerusalem
Primary Gospels	Matthew and Luke	Matthew Mark Luke John	John	Matthew and Mark	Matthew and Mark	Luke and John	Luke	Matthew Mark Luke John
Years in Christ's Life	About 30 years			Approximately 3½ years				

Period One: The Early Years of Jesus Christ

A.　The Preview of Christ (John 1:1-18; Matt. 1:1-17: Luke 3:23-38).

1.　His eternality. The gospel of John begins the account of the life of Christ by making it abundantly clear that before Jesus was born at Bethlehem, He already existed. Jesus ("the Word") was the great Creator God who took on flesh, becoming a man, in order that He might provide salvation for a lost and sinful human race. Jesus was the God-man. (See appendix, *Note A: The Person of Jesus Christ.*)

2.　His ancestry. Because Jesus was not only the Eternal God, but also a man, He obviously entered the human race through a specific family. But not any family would do. Jesus, being Israel's long awaited Messiah had to be a descendant of Abraham, but more specifically of the family of David. Matthew began his gospel by immediately establishing that Jesus of Nazareth was indeed of the right family and thus had a legal claim to the throne of David. Matthew did this by giving the genealogy of Joseph. Luke's genealogy is probably that of Mary, because Luke already stated in his gospel that Jesus was the son of Mary only. It is more likely that Luke is giving the *real* (and not the legal) genealogy of Jesus, because Luke emphasizes Jesus' humanity.[19]

B.　The Birth of Christ (Matt. 1:18-25; Luke 1:5–2:39).

1.　The annunciation to Mary. Breaking the silence of four centuries, the angel Gabriel came from God announcing the births of John the Baptist and Jesus. After announcing the birth of John the Baptist, Messiah's forerunner, Gabriel appeared to a young girl by the name of Mary. She was engaged to a man named Joseph. Both Mary and Joseph were from the tribe of Judah and the line of King David and both were godly people.

Mary was informed that she had been chosen by God (Mary had "found favor with God") to be the mother of Israel's Messiah. Gabriel told Mary that the conception of the child would be a miraculous thing. Normal sexual relations would not be involved,

19.　A. T. Robertson, *A Harmony of the Gospels for Students of the Life of Christ* (New York: Harper, 1922), p. 259; Norval Geldenhuys, *Commentary on the Gospel of Luke* (Grand Rapids: Eerdmans, 1966), p. 152.

but rather the Creator God would generate life within her womb. Her child would not only be her physical son (truly man), but He would be the Son of God (truly deity). Gabriel also informed her about the work of her son. He was to be called Jesus ("the Lord is salvation"), which pictured His great work of redeeming mankind. He would reign on the throne of David over the nation of Israel in a marvelous kingdom. This declaration by Gabriel reflects the many Old Testament promises that Messiah would reign upon the earth in a glorious kingdom, in fulfillment of the great Davidic Covenant (2 Sam. 7).

2. The annunciation to Joseph. Several months later an angel (probably Gabriel) appeared to Joseph informing him of two things. First, he told Joseph that the pregnancy of Mary was in fact supernatural, and second, he was to marry Mary immediately. By marrying her, Joseph would become the protector and provider for Mary and the newborn baby.

3. The location of nativity. Luke states that God used a Roman decree to move Joseph and Mary from Nazareth to Bethlehem in order to fulfill the prophecy regarding the birthplace of the Messiah (Mic. 5:2). Upon arriving at Bethlehem, Mary gave birth to her son. But because the overcrowded town had no housing available, they had to take refuge in one of the limestone caves that dot the area. Here Mary gave birth to Jesus and placed Him in a manger (a feeding trough) and here some shepherds, who had been informed by angels of Messiah's birth, found Him.

C. The Youth of Christ.

1. In Egypt. After His birth near Bethlehem, Joseph and Mary moved into Bethlehem and lived there for about a year. It was at this time that wise men from the East arrived, coming to worship Israel's Messiah. They eventually found the young child living in a house in Bethlehem and gave valuable gifts to Him. These wise men had innocently informed King Herod of the birth of Israel's king. As a result of this news, Herod tried to eliminate Jesus by killing all the young children of Bethlehem. In order to avoid Herod's decree, Joseph, Mary, and Jesus fled to Egypt.

2. In Nazareth. Following a short period in Egypt, the family was directed by God to return to Palestine and settle in the Gal-

ilean town of Nazareth. Here Jesus learned the carpentry trade from Joseph. During the next twenty-five to thirty years, Jesus lived a normal life, growing and developing normally. Joseph probably died during the years of Jesus' early manhood, placing Jesus in the position of responsibility for the family.

Period Two: The Preparation For the Ministry of Jesus Christ

A. The Forerunner of Christ (Matt. 3:1-12; Mark 1:1-8; Luke 3:1-18; John 1:19-34).

1. John's birth. In fulfillment of the Old Testament prophets Isaiah and Malachi, John the Baptist was born. The angel Gabriel had appeared to an aged priest named Zacharias and informed him that he and his elderly wife Elizabeth were going to have a son. The agedness of these two, plus other circumstances that surrounded the birth of John the Baptist, alerted the godly in Israel that God was at work in the midst of His people.

2. John's purpose. The ministry of John the Baptist was a separatist movement; that is, it was outside the established religion of Judaism, and it did not have the official approval of the religious leaders. John declared that he was not the Messiah but that he was simply ''the voice of one crying in the wilderness'' (Isa. 40:3). John's message was designed to prepare the nation of Israel for the prophesied Messiah. The nation was to repent of (change its attitude and turn away from) its sins and identify itself with the Messiah, who was coming to establish His kingdom. That kingdom, John declared, was ''at hand.'' What kingdom? The kingdom that fulfilled the great Davidic and Abrahamic Covenants (2 Sam. 7; Gen. 12, 15, 17). It was to be a literal, earthly kingdom that Messiah would rule over (note again Gabriel's statement in Luke 1:32-33). Although there would be spiritual aspects to this kingdom, it was not a ''spiritual kingdom'' (that is, the rule of God in the hearts of His people). A ''spiritual kingdom'' had always existed. But John was announcing the nearness of another aspect of the kingdom: the earthly kingdom of Messiah. The actual arrival of this earthly kingdom depended upon a positive, godly response by the people of Israel. Only Israel's unrepentance and rejection could stop it from coming at that time (which is what

happened). John the Baptist's message was designed to bring about that needed repentance.

3. John's baptism. John's ministry included water baptism as an external sign of inward repentance. (John did not originate the methodology of water baptism, as it was used by other groups at that time.) His baptism was one of repentance. His baptism did not remove sins (the removal of sin is based on blood, not water), but was the outward declaration that repentance had taken place in the heart. John taught the people that Messiah would baptize them in the Holy Spirit and with fire; that is, all the people would be "baptized" by Messiah, either with life (the Spirit) or with judgment (the fire).

John's ministry had a great impact on the nation of Israel and he fulfilled his ministry of alerting Israel to the fact that Messiah had come.

B. The Baptism of Christ (Matt. 3:13-17; Mark 1:9-11; Luke 3:21-23).

1. A fulfillment. When Jesus came to the Jordan River to be baptized by John, John strongly objected to the idea of Jesus being baptized by him. John was persuaded, however, when he came to understand that his ministry was really an extension of the Old Testament requirements for the godly Israelite. Just as it was necessary for Jesus to be circumcised, tithe, and attend the prescribed feasts, so it was necessary for Him to be baptized. John understood that Jesus did not have anything to repent of but did not realize at first that Jesus needed to be baptized to fulfill all of the "law's" requirements.

2. An anointing. The baptism of Jesus was also the occasion for His induction into the office of king. The Holy Spirit came visibly on Jesus at His baptism, anointing Him. Just as kings in the Old Testament were anointed with oil (symbolizing the Holy Spirit) at the time of their inauguration, so Jesus was anointed by the Spirit Himself as He was inaugurated as Israel's king, fulfilling the Davidic Covenant. The dove fulfilled Isaiah 42:1 and the voice from heaven was a kind of coronation formula for the king (Ps. 2:7-8). Jesus spoke of His anointing later on in His ministry (cf. Luke 4:18 with Isa. 61:1).

C.   The Temptation of Christ (Matt. 4:1-11; Mark 1:12-13; Luke 4:1-13).

The final part of His preparation came in the temptation experience. After Jesus was baptized by John, He was immediately led by the Spirit into the wilderness where He was tempted by Satan for a period of forty days. The temptations were far more extensive than the three recorded by the synoptic gospels. Luke is clear that the temptation experience went on throughout the entire forty-day period. In fact, Satan did not stop testing the Lord Jesus in the wilderness but continued on throughout His life (cf. Luke 4:13 with Hebrews 2:18; 4:15).

But information about this specific time of temptation was given in order to present unmistakable evidence that Jesus was morally and spiritually qualified to be the Messiah and the redeemer of mankind. Jesus met Satan in the most unfavorable circumstances and came out victorious.

With John's preparatory ministry nearly completed and with the personal preparation of Jesus in the baptism and temptation experiences over the Lord Jesus was ready to begin His own ministry.

Period Three: The Early Ministry of Jesus Christ

A.   The First Disciples (John 1:29-51).

Jesus began His ministry in the same area in which He had been baptized, the region around the Jordan River. His first concern was to begin to surround Himself with men who could help Him establish His much-prophesied and long-awaited earthly kingdom. His first followers were men who had been disciples of John the Baptist. They were regenerated men with a heart for the things of God. The five mentioned in this Scripture text were joined later by hundreds of others who would be called disciples of Jesus Christ (The term *disciple* generally has the idea of a "learner" or a "follower.") At first, Jesus' closest disciples only accompanied Him occasionally in His ministry. After a time with Him, they would then return to their employment. Later He would call them to come and join Him again for a short time in His work. (Only later would twelve be selected to be with Him all the time.)

B.   The Galilean Ministry (John 2:1-12; 4:43-54).

Christ's early ministry lasted for about one year, and Jesus moved about to all places in Palestine where potential believers might be found. He began working miracles designed to awaken the people to the fact that Messiah had indeed come. He worked His first miracle at Cana of Galilee, where He changed water into wine.

C.   The Judean Ministry (John 2:13–3:36).

After spending some time in the Galilee region, Jesus returned to Judea. Upon arriving at the Jerusalem Temple, He was disgusted with the flagrant merchandising going on there. He "cleansed" His Father's house and in doing so alerted the religious leaders to His presence. He worked a number of miracles in Jerusalem during those days, which aroused the interest of Nicodemus, one of the Jewish leaders. In the now-famous discussion with this man, Jesus made it clear that the kingdom was entered only through the new birth. It was the cleansing and regenerating work of the Spirit which would bring such a new birth into the life of a believing man.

D.   The Samarian Ministry (John 4:1-42).

The first year of Jesus' ministry was concluded by the account of His encounter with a woman of Samaria. Jesus confronted this woman with her sin and her need of a savior. She and many others from her town believed in the Lord Jesus Christ. Jesus made a very clear declaration to this woman that He was the Messiah that many were waiting for.

Period Four: The Galilean Ministry of Jesus Christ

A.   The Tribute of Jesus (Matt. 11:2-19; Mark 6:17-30; Luke 3:19-20).

When John the Baptist was jailed by wicked Herod Antipas, Jesus went to Galilee and made Capernaum the base for His next year of ministry. John the Baptist was arrested sometime during the first year of Christ's ministry and remained in prison for more than a year before he was executed. John was confused over his imprisonment and the fact that the kingdom had not come yet. But

Jesus assured John that He was indeed the Messiah, giving John needed comfort. Jesus testified that John the Baptist was a great man in God's eyes. The death of John was an ominous sign of things to come.

THE PROVINCE OF GALILEE

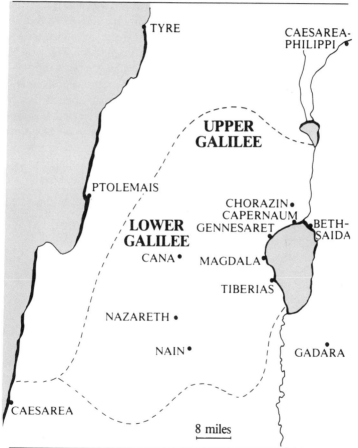

TYRE

CAESAREA-
PHILIPPI

**UPPER
GALILEE**

PTOLEMAIS

CHORAZIN
CAPERNAUM
GENNESARET
BETH-
SAIDA

**LOWER
GALILEE**

CANA

MAGDALA

TIBERIAS

NAZARETH

NAIN

GADARA

CAESAREA

8 miles

B.   The Disciples of Jesus (Matt. 4:18-22; 10:1-42; Mark 2:13-14; Luke 5:1-11; 6:12-16; 8:1).

At this point in the gospel narratives the ministry of Christ is nearly halfway completed. During the first half of His ministry the Lord Jesus had many disciples who would surround Him as He taught and moved from place to place. After a short period of time they would return to their occupations and family life. The four fishermen are an example of this. Mark 1:16-20 records the first time Jesus came to the shores of Galilee and requested that the four follow Him. (Remember that the four were already believers and had already spent time with Christ in John 1:35-51.) After ministering with Jesus for a time they returned to their fishing business. Later in Luke 5:1-11, Jesus again invited them to join Him, and the cycle was repeated. Only after spending a night in prayer were twelve men selected from the ranks of the followers of Christ to accompany Him permanently. It was during the last half of Christ's ministry that these men were with Him all the time. (See appendix, *Note B: The Apostles of Jesus Christ.*)

C.   The Teachings of Jesus (Matt. 5:1–7:29; 13:1-52; Luke 4:16-32; John 5:1-47).

Some of Christ's greatest teachings were given during this period of His ministry—teachings such as the Sermon on the Mount, the parables of the kingdom, and the discourse on Christ's equality with the Father. But Jesus was not just another teacher, disseminating religious truth. As He spoke on a wide range of theological and practical subjects, the reaction of people was that "never did a man speak the way this man speaks" (John 7:46). It was common knowledge that Jesus was "mighty in . . . word" (Luke 24:19) and that He spoke as one who had authority, unlike the teachers of His day (Matt. 7:29). The people who heard Him were constantly "amazed" at His teachings (Mark 10:24; Matt. 7:28). Jesus' instruction was not only powerful but His words were gracious with the result that the crowds "enjoyed listening to Him" (Mark 12:37; Luke 4:22). He was clearly in a class by Himself when it came to setting forth the truth of God.

D. The Miracles of Jesus (Matt. 8:23–9:34; Mark 1:21–2:12; 3:1-6; Luke 7:1-17; John 4:46–5:9).

Jesus was known as one who was mighty in deeds as well as words. During this period there was probably the greatest demonstration of Christ's miracles. These miracles were designed by God to authenticate the Person and the message of the Lord Jesus. Many men had come claiming to be Israel's Messiah, but only Jesus backed up His messianic claim with these demonstrations of the power of God.

His miracles showed His authority over nature, demons, death, and a wide range of human infirmities. God gave to men all the evidence they needed to see that Jesus was the Christ, the Son of the Living God. (See appendix, *Note C: Miracles in the Gospels and Acts.*)

E. The Opposition to Jesus (Matt. 11:20-30; 12:1-14, 22-45; Mark 6:1-6; John 5:10-47).

1. Its origins. At first the leaders and the people of Israel were generally positive about Jesus of Nazareth (e.g. John 3:2). But as time went on the leaders began to resist and oppose Jesus, and they had a great influence on the people. Two issues particularly brought about the leadership's opposition. First, they viewed Jesus as one who broke God's law because He "worked" on the Sabbath when He healed people. The Sabbath day healings were a constant source of irritation to the leaders. (Jesus, of course, was only breaking their traditions and not God's law.) Second, Jesus' claims of equality with the Father enraged them. On more than one occasion they picked up stones to stone Him for His "blasphemy." While other issues had a part in their rejection of Jesus, these two matters were primary.

2. Its results. A most serious result of their opposition to Christ occurred when the leaders refused to admit that Christ's miracles were done in God's power. (The climatic result of their opposition would take place later when they crucified Jesus.) Instead they claimed that Jesus' miracles were performed in the power of Satan (Matt. 12:22-37). These men rejected the clear evidence given by the Spirit of God that Jesus of Nazareth was their Messiah. Jesus responded to them by warning them that there was

no further evidence that would come from God and that the nation of Israel faced God's judgment. This amazing rejection of the Spirit's testimony to Christ brought about a change in Christ's ministry.

F. The Changes in Jesus' Ministry (Matt. 12:38–13:52).

With this "official" rejection by the leaders of Israel, Jesus' ministry changed noticeably. First, His miracles were no longer designed to be testimonies to the nation generally, but only evidences to individuals. Second, He began to speak in parables. Up to this point He had spoken "clearly" and did not use parables. Parables were now employed in order to communicate truth to believers while at the same time hiding truth from unbelievers. Third, the focus and emphasis of His ministry shifted from off the nation and on to His disciples. And fourth, the subject matter of His teachings changed somewhat. Added to His teachings on subjects like prayer and salvation were new discussions on the church and His death.

Period Five: The Training of the Twelve Apostles of Jesus Christ

A. Jesus' Withdrawal with the Twelve (Matt. 15:21-38; John 6:1-3).

When the religious leaders of Israel rejected Him and His offer of the kingdom, Jesus began to withdraw somewhat from public view. Some of His time was spent in geographic areas other than Galilee or Judea in order to avoid the harassment of the Jewish leaders. Outside of their jurisdiction He had a greater freedom to teach His followers. So He now turned His attention in a greater way to His chosen ones. It was necessary that He prepare them for their new role, as part of the foundation of the church that He was going to build (Eph. 2:20). Since the King and His kingdom had been rejected, the church would be established, and these men would be a key part of it.

B. Jesus' Focus on the Twelve (Matt. 16:21-26; Mark 6:31-52; 9:30-32; Luke 9:28-52; John 6:4-71).

The Twelve were taught many things during this period. Even though Jesus still ministered to large groups of people, His emphasis in both His words and His works was on the Twelve. Greater emphasis was placed on certain issues, such as discipleship, truth and error, and the coming death and resurrection of Christ.

Because of the rising opposition and rejection of Jesus, there was a need to encourage both Jesus and the Twelve. In this setting, Jesus went up on a mountain and was transfigured—His glory being revealed to three of His men. The revelation of His glory coupled with the voice of the Father was a needed reminder to them that Jesus was indeed Israel's Messiah even though the nation rejected that fact.

Period Six: The Judean Ministry of Jesus Christ

A. The Opposition to Jesus (Luke 11:14-36; 13:10-21; John 7:2-52; 8:12-59; 9:13-34; 10:19-21).

It is now six months before the crucifixion. Jesus went to Jerusalem for the Feast of Tabernacles (September/October). Opposition to Christ steadily increased during this period, and if the opportunity had presented itself, the Jewish leaders would have killed Him. But, as John states, His "hour had not yet come." While the leadership was against Him, the people were confused and quite divided in their viewpoint of Him. Some, following the position of the leaders, believed Him to be a false teacher. Others, while not concluding that Jesus was Messiah or the Son of God, viewed Him as a good man or as a prophet of God.

B. The Teachings of Jesus (Luke 10:1–11:13; John 8:2–10:31).

Some of Jesus' best-known teachings came from this period, such as the parable of the Good Samaritan and the "Lord's Prayer." He claimed to be the Light of the world, the Good Shepherd, and the great I Am. His teachings were carried to many others during this period through the ministry of the Seventy, whom He sent out two by two.

Period Seven: The Perean Ministry of Jesus Christ

A. Notable Events (John 10:40-42; 11:45-54).

Approximately three or four months before His crucifixion, Jesus withdrew across the Jordan River into the region of Perea.

He did return to Judea during this period, but the time was primarily spent in Perea (John 10:40). It was wise to get outside of the jurisdiction of the Great Sanhedrin because this group was determined to put Jesus to death.

B.   Notable Miracles (Luke 17:11-2l; 18:35-43; John 11:17-44).

Awesome displays of Christ's power were still seen in the last few months of His earthly ministry. The healing of blind Bartimaeus and the healing of the ten lepers occurred during this period. However, the most notable miracle was the raising of Lazarus from the dead. But even in that spectacular miracle the great division of attitude about Jesus was seen. Many believed, but others wanted to put Lazarus to death, along with the Lord Jesus.

C.   Notable Teachings (Luke 13:22–19:28).

A large number of parables were spoken during this period, as Jesus desired to communicate truth to believers while concealing the truth from the unbelievers. Parables given during this time included such well known ones as the lost sheep, the prodigal son, the unjust steward, and the unrighteous judge. Again the Lord spoke about discipleship, the delay of His kingdom, and His upcoming death and resurrection.

Period Eight: The Last Days of Jesus Christ

A.   His Sufferings.

Approximately twenty-five percent of the gospel records deal with the final, crucial eight days of Christ's life. The opposition against Christ reached its peak during the week of the Passover feast. The diabolical hatred of Jesus by the religious leaders was again and again revealed. Jesus answered all of their devious questions with great wisdom and discernment, yet they still wanted to destroy Him. Jesus gave His followers more important information in such teachings as the Upper Room discourse and the Olivet discourse. The gospel writers give us a glimpse of many events in those hours before the crucifixion, as Jesus went to the Garden of Gethsemane, prayed, and was arrested there, and as He faced the trials of the Jews and the Romans, and was condemned to die. They recorded the historical aspects of the single most important event in the story of mankind, the sacrificial death of the Son of God.

B. His Victory.

The gospel writers followed the story of Christ's sufferings with the accounts of His glorious triumph over Satan, sin, and death as He arose from the dead, appeared alive for forty days, and ascended into heaven. New life is now offered to mankind, and that is the "good news" that the gospel writers communicate to us.

THE RESURRECTION APPEARANCES OF CHRIST

#	Appeared to	Geographic Location	Time	Scriptures
1	Mary Magdalene	Jerusalem	Sunday	Mark 16:9-11 John 20:11-18
2	Some other women	Jerusalem	Sunday	Matthew 28:9-10
3	Peter	Jerusalem	Sunday	Luke 24:34 1 Corinthians 15:5
4	Emmaus disciples	Emmaus	Sunday	Luke 24:13-35
5	10 disciples	Jerusalem	Sunday	Mark 16:14 Luke 24:26-43 John 20:19-25
6	11 disciples	Jerusalem	A week later	John 20:26-31 1 Corinthians 15:5
7	7 disciples	Galilee	?	John 21:1-25
8	500 at one time	?	?	1 Corinthians 15:6
9	James (brother of Jesus)	?	?	1 Corinthians 15:7
10	11 disciples	Galilee	?	Matthew 28:16-20 Mark 16:15-18
11	11 disciples	Jerusalem	40 days later	Luke 24:44-53 Acts 1:3-12

CHRONOLOGY OF PASSION WEEK

Event	Day	Scriptures
Triumphal entry into Jerusalem	Sunday	Matthew 21:1-17; Mark 11:1-11; Luke 19:29-44; John 12:12-19
The cursing of the fig tree	Monday	Matthew 21:18-19; Mark 11:12-14
The cleansing of the Temple	Monday	Matthew 21:12-13; Mark 11:15-18; Luke 19:45-48
Debates with the religious leaders	Tuesday	Matthew 21:23—23:39; Mark 11:27—12:40; Luke 20:1-47
The Olivet Discourse	Tuesday	Matthew 24:1—25:46; Mark 13:1-37; Luke 21:5-36
Judas betrays the Lord	Tuesday	Matthew 26:14-16; Mark 14:10-11; Luke 22:3-6
No recorded events. Jesus at Bethany?	Wednesday	— — —
The Last Supper	Thursday	Matthew 26:17-29; Mark 14:12-25; Luke 22:7-20; John 13:1
The Upper Room Discourse	Thursday	John 13:2—14:31
Teachings on the way to Gethsemane	Thursday	John 15:1—18:1
In the Garden of Gethsemane	Thursday/ Friday	Matthew 25:30-46; Mark 14:26-42; Luke 22:39-46
Jesus is betrayed and arrested	Friday	Matthew 26:47-56; Mark 14:43-52; Luke 22:47-53; John 18:2-12

CHRONOLOGY OF PASSION WEEK (continued)

Event	Day	Scriptures
The trials of Jesus —before Annas —before Caiaphas —before the Sanhedrin —before Pilate —before Herod —before Pilate	Friday	John 18:13-24 Matthew 26:57-68; Mark 14:53-65; Luke 22:42 Matthew 27:1; Mark 15:1; Luke 22:66-71 Matthew 27:1, 11-14; Mark 15:1-5; Luke 23:1-5; John 18:28-38 Luke 23:6-12 Matthew 27:15-26; Mark 15:6-15; Luke 23:13-25; John 18:28— 19:16
The crucifixion of Christ	Friday	Matthew 27:27-56; Mark 15:16-41; Luke 23:26-49; John 19:17-30
The sayings from the Cross —Father, forgive . . . —Today, you shall be . . . —Woman, behold . . . —My God, My God . . . —I am thirsty. —It is finished. —Father, into Thy . . .	Friday	 Luke 23:34 Luke 23:43 John 19:26-27 Matthew 27:46; Mark 15:34 John 19:28 John 19:30 Luke 23:46
Jesus is buried	Friday	Mark 15:42-45; John 19:31-38

5

MATTHEW

INTRODUCTION TO MATTHEW

A. AUTHORSHIP OF MATTHEW

Since none of the gospel writers identify themselves in their writings, it is necessary to rely on the early church Fathers as well as on evidence that is within the gospels themselves. In the case of the first gospel, the church Fathers from earliest times unanimously testify that Matthew, the apostle of Christ, wrote it. "From earliest times, Matthew was recognized as the author of this gospel. A fragment from a lost work of Papias, Bishop of Hierapolis in Phrygia, about A.D. 130, is the earliest evidence."[1]

And many others, such as Justin Martyr, Irenaeus, and Jerome, agree that the first gospel was penned by Matthew. Also, although not being conclusive evidence, it is noteworthy that all the early copies of the first gospel have the heading "according to Matthew."[2]

In the gospel records there is very little specific information about the life and relationships of Matthew (who is also called Levi). He obviously is included in all the gospel texts where the Twelve were involved in the Lord's ministry. But there are just a few places where he is mentioned by name.

Before following Christ, Matthew was a tax collector for the Roman government. Tax collectors were highly unpopular with

1. Arthur Robertson, *Matthew* (Chicago: Moody, 1983), p. 8.
2. John F. Walvoord, *Matthew: Thy Kingdom Come* (Chicago: Moody, 1968), p. 9.

the Jews. They were employed by Rome and were generally regarded as thieves. The tax collectors (also called publicans) could assign an inflated value to the goods being taxed and thus raise the taxes of an individual. This was commonly done, and most tax collectors became wealthy from pocketing the extra revenue. The Jews, therefore, looked upon Jewish tax collectors as traitors to Israel, as well as thieves. Matthew had his tax collection booth on the busiest road in Palestine, the only ''truly international road of all those which passed through Palestine.''[3] This site, near Capernaum, not only brought great wealth to Matthew but also put him in a position where he would have had numerous exposures to the Lord Jesus. Matthew had undoubtedly heard Jesus and had been drawn to Him. Jesus knew that he was ripe for discipleship and called Matthew to join Him. Matthew left everything and followed Jesus (Luke 5:27-29).

> Matthew must have been the richest of the apostles. We should not miss the quiet heroism involved in this. If following Jesus had not worked out for the fishermen, they could have returned to their trade without difficulty. But when Levi walked out of his job he was through. They would surely never take back a man who had simply abandoned his tax office. His following of Jesus was a final commitment.[4]

After his call to follow Christ, he invited many of his fellow tax collectors to come and meet Jesus (Matt. 9:10-13). The only other places where Matthew's name is mentioned is in the four lists of the twelve apostles (Matt. 10:3; Mark 3:18; Luke 6:15; Acts 1:13).

The contents of the gospel of Matthew points to the possibility of it being written by Matthew, the tax collector.

> The skillful organization of the Gospel agrees with the probable interests and abilities of a tax collector such as the

3. Alfred Edersheim, *Sketches of Jewish Social Life in the Days of Christ* (Grand Rapids: Eerdmans, 1967), p. 42.
4. Leon Morris, *The Gospel According to St. Luke* (Grand Rapids: Eerdmans, 1982), p. 119.

apostle Matthew had been. So also does the fact that this is the only Gospel to contain the story of Jesus' paying the temple tax (17:24-27). The account of the call of Matthew to discipleship uses the apostolic name ''Matthew'' rather than the name ''Levi,'' used by Mark and Luke, and omits the possessive pronoun ''his,'' used with ''house (home)'' by Mark and Luke in describing the place where Matthew entertained Jesus at dinner. . . . These incidental details may well constitute telltale indications of Matthaean authorship and thus support the early church tradition.[5]

Over the years some scholars have debated the idea that Matthew's gospel was originally written in Hebrew and then was translated into Greek. This possibility is based on a statement made by Papias, an early church Father, who stated that Matthew recorded Christ's sayings in Hebrew.[6] But other scholars have pointed out that it is unlikely that Papias was referring to our gospel of Matthew. First, the gospel of Matthew, which is written in Greek, bears ''none of the characteristics of a translated work.''[7] Second, no such Hebrew (or Aramaic) gospel has been found. Third, Matthew could have written many of Christ's sayings in Hebrew for the benefit of the Jews without such a collection being the same as (or the basis of) his Greek gospel.

Conservative scholarship has agreed that whether or not there was an earlier Hebrew version, the present Greek version was Matthew's own work and that it is the inspired Word of God. Whatever earlier materials Matthew may have produced in his native tongue, the point is that the Greek gospel was inspired of God and bears the authority of being the Word of God.[8]

5. Robert H. Gundry, *A Survey of the New Testament*, rev. ed. (Grand Rapids: Zondervan, 1981), pp. 82-83.
6. W. Graham Scroggie, *A Guide to the Gospels* (Old Tappan, N. J.: Revell, 1962), pp. 131-33.
7. Walvoord, *Matthew: Thy Kingdom Come,* p. 10.
8. Ibid., p. 11.

B.   PLACE AND DATE OF MATTHEW

Conservative scholars are generally agreed that Matthew wrote prior to the destruction of Jerusalem in A.D. 70, because he speaks of that event as future. However, it is difficult to give an exact date for the writing.

The issue of the date of writing partly depends on whether or not Matthew was written before Mark, and thus was the very first gospel written. (See the discussion of the synoptic problem on pages 46-48.) Modern scholarship has generally held to the priority of Mark's gospel, believing that both Matthew and Luke borrowed heavily from Mark. But the evidence put forward for the priority of Mark is not as strong as many would suggest.[9] There is strong evidence from the church Fathers for the priority of Matthew. Their testimony is quite clear that Matthew was the first gospel written, followed by Mark, Luke, and John. Also it is logical that Matthew would be written early (and possibly first), because there was an immediate need for a gospel that was directed to the Jew, and Matthew's gospel had a Jewish audience in view.

Although an exact date is impossible to give, a date somewhere around A.D. 45-55 would be reasonable. It is also impossible to give the location of the writing, because the travels of Matthew are uncertain. Many hold to Jerusalem as the place where this gospel was written, whereas others suggest Antioch of Syria as a possibility.

C.   PURPOSE OF MATTHEW

Matthew was written to the Jews to demonstrate that Jesus of Nazareth is the King of the Jews. Matthew formed a connecting link between the Old Testament books and the writings of the New Testament. Matthew shows how the prophecies of the Old Testament were fulfilled in the Person and work of Jesus Christ.

9. Robert L. Thomas and Stanley N. Gundry, *A Harmony of the Gospels* (Chicago: Moody, 1978), pp. 274-79.

D.   BASIC OUTLINE OF MATTHEW

    I. The Presentation of Jesus the King (1:1–4:11)
       A. The Birth of the King (1:1–2:23)
       B. The Announcer of the King (3:1–l2)
       C. The Approval of the King (3:13–4:11)
    II. The Teachings of the King (4:12–7:29)
       A. The Ministry of the King (4:l2-25)
       B. The Sermon of the King (5:1–7:29)
    III. The Power of Jesus the King (8:1–11:1)
       A. His Power over Sickness (8:1-13)
       B. His Power over Disease and Demons (8:14-17)
       C. His Power over Men, Nature, and Demons (8:18-34)
       D. His Power to Heal and Forgive (9:1-17)
       E. His Power over Death (9:18-26)
       F. His Power over Physical and Spiritual Blindness (9:27-38)
       G. His Power to Proclaim the Good News (10:1–11:1)
    IV. The Opposition to Jesus the King (11:2–16:12)
       A. The Rejection of the King (11:2–12:50)
       B. The Parables of the Kingdom (13:1-52)
       C. Further Rejection of the King (13:53–16:12)
    V. The Preparation of the Disciples in View of the Rejection (16:13–20:34)
       A. Revelations in View of the Rejection (16:13–17:21)
       B. Instructions in View of the Rejection (17:22–20:34)
    VI. The Final Presentation of the King and the Final Rejection (21:1–27:66)
       A. The Public Ministry (2l:1-22)
       B. The Conflict with the Leaders of Israel (21:23–22:46)
       C. The Rejection of the Nation by the King (23:1-39)
       D. The Prophecies of the King (24:1–25:46)
       E. The Death of the King (26:1–27:66)

VII. The Great Proof of Jesus the King's Right to be King
(28:1-20)
A. The Resurrection Appearances (28:1-10)
B. The Attempted Cover-up (28:11-15)
C. The Great Commission (28:16-20)

E. THEME OF MATTHEW

Each of the gospel writers view the Lord Jesus Christ from a distinct perspective. Matthew presents Jesus of Nazareth as the Messiah, the King of the Jews. Matthew develops his theme of Jesus as King from the very beginning of his gospel. He shows that Jesus has the right ancestry to be king, because He comes from the royal line of King David. Matthew reaches back again and again into the Old Testament to demonstrate that Jesus fulfills the prophecies concerning the Messiah.

Matthew records the presentation to Israel of the King and the offer of His kingdom to them. But he reveals that Israel rejected her King and His kingdom in spite of the words and works that verified His claims. And even though that generation of Israelites rejected its king, Matthew shows his readers that the King will return one day to rule in great power and glory.

> More than any other of the Gospels, Matthew's is allied with the Hebrew Scriptures in theme and tone; their subjects are its subjects, the Messiah, Israel, the Law, the Kingdom, and Prophecy. Jewish ideas and terms characterize the whole record. Its witness would not have impressed either the Roman, for whom Mark wrote, or the Greek, for whom Luke wrote, but to Jews its significance would be inescapable.[10]

F. SPECIAL CONSIDERATIONS ON MATTHEW

1. Matthew's unique content
Each of the gospel writers selected material from the life of Christ to fit their own purposes. Naturally, some accounts or teachings would be selected by more than one author. (For exam-

10. Scroggie, *A Guide to the Gospels,* p. 248.

ple, all four of the gospel writers chose to include the miraculous "feeding of the 5,000.") But other material is found in just one gospel. In the case of Matthew, about forty-two percent of his material is unique; that is, forty-two percent is found nowhere else but Matthew. This forty-two percent includes miracles, teachings, and events.

Jesus worked hundreds of miracles, but only thirty-six are specifically detailed in the gospels. Out of those thirty-six miracles, Matthew records twenty, plus twelve passages that summarize Jesus' miracles (for example, 4:23-24; 8:16; 9:35). Out of the twenty miracles recorded by Matthew, only four are unique to his gospel: the healing of the two blind men (9:27-31), healing of the dumb demoniac (9:32-33), the deliverance of the blind and dumb demoniac (12:22), and the fish with the coin in its mouth (17:24-27).[11]

About 60 percent of Matthew's gospel is devoted to the teachings of the Lord Jesus. There are six major discourses in Matthew. It is difficult to determine how much of these discourses are totally unique to Matthew because many of the subjects given in these discourses are recorded in the other gospels. But the length of these discourses make Matthew different from Mark and Luke. (John also records lengthy teachings of Christ, but they are different discourses.) The six major discourses in Matthew are: the Sermon on the Mount (5:1–7:29), the charge to the twelve apostles (10:1-42), the kingdom parables (13:1-52), the teaching on greatness and forgiveness (18:1-35), the rebuke of the religious leaders (23:1-39), and the Olivet discourse (24:1–25:46).

There are twelve parables in Matthew that are unique, the majority of which are embedded in the six major discourses mentioned above. However, three are not in those major discourses. They are: the laborers hired for work in the vineyard (20:1-16), the man who called his two sons to work (21:28-32), and the king's wedding feast (22:1-14).

Matthew also includes certain events in his gospel that are not found elsewhere. Some of his unique contributions are:

11. Ibid., pp. 286-87.

- (a) The genealogy of Christ (1:1-17)
- (b) The story of the wise men (2:1-12)
- (c) The slaughter of the babies of Bethlehem (2:16-18)
- (d) The taking of the baby Jesus to Egypt (2:13-15, 19-23)
- (e) Peter's experience of walking on the water (14:28-33)
- (f) Christ's reply to Peter's confession (16:17-19)
- (g) Events related to Judas Iscariot (26:14-16; 27:3-10)
- (h) Events connected with the Resurrection (27:51-53)
- (i) The women's watch at the tomb (27:57-61)
- (j) The bribing of the soldiers at the tomb (28:11-15)
- (k) Christ's appearance to the women (28:9-10)

2. Matthew's use of the Old Testament

More than any other gospel writer, Matthew appealed to the Old Testament Scriptures. There are fifty-three direct quotations and seventy-six allusions to Old Testament language.[12] (There is some disagreement on the exact total). The majority of the quotes and allusions come from the lips of the Lord Jesus (eighty-nine out of the one hundred twenty-nine). The rest are part of Matthew's narrative.

It is interesting to note that in the vast majority of the quotes, the Old Testament was employed by Matthew and Christ in a literal sense, paying attention to the grammatical and historical meaning. "By far the major use of the Old Testament in Matthew was in its literal sense, without the allegorizing that characterized rabbinical exegesis. The comparatively few typological uses, to be found in the writer's own narrative portions, are not far-fetched, but reflect a sensitivity to the nature of prophecy."[13]

3. Matthew's use of the word *kingdom*

Since Matthew emphasizes Jesus as the King, it is not surprising that his gospel speaks often of the kingdom (about thirty-

12. Ibid., pp. 268-70.
13. Homer Kent, Jr., "Matthew's Use of the Old Testament," *Bibliotheca Sacra* 121 (January-March, 1964): 43.

eight times). The word for kingdom is the Greek word *basileia*. It is a noun that has the idea of "sovereignty," "dominion" or "rule."[14] As it is used in the Scriptures, it contains three basic elements: "First, a *ruler* with adequate authority and power; second, a *realm* of subjects to be ruled; and third, the actual exercise of the function of rulership."[15]

Generally the "kingdom" refers to God's rule over His creation. There are different aspects of this kingdom that are seen in Matthew.

(a) There is a spiritual kingdom (e.g., 6:33; 19:23). "The spiritual kingdom, which is closely related with God's universal kingdom, is composed of the elect of all ages, who have experienced a new birth by the power of the Holy Spirit. This kingdom can not be entered apart from such a new birth."[16] This aspect of the kingdom is always present, since the redeemed are always present.

(b) The word *kingdom* also has to do with the literal, earthly kingdom of the Messiah (also called the " millennium"). This earthly kingdom is a fulfillment of the covenant God made with King David (2 Sam. 7). It is the Lord Jesus who will, in the future, reign as king fulfilling God's promise. This phase of the kingdom was proclaimed to be "at hand" when Jesus came the first time (3:2; 4:17; 10:5-7). It was this aspect of the kingdom that was offered to Israel and was subsequently rejected by her. Although this earthly kingdom has a spiritual part to it, it is primarily a literal rather than an abstract concept. The Jews of Jesus' day knew that this kingdom was not present, but that it would come eventually.

(c) Another meaning of *kingdom*, as used by Matthew, is its mystery aspect as expressed in the kingdom parables (13:1-52). This form of the kingdom had not been revealed up to that point. But when Israel rejected Jesus as her Messiah-King, the offer of the literal kingdom was taken from that generation of Israel-

14. W. E. Vine, *An Expository Dictionary of New Testament Words* (London: Oliphants, 1963) 2:294.
15. Alva McClain, *The Greatness of the Kingdom* (Chicago: Moody, 1968), p. 17.
16. J. Dwight Pentecost, *Things to Come* (Grand Rapids: Dunham, 1964), p. 142.

ites (21:43) and another form of God's kingdom was introduced. There was a time period for the existence of this form of the kingdom.

> The time period covered by the parables in Matthew 13 extends from the time of Israel's rejection until Israel's future reception of the Messiah. This means this program began while Christ was still on the earth, and it will extend until His return to the earth when He comes in power and great glory. This period includes within it the period from Pentecost in Acts 2 to the Rapture, that is, the age of grace. . . . Although this period includes the church age, it extends beyond it, for the parables of Matthew 13 precede Pentecost and extend beyond the Rapture. . . . they show the hitherto unrevealed form in which God's theocratic rule would be exerted in a previously unrevealed age necessitated by Israel's rejection of Christ.[17]

It is true, therefore, that Matthew speaks of a present kingdom, but also of a form of the kingdom that is yet future. Jesus is king now, but His kingship lies in the future also.

A SUMMARY OF MATTHEW

I. The Presentation of Jesus the King (1:1–4:11)
    A. The Birth of the King (1:1–2:23)
    In order to establish clearly Jesus' claim to be Israel's king, Matthew begins his gospel by showing that Jesus' lineage was that of the kingly line of David (1:1-17). Beginning with Abraham and continuing on to David and then through to Joseph (who was Jesus' *legal* father), Matthew demonstrates that Jesus indeed had a legal claim to the throne. (Luke's genealogy traces the actual bloodline of Jesus back to David through Mary.)[18] Genealogically, Jesus of Nazareth was qualified to be Israel's king.

    In discussing the birth itself, Matthew twice states that Mary's conception was "of the Holy Spirit" (1:18, 20). Jesus was born of the virgin Mary and this was seen as a clear fulfill-

---

17. J. Dwight Pentecost, *The Words and Works of Jesus Christ* (Grand Rapids: Zondervan, 1981), p. 214.
18. Thomas and Gundry, *Harmony*, pp. 313-19.

ment of Isaiah 7:14. In the story, it is not clear what Mary did or did not tell Joseph about her pregnancy. It is clear that righteous Joseph did not accept her story and had determined to divorce (break the binding engagement contract) Mary privately, probably with the minimum number of two witnesses. Before he was able to divorce her, an angel appeared to Joseph confirming Mary's story and instructing Joseph to give Mary protection by immediately marrying her. Twice the instruction was given to name the baby *Jesus*, which means "Jehovah saves." Matthew's genealogy may have suggested to some that Jesus was to be a political leader and deliverer only, but the emphasis on His name was declaring that Messiah would also deliver His people spiritually by bringing them redemption (the New Covenant).

Sometime after the birth of Jesus, wise men (magi) from the East came seeking the newborn king of the Jews (2:1-12). These men, who were experts in studying the stars, had apparently been granted a supernatural sign in the heavens and had identified it as Messiah's star (2:2). The wise men assumed that Jerusalem was the place to go, and anticipated receiving additional information there. (It seems they were not familiar with Micah 5:2, which gives the birthplace of Messiah.) Eventually the wise men found the child Jesus in a house in Bethlehem and worshiped Him, presenting Him with valuable gifts. (This event probably took place a year or so after the birth of Jesus.) It may be that Matthew included this story of these Gentiles from the East coming to worship the Jew's king because it is an excellent picture of what will be the situation in the millennial kingdom when the Gentiles worship the Messiah of Israel.

Because of King Herod's hatred for this newborn "rival" to his throne, the wise men were instructed to return home without informing Herod of the exact location where Jesus could be found. In a rage, King Herod tried to eliminate Jesus by destroying all the very young children of Bethlehem (2:13-18). But Joseph had been warned in a dream to flee to Egypt with Mary and Jesus. Later, upon returning from Egypt, Joseph was instructed to stay away from Judea and return to Galilee to live (2:19-23).

B. The Announcer of the King (3:1-12)

Nothing is given in Matthew about the childhood of Jesus. His account picked up the story some thirty years after the birth narrative. Matthew's gospel focuses next on the ministry of John the Baptist. John came announcing the nearness of Messiah's kingdom. This kingdom was not present but was "at hand" (3:2). John's message boldly proclaimed that personal repentance was necessary in order to be part of this kingdom. The Jews assumed that because they were God's chosen people, of the bloodline of Abraham, that they were automatically part of Messiah's kingdom (3:8-9). John baptized those who did repent of their sins in preparation for Messiah's coming.

C. The Approval of the King (3:13–4:11)

When Jesus appeared at the Jordan River to be baptized, John resisted the idea, knowing that Jesus had nothing to repent of. But Jesus pointed out to John that He needed to be baptized because He needed to fulfill all of God's righteous requirements (3:15). Jesus had been circumcised, paid His tithes, attended the annual feasts—and everything else prescribed by the law had been obeyed. John's baptism was an addition to the requirements of God and Jesus needed to fulfill all God's requirements. John saw the wisdom of His reasoning and baptized Jesus. When Jesus came up out of the water, the Holy Spirit in the form of a dove came upon Him. Just as kings were anointed with oil in the Old Testament (symbolizing the Holy Spirit coming upon them), so Jesus was being set apart as Israel's king on this occasion. He did not receive the symbolic anointing oil, but rather received the reality of the Spirit's fullness (cf. John 3:34).

After the baptism, Jesus was led by the same Holy Spirit into the Judean wilderness to be tested by Satan. He passed the tests and revealed that He was morally and spiritually qualified to be Israel's king.

II. The Teachings of the King (4:12–7:29)

A. The Ministry of the King (4:12-25)

Matthew began his discussion of the ministry of Christ with Jesus' return to Galilee and the establishing of His "base of operations'' at Capernaum. Approximately one year had gone by since the temptation of Jesus. Matthew summarized that year by noting that Jesus called disciples to assist Him in the ministry and that Jesus was preaching and performing many miracles.

B. The Sermon of the King (5:1–7:29)

John the Baptist had declared the nearness of Messiah's kingdom and the need to repent in order for that kingdom to come. In the Sermon on the Mount (5:1–7:29), Jesus the king taught the people of Israel how to get into His kingdom. He made it clear that they had to be righteous (5:20) even to the point of being perfect (5:48). In the Beatitudes (5:3-12), He taught the need to sorrow for sin and to recognize their total spiritual poverty if they were to be part of His kingdom. (Note that entrance into any facet of God's kingdom is based on faith.) In the Sermon, many of the requirements and rewards of kingdom living are given. This great message of King Jesus has many applications to life today, but the message is primarily directed to the Jews of Jesus' day in relationship to the coming Messianic kingdom.

III. The Power of Jesus the King (8:1–11:1)

In this section Matthew gives examples of Christ's power and authority. There is no chronological order in this section as he takes examples from various times in the ministry of Christ and brings them together in this section. His authority over men and His power over demons and disease are noted.

The miracles of Christ were designed to alert the leaders of Israel to the fact that Messiah had come. (See appendix, *Note C: Miracles in the Gospels and Acts.*) For example, when He healed a leper (8:2-4), Jesus instructed the man to show himself to the priest as the law prescribed. This would be a witness to the priest of Messiah's presence. When Jesus healed a paralytic (9:1-8), it was to verify His claim that He had the authority to forgive sins. Those who heard Him understood the seriousness of such a claim.

The miracles of the King also were a foreshadowing of His kingdom. Isaiah 35 and other prophetic passages said that disease and deformity would be absent in Messiah's kingdom. It is not suprising, therefore, to observe that Christ's miracles often had to do with the blind seeing, the lame walking, the deaf hearing, and other kinds of disease and deformity being removed (e.g. 8:14-17; 9:1-7, 32-35). Also, Messiah's kingdom would flourish without the presence of Satan and his forces. During the millennial kingdom Satan and the demons will be placed into the abyss where they will have no influence (Rev. 20:1-3). Many of Christ's miracles reflected that reality yet to come. Again and again His power and authority over demons was evidenced. (e.g. 8:16, 28-34).

In this section, the need for faith is again emphasized. The blessings of the coming kingdom are inseparably linked to personal faith (e.g. 8:9-13, 26; 9:2, 22, 29).

IV. The Opposition to Jesus the King (11:2–16:12)
    A. The Rejection of the King (11:2–12:50)

During all of His ministry the Lord Jesus had experienced resistance by some in Israel. But now the opposition had increased greatly and come to a significant level. Matthew begins this section by speaking of the rejection of Messiah's forerunner, John the Baptist (11:2-19). And in light of the opposition to John the Baptist and to Himself, Jesus "began" to pronounce woe on those who had heard His words and had seen His works (11:20). The opposition increased as the religious leaders charged Him with being a lawbreaker, because He "broke" the law of the Sabbath (12:1-14; cf. John 5:1-18). (Actually Jesus only broke their traditions related to the Sabbath.) This was a key issue in the rejection of Jesus by the Pharisees.

A critical moment arrived in Christ's ministry when Jesus met a man who was blind and dumb as a result of demonic activity. Jesus powerfully cast out the demon and thus removed the blindness and dumbness of the man. This spectacular demonstration of the power of God was rejected by the Pharisees. They did not deny that a miracle had taken place, but they said that Jesus did His miracles in the power of Satan (12:22-24).

> In this charge the vindictive opposition of the religious rulers of Israel reached a new plateau beyond which it could not go. . . . to admit the genuineness of His miracles, which had been foretold in their own Scriptures, and then to charge Him with having done these things by the powers of hell, thus as-

cribing wickedness to their own incarnate Messiah—this was something new and terrible among the many sins of the chosen nation. And the charge provoked from the Son of God an ultimatum of such unparalleled severity that it stands alone in the gospel records as an appropriate witness to the awful possibilities of human sin in the face of the light of God's grace.[19]

Once the leaders took this position that Jesus' miracles were done in the power of Satan and that He was a representative of the Devil, the course of opposition was clearly charted. "This incident, then, marked the great turning point in the life of Christ. From this point on to the cross the nation is viewed in the Gospels as having rejected Christ as Messiah. The unofficial rejection by the leaders would become official when finalized at the cross."[20]

The consequences of this decision not only affected the future of the nation but also altered the ministry of Christ in several ways. First, Christ's teaching methods changed. He now began to use parables, whereas before He "spoke plainly." Second, His miracles were no longer designed to be signs for the nation but were for the benefit of individuals. Third, the focus of His ministry shifted from the large crowds and onto His chosen followers. And fourth, Jesus began to speak of the church and His death and began to teach in light of the rejection.

B. The Parables of the Kingdom (13:1-52)

An important question would now have arisen: "Because Israel has rejected the Messiah, what will happen to the kingdom program?" The Messianic kingdom was part of an irrevocable covenant and, therefore, it could not simply be abandoned. Matthew 13 outlines the kingdom program in light of the rejection of Christ. This aspect of the kingdom (in Matthew 13) was not revealed in the Old Testament and so is referred to as "the mysteries of the kingdom" (13:11). This aspect of the kingdom of God began at the rejection of Christ and will continue on until the Second Coming of Christ.

There were nine parables given by Christ in this section with the first five spoken publicly and the final four addressed to just

19. McClain, *The Greatness of the Kingdom*, p. 313.
20. Pentecost, *Words and Works*, p. 208.

the disciples in a house. These parables teach that there will be a sowing of the Word of God throughout this period, but that there will also be a counter sowing by Satan's forces. The kingdom will grow large outwardly during this age, but there will be inner corruption of doctrine. Nevertheless, the Lord will buy for Himself a peculiar treasure (Israel) and a priceless treasure (the church). This age will end in separation and judgment.

C. Further Rejection of the King (13:53–16:12)

In spite of Jesus' clear teaching and great miracle working, the opposition continued to grow. The people of Nazareth rejected Him (13:53-58), Herod Antipas put John the Baptist to death (14:1-13), and the leaders of Israel continued their assault on Him (15:1-14; 16:1-12). At this point Jesus began to withdraw with His disciples to places outside the jurisdiction of the Jews.

V. The Preparation of the Disciples in View of the Rejection (16:13–20:34)

With the opposition growing and with the cross looming in the near future, Jesus taught His men many needed truths. He revealed again that He was Messiah, the Son of God (16:13-16), but that He must die (16:21-26). He spoke of the church that was going to be built (16:17-20), as well as a wide variety of other topics, such as forgiveness, divorce, and spiritual authority (17:22–20:34). Perhaps the most significant lesson was taught at the Transfiguration, where three of the disciples saw something of Jesus' glory (16:28–17:9). This event showed that God approved of Jesus even though men rejected Him and it was also a foreshadowing of the glory of Christ when the Messianic kingdom comes. It must have been a great encouragement to Jesus and His followers and something they never forgot (cf. 2 Pet. 1:16-18).

VI. The Final Presentation of the King and the Final Rejection (21:1–27:66)

A. The Public Ministry (21:1-22)

With the Passover feast only a few days away, Jesus returned to Jerusalem to formally present Himself as Messiah. The "triumphal entry" was the public declaration that He was Israel's king, fulfilling Zechariah 9:9 (21:1-17). Furthermore, His cleansing of the Temple was part of His formal presentation as He possessed the Father's Temple in the name of the Father (21:12-13). He healed the sick, thus demonstrating once again His authority (21:14). And the final act of His presentation was to receive praise from the people (21:15-17). But because He had been rejected already, He withdrew from Jerusalem. His cursing of the fig tree was a symbolic act. That generation of Israelites, represented by the fig tree, was under the judgment of God.[21]

B. The Conflict with the Leaders of Israel (21:23–22:46)

On Tuesday of the final week, the leadership of Israel pointedly challenged the authority and the teachings of Jesus. Jesus responded to their questions with amazing insight, but also with serious warnings of the extreme danger that the leaders and the nation were in.

C. The Rejection of the Nation by the King (23:1-39)

In response to His rejection by the scribes and the Pharisees, the Lord Jesus delivered one of the most blistering denunciations of these men in all of the gospel records. He publicly rebuked them for their pride, hypocrisy, and spiritual blindness. But even in His message of judgment, the Lord's compassion was seen (23:37-39).

D. The Prophecies of the King (24:1–25:46)

After His conflict with the leaders, Jesus left Jerusalem and crossed over the brook Kidron and sat down on the Mount of Olives. Here the disciples asked Him a series of questions about the future and about His coming to rule. The Lord Jesus responded with the "Olivet Discourse," the only lengthy prophetic sermon recorded in the gospels. The basic outline of this discourse is as follows.

1. The setting of the sermon (24:1-3)
2. The first half of the Tribulation period (24:4-8)
3. The second half of the Tribulation period (24:9-25)
4. The Second Coming of Christ (24:26-30)
5. The gathering of Israel at the end (24:31)
6. A parenthetical exhortation to watchfulness (24:32-51)
7. Judgments of the living at the end of the Tribulation (25:1-46)

---

21. Pentecost, *Things to Come,* p. 460.

E. The Death of the King (26:1–27:66)

Along with the other gospel writers, Matthew records many of the events preceding the crucifixion of Christ, including the betrayal by Judas, the arrest in Gethsemane and the trials before the Jews and the Romans (see the chart on pages 72-73).

A climax to Matthew's gospel is reached when he records the placing of the superscription ''THIS IS JESUS THE KING OF THE JEWS'' (27:37) above the cross. That superscription, placed there by the Roman governor Pilate, spoke volumes about the reality of what was happening in Israel.

VII. The Great Proof of Jesus the King's Right to Be King (28:1-20)

The resurrection of Jesus Christ was (and is) the great proof of the Father's acceptance of Christ's work and of Christ's right to rule. His claims were clearly demonstrated to be valid because of the resurrection (see the chart on page 71 for the resurrection appearances of Christ). One day Jesus will return to claim His kingdom as ''King of kings and Lord of lords'' (Rev. 19:16). But until that day, His followers are to go out with His authority and proclaim the good news (28:19-20).

NEW TESTAMENT JERUSALEM

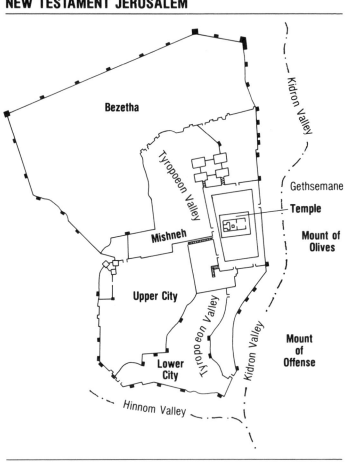

6

MARK

Introduction to Mark

A.   AUTHORSHIP OF MARK

Although there is no statement of authorship within the second gospel, the witness of the early church uniformly assigns it to Mark. Papias, Irenaeus, Clement of Alexandria, Origen, and Jerome all state that Mark wrote this gospel.

> [This tradition of Mark as the author] goes back to the beginning of the second century and is derived from the three centers of early Christianity, Asia, Rome (with Gaul), and Alexandria. The validity of this tradition is strengthened by the fact that there is no reason it should have been assigned to a minor character like Mark if he did not write it. The ancient caption to this gospel, *Kata Markon* (''according to Mark'') supports this uniform tradition.[1]

Mark is first mentioned by name in Acts 12:12 (''John who was also called Mark''). Like many in his day he was known by two names. John was his Hebrew name and Mark (Marcus) was his Latin name. Three times in the New Testament he is mentioned with both names being used (Acts 12:12, 25; 15:37); twice he is spoken of as John (Acts 13:5, 13); and five times as Mark (Acts 15:39; Col. 4:10; Philemon 24; 2 Tim. 4:11; 1 Pet. 5:13). Though not mentioned by name, many commentators believe that

---

1. D. Edmond Hiebert, *The Gospel of Mark* (Chicago: Moody, 1974), p.11.

Mark was the "young man" who fled from the Garden of Gethsemane on the night of the Lord's arrest there (Mark 14:51-52).

Mark lived in Jerusalem and was the son of a widow who
lived there also. Apparently his mother was fairly wealthy. "It is
very probable that his mother was a person of some substance
since, according to Acts xii, her house was regarded as a *rendez-
vous* for many members of the primitive Church."[2]

Mark was a nephew of the well-known church leader, Barnabas (Col. 4:10). When Barnabas and Paul left Jerusalem to return
to Antioch of Syria after the so-called famine visit, they brought
Mark with them (Acts 12:25). Then, when Paul and Barnabas left
on their first missionary journey, Mark went along as their helper
(Acts 13:5). However, for reasons unknown, he abandoned the
missionary expedition before the work was done, much to Paul's
displeasure. Later, when a second missionary journey was proposed by Paul, Barnabas wanted to take Mark again. Paul refused
and the two parted company with Barnabas taking Mark on a missionary journey to Cyprus (Acts 15:36-39).

About eleven years went by before Mark is again mentioned
in Scripture. By that time Mark had proved himself to Paul and
was called a "fellow worker" (Philemon 24). At that time Paul
also wrote to members of the church at Colossae and sent greetings to them from Mark (Col. 4:10). When Paul was released
from his Roman imprisonment (where he wrote Colossians and
Philemon), he left Rome, but apparently Mark stayed there and
ministered among the believers there. Mark then joined with the
apostle Peter when he came to Rome (1 Pet. 5:13). "This association with both Peter and Paul is a most significant feature about
him."[3] After this Mark is again mentioned by Paul as Paul faced
death in his second Roman imprisonment (2 Tim. 4:11). Paul
viewed him as "useful" for service. It is quite evident that Mark
overcame initial failure and became a valued minister of the gospel of Christ.

2. Donald Guthrie, *New Testament Introduction* (London: Tyndale, 1966), p. 67.
3. Ibid.

B. PLACE AND DATE OF MARK

Although several dates have been suggested for the gospel of Mark, a date of about A.D. 64-68 seems probable. This is based to a large extent on a statement made by the church Father Irenaeus. He stated that Mark wrote the gospel after the death of Peter. Since Peter died in the persecutions of the Emperor Nero (which began in A.D. 63), the earliest date would be A.D. 64.

It is generally accepted that Mark wrote his gospel in Rome with a Roman audience in mind. This was the uniform view of the early church and the content of the gospel of Mark would be supportive of such a tradition. "He translated Aramaic expressions for the benefit of his readers (3:17; 5:41; 7:34; 14:36; 15:34). Even more indicatively, he explained Greek expressions by their Latin equivalents (12:42; 15:16) and used a number of other Latin terms."[4] "More substantial evidence for a Roman origin comes from Mark's reference to Simon of Cyrene as 'the father of Alexander and Rufus'(15:21). This is most naturally to be understood as meaning that these men were personally known to Mark's readers. Romans 16:13 indicates that Rufus was a member of the church at Rome."[5]

C. PURPOSE OF MARK

Mark's purpose in writing his gospel was to give to the Romans a view of Jesus Christ that would fit their way of thinking. He wished to present the Savior, the Son of God, in such a way that they would be won to Him (1:1). Clement of Alexandria (a church Father of the late second century) said that the gospel of Mark was written in response to a request by the Romans for a written account of Christ's life and ministry. The Romans were (it is said) so moved by the oral preaching of the gospel that they wanted it in writing so that they could go over it again and again.[6]

4. Robert H. Gundry, *A Survey of the New Testament*, rev. ed. (Grand Rapids: Zondervan, 1981), p. 79.
5. Hiebert, *The Gospel of Mark*, p. 15.
6. W. Graham Scroggie, *A Guide to the Gospels* (Old Tappan, N. J.: Revell, 1962), p. 185.

D. BASIC OUTLINE OF MARK

    I. The Presentation of the Lord's Servant (1:1-13)
      A. His Forerunner, John the Baptist (1:1-8)
      B. His Baptism (1:9-11)
      C. His Temptation (1:12-13)
    II. The Manifestation of the Lord's Servant (1:14–3:6)
      A. His Preaching Ministry in Galilee (1:14-22)
      B. His Healing Ministry in Galilee (1:23-45)
      C. His Conflicts with the Scribes (2:1–3:6)
    III. The Opposition to the Lord's Servant (3:7–8:13)
      A. The Increasing Popularity of the Servant (3:7-20)
      B. The Increasing Opposition to the Servant (3:21-35)
      C. The Teaching in Light of the Opposition (4:1-34)
      D. The Many Works of the Servant (4:35–8:13)
    IV. The Instructions to the Disciples in View of the Opposition (8:14–10:52)
      A. Instructions in Galilee (8:14–9:50)
      B. Instructions on the Way to Jerusalem (10:1-52)
    V. The Rejection of the Lord's Servant (11:1–15:47)
      A. His Triumphal Entry into Jerusalem (11:1-26)
      B. His Disputes with the Leaders (11:27–12:44)
      C. His Prophetic Teaching (13:1-37)
      D. The Preparatory Events (14:1-11)
      E. The Passover Meal (14:12-25)
      F. The Garden of Gethsemane (14:26-52)
      G. The Trials of Jesus (14:53–15:20)
      H. The Crucifixion (15:21-41)
      I. The Burial (15:42-47)
    VI. The Resurrection of the Lord's Servant (16:1-20)

E. THEME OF MARK

Jesus is presented as the ''Servant of the Lord,'' a theme found in the Old Testament prophets (e.g., Isa. 42:1, 53:1-11; Zech. 3:8). Mark wrote a gospel that emphasized what Christ did, as the Servant of the Lord. This would appeal to the Roman who was a man of action with little concern for Hebrew prophecy or

Greek philosophy. Mark emphasized the powerful deeds of Christ and had relatively little to say about the words of Christ. (People are interested in what a servant can do, but are not particularly interested in what a servant says.) Christ's mighty miracles and helpful ministries to people are the focus of this gospel. Mark 10:45 is both a climax and a summary of this gospel: "The Son of Man did not come to be served, but to serve, and to give His life a ransom for many."

F. SPECIAL CONSIDERATIONS ON MARK

1. Mark's writing style

Mark's gospel is a gospel of action, perhaps reflecting the personality of his mentor, the apostle Peter. Mark wanted to communicate the amazing, relentless activity of Jesus Christ rather than His teachings. As a result, Mark's writing is brief, abrupt, vivid, and very much to the point. In the 678 verses that constitute Mark's gospel, the word *and* is used more than 1,300 times, giving the impression that Mark is in a hurry to tell his story. More than 40 times he states that something took place "immediately" or "straightway." About 150 times Mark uses the *historic present* tense of the verb. The historic present is a more vivid way of relating an event—representing an action as presently going on and not yet finished. For example, Mark said that "Jesus seeing their faith" (2:5); and "hearing this, Jesus said" (2:17). (In contrast, Matthew and Luke, describing the same event as Mark, would usually use the simple past tense to indicate that an event had happened.)

Mark's style is, therefore, quite forceful. Also, he used double negatives for emphasis, picturesque detail, and vivid statements to communicate his message graphically. The striking brevity of this gospel, coupled with its descriptive style, would have spoken to the Roman mind.

2. The content of Mark's gospel

The gospel of Mark is not only the shortest gospel, but it also has the least amount of unique material in it. It is estimated that only seven percent of Mark's material is unique to his gospel, with ninety-three percent of Mark's material found in the other gospels. The fifty or so verses that are unique to Mark are scattered throughout the gospel. They add detail to the parallel accounts found in the other gospels. Only two miracles are unique to Mark: (1) the healing of the deaf and dumb man (7:31-37), and (2) the healing of the blind man at Bethsaida (8:22-26). Only two parables are unique to Mark: (1) the sprouting seed (4:26-29), and (2) the doorkeeper (13:34-37). There are no major discourses of Christ found only in Mark.

3. Mark's relationship with the apostle Peter

Bible scholars are in general agreement that Mark's gospel is, in a sense, the apostle Peter's gospel. Although not everything came from Peter, the strong tradition has been that Peter was the greatest influence on Mark in the penning of the second gospel. Early tradition declared that Mark was the "interpreter" of Peter, writing down the words and deeds of the Lord Jesus Christ as Peter related them.[7] The idea being that as Mark accompanied Peter, he wrote down Peter's messages.

> The general outline of this gospel conforms to the outline of the gospel story as given by Peter in Acts 10:34-43. Thus there may be some ground for regarding the gospel as a catechetical expansion of the preaching of the Apostle Peter. But there is no need to assume that when Mark commenced the writing of his gospel, he deliberately restricted himself to a reproduction of Peter's preaching. It must be remembered that Mark was acquainted with the preaching of the apostles in Jerusalem from early days. Peter's preaching indeed was the main source upon which he drew, but he also knew considerable about Jesus before he became Peter's assistant.[8]

In 1 Peter 5:13, the apostle Peter spoke of Mark as his "son." And Acts 12:12-17 says that Peter was well-known in the household of Mark, as that text describes how the servant-girl Rhoda recognized Peter's voice. This would certainly suggest that Mark knew Peter and his preaching from the earliest days of the church, as Peter was apparently a frequent visitor in the home.

7. Guthrie, *New Testament Introduction*, p. 66.
8. Hiebert, *The Gospel of Mark*, p. 14.

SUMMARY OF MARK

I. The Presentation of the Lord's Servant (1:1-13)

In harmony with his theme of Jesus as the Servant, Mark hurriedly introduces the ministry of Christ. He does not mention Christ's preexistence, ancestry, birth, or His early years. These matters would be relatively unimportant for a servant, since the interest is always on what a servant can do, not where he came from. In an abbreviated manner Mark quickly summarizes the ministry of John the Baptist and the baptism and temptation of Christ in order to get into the work of Jesus, the Servant of the Lord. (Note that Luke devotes 183 verses to this same material that Mark summarizes in 13 verses.)

II. The Manifestation of the Lord's Servant (1:14–3:6)

In this section Mark picks up the ministry of Christ when it is about one year along. He summarizes Christ's preaching (1:14-15), speaks of a calling of the four fishermen (1:16-20), and then begins to relate a number of Christ's miracles (such as the healing of a paralytic and the cleansing of a leper). These and other miracles were a clear demonstration of Christ's authority.

III. The Opposition to the Lord's Servant (3:7–8:13)

Although this section continues to relate Christ's powerful deeds, it also reveals the mounting opposition to the Lord Jesus. The critical charge of His enemies that He was working miracles in the power of Satan is found here (3:22-30), as is the rejection of Jesus by the people of Nazareth (6:1-6). This section reveals that as Jesus was becoming well known, many people came to believe in Him, but it also shows that many of the religious leaders were standing against Him.

IV. The Instructions to the Disciples in View of the Opposition (8:14–10:52)

As opposition increased Jesus spoke more often of His death and the need to face the rigid requirements of true discipleship. Much of His teaching was in answer to questions posed by His disciples (e.g. 9:11 and 9:18), or in situations where the disciples obviously needed instruction (e.g. 8:32-38; 10:35-45). On other occasions events were teaching devices used by the Lord (such as the Transfiguration, 9:2-8, and the curing of the epileptic boy, 9:17-29).

V. The Rejection of the Lord's Servant (11:1–15:47)

As with the other gospels, Mark's focus is on the last week of Christ's life when the rejection of the Lord Jesus climaxes at the crucifixion. Mark, along with the other gospels, relates the events of the triumphal entry, the arrest in Gethsemane, the trials of Christ, and other matters leading up to the death of Christ. Mark views the death of Christ as the greatest work of the Servant of the Lord. Although Mark does not add much new detail here, he does give some helpful time notations, which aids our understanding of the sequence of events in the Passion Week.

VI. The Resurrection of the Lord's Servant (16:1-20)

Mark ends his gospel with this great proof that Jesus is able to save— He rose from the grave! He records the appearance of angels to the women and the declaration that the Lord Jesus has risen from the dead.

Note: Mark 16:9-20 is a disputed section of Scripture because it is missing from some early Greek manuscripts. Based on that manuscript evidence and the statements of some church Fathers, many scholars believe these verses are not authentic but instead were added later. Many other scholars view these verses as Scripture because the majority of ancient manuscripts includes them.

> These last twelve verses of Mark are not found in the two oldest Greek manuscripts of the New Testament, Vaticanus and Sinaiticus (fourth century). Eusebius, writing in the same century, says that they were lacking ''in almost all the existent copies of the Gospel . . . the accurate ones at all events.'' Jerome (about A.D. 400) says that they were found ''in a few Gospels'' and were missing in ''almost all the Greek copies.''[9]

There are in the manuscripts of Mark several different endings to the gospel. It is uncertain, therefore, if the gospel of Mark

9. Ralph Earle, *Mark* (Chicago: Moody, 1970), p. 126.

ends at 16:8 or if one of the variations might reflect the true ending of this gospel. Currently there is no definitive answer to this problem. It should be observed, however, that this is a textual problem and not an issue of inspiration. The question is not the inspiration of Mark's gospel (it is inspired of God), but rather if 16:9-20 was part of that original, inspired gospel. It should also be noted that the essential contents of 16:9-20 are found in other portions of the Scriptures.

7

LUKE

Introduction to Luke

A.   Authorship of Luke

From earliest times the church has held that the third gospel was written by Luke, even though his name is not mentioned in the gospel itself. Most scholars are in agreement that the author of the third gospel is the same individual who penned the book of Acts. Both books are written to someone named Theophilus, both are similar in language and style, and the latter refers to the former.[1] It is also clear that the writer of these two books was a companion of the apostle Paul, as the "we" sections of Acts indicate (Acts 16:10, 11; 20:5; 21:1). In these sections of Acts, the author is personally involved in the journeys of Paul. The question then becomes one of identifying the right companion of Paul, and thus identifying the author of these two books. Luke was a close companion of Paul as several Scriptures indicate (Col. 4:12-14; 2 Tim. 4:11; Philem. 24). After noting all of Paul's known companions and after analyzing all the historical data, Luke is the one who best fits the scriptural information.[2]

Tradition also affirms the author to be Luke. There is unanimous testimony from the early church Fathers that Luke, who was from Antioch of Syria, wrote the third gospel. Irenaeus (about

1. Norval Geldenhuys, *Commentary on the Gospel of Luke* (Grand Rapids: Eerdmans, 1966), p. 15.
2. Leon Morris, *The Gospel According to St. Luke* (Grand Rapids: Eerdmans, 1982), pp. 16-17.

A.D. 185), Justin Martyr (about A.D. 150), the Muratorian Canon (about A.D. 195), and a number of other sources agree that the author of the third gospel was Luke.[3]

Medical language points to Luke the physician as being the author. Being a physician, Luke was well educated and thus capable of writing in the good Greek style of this gospel and the book of Acts. Some have suggested that since Luke was from Antioch of Syria, he probably would have gone to the closest university for his training, and that was at Tarsus. It is further suggested that Luke came to a knowledge of the Savior while there, being influenced by another young intellectual from Tarsus, one by the name of Saul. This, of course, is speculation, though it is within the realm of possibility.

Luke was a close friend and companion of the apostle Paul. Luke joined Paul at Troas on Paul's second missionary journey. On that journey, Luke evidently stayed at Philippi (Acts 16), after Paul founded the church there, and was a key in the ministry of that new church. Paul continued on his journey but returned to Philippi some six years later on his third missionary trip. At that time, Luke rejoined him and journeyed on to Palestine with him. During that six-year period at Philippi, Luke not only ministered to the church there but evidently was Paul's representative in Macedonia. Some believe that Luke is the "brother" noted for his excellence in the gospel ministry in that area (2 Cor. 8:18).[4] Luke remained with Paul for the two years of Paul's imprisonment at Caesarea and then accompanied him to Rome (Acts 28).

Luke himself was a Gentile believer, as the context of Colossians 4 would indicate. (Luke was not included in the list of those of the "circumcision"—that is, Jews.) Luke is therefore the only Gentile writer of Scripture. The two books that he wrote amount to about twenty-five percent of the New Testament.

---

3. W. Graham Scroggie, *A Guide to the Gospels* (Old Tappan, N. J.: Revell, 1962), p. 335.
4. Merrill C. Tenney, *New Testament Survey* (Grand Rapids: Eerdmans, 1961), p. 173.

B. PLACE AND DATE OF LUKE

Unlike many of the books in the New Testament, the exact date of Luke is difficult to determine. Over the years a number of possibilities have been suggested. Of these possibilities, two are most probable. One view is that Luke was written around A.D. 58 from the city of Caesarea while Paul was imprisoned there. A second possibility is that it was written from Rome shortly before A.D. 65. Most scholars believe that the book of Acts was written before the fall of Jerusalem in A.D. 70 and Luke's gospel was written before Acts. Therefore, a date of A.D. 58 or A.D. 65 would be possible.

C. PURPOSE OF LUKE

In the introduction to his gospel, Luke explains clearly his purpose for writing. He wrote to present an historically accurate and chronologically correct account of the life and ministry of Jesus Christ. He wanted his readers to be well grounded in their faith.

D. BASIC OUTLINE OF LUKE

    I. The Prologue of Luke's Gospel (1:1-4)
    II. The Coming of Jesus the Son of Man (1:5–4:13)
        A. His Entrance into the World (1:5–2:52)
        B. His Presentation to Israel (3:1–4:13)
    III. The Ministry of Jesus the Son of Man (4:14–9:50)
        A. His Ministry Begins (4:14-30)
        B. His Authority Demonstrated (4:31–6:11)
        C. His Disciples Chosen (6:12-49)
        D. His Multifaceted Ministry (7:1–9:50)
    IV. The Ministry of Jesus the Son of Man in Times of Rejection (9:51–19:27)
        A. His Final Journey to Jerusalem (9:51-62)
        B. His Instruction in View of His Rejection (10:1–19:27)

V. The Suffering and Sacrifice of Jesus the Son of Man
   (19:28–23:56)
   A. His Triumphal Entry (19:28-44)
   B. His Debates with the Leaders (19:45–21:38)
   C. His Betrayal and Arrest (22:1-54)
   D. His Trials (22:54–23:25)
   E. His Death (23:26-56)
VI. The Final Authentication of Jesus the Son of Man (24:1-
   53)
   A. His Empty Tomb (24:1-12)
   B. His Emmaus Disciples (24:13-35)
   C. His Resurrection Appearances (24:36-49)
   D. His Ascension into Heaven (24:50-53)

E.   THEME OF LUKE

The four gospels view Jesus Christ from four different van-
tage points. Luke views Jesus Christ as a man, a real human being. Jesus Christ was the perfect man—a picture of unfallen man.
Luke uses the phrase ''son of man'' twenty-four times in his gospel. This title is the one that Jesus used most frequently of Himself. The phrase ''son of man'' emphasizes His humanity, and
Jesus used it especially when referring to His suffering and death.
It is also clear that Jesus used the expression because of its important connection with Daniel 7:13, where the phrase is obviously
messianic. This was a phrase, therefore, that emphasized both His
humanity and His messiahship.[5]

Luke seems to have a special audience in mind as he writes,
namely the Greek. Luke's approach and view of Christ would appeal to the Greek, who was constantly looking for the ideal man.
Luke presents and describes the sinless, perfect ''son of man.''

Luke's gospel brings out the wider implications of the gospel
of Jesus Christ—salvation is not just for the Jew, but it is also for
the Gentile.

5. Geldenhuys, *Gospel of Luke*, p. 352.

F.   SPECIAL CONSIDERATIONS ON LUKE

Each of the four gospels has unique features as each tells its story of the life of Jesus Christ. More than fifty percent of Luke's gospel is unique, containing materials found nowhere else. Without Luke, certain periods of Christ's life would be unknown to us. Luke alone gives certain important chronological notations (2:1; 3:2; 3:23). Luke has a greater focus on individuals than do the other gospels. For example, Luke mentions thirteen women not found in the other gospels. It can also be said that Luke's gospel has a more comprehensive range than the others. It begins with the announcements concerning the births of John the Baptist and Jesus, and ends with a reference to the ascension of Christ.

1. Miracles that are unique to Luke

It is impossible to say how many miracles Jesus Christ performed during His ministry. That is because many are referred to collectively and because many were probably never recorded (John 20:30; 21:25). There are thirty-six miracles specifically detailed in the gospels, twenty of which are found in Luke. Of the twenty in Luke, the following seven are unique to this gospel.[6]

   (a)   The miraculous catch of fish (5:1-11)
   (b)   The raising of the widow's son (7:11-17)
   (c)   The casting out of a demon (11:14)
   (d)   The healing of a crippled woman (13:10-17)
   (e)   The healing of a man with dropsy (14:1-4)
   (f)   The healing of the ten lepers (17:11-19)
   (g)   The restoring of Malchus' ear (22:49-51)

2. Parables that are unique to Luke

The teachings of Jesus were full of illustrations from life. Many of Christ's illustrations could be classified as parables. But of those that are extended narratives there are some fifty-one ''parables'' spoken by Christ. Needless to say, this number is not fixed because there is much disagreement as to what constitutes a parable. However, of the fifty-one so classified, thirty-five are found in Luke, and the following nineteen of those are unique to his gospel.

6. Scroggie, *A Guide to the Gospels,* pp. 349-53.

(a)   The two debtors (7:41)
(b)   The good Samaritan (10:30)
(c)   The friend at midnight (11:5)
(d)   The rich fool (12:13)
(e)   The watching servants (12:35)
(f)   The faithful steward (12:41)
(g)   The barren fig tree (13:6)
(h)   The chief seats (14:7)
(i)   The great supper (14:16)
(j)   The unfinished tower (14:28)
(k)   The unwaged war (14:31)
(l)   The lost coin (15:8)
(m) The prodigal son (15:11)
(n)   The unfaithful steward (16:1)
(o)   The rich man and Lazarus (?) (16:19)
(p)   The unprofitable servants (17:7)
(q)   The unrighteous judge (18:1)
(r)   The Pharisee and the publican (18:9)
(s)   The pounds (19:11)

3. Events that are unique to Luke

Some occurrences in Christ's life and some of His recorded teachings are very similar. However, in spite of their close similarity to one another, a careful analysis reveals that they took place at different times or locations. Listed below is a group of events that are not in the category of parables or miracles but are incidents recorded only by Luke.

(a)   The announcements of the births of John and Jesus (1:5-56)
(b)   The accounts of the births of John and Jesus (1:57–2:20)
(c)   The presentation of the baby Jesus in the Temple (2:21-38)
(d)   The story of Jesus at age twelve (2:39-52)
(e)   The dating of the start of John the Baptist's ministry (3:1-2)
(f)   The impact of John's ministry (3:10-15)
(g)   The genealogy of Jesus (3:23-38)

(h) Christ's rejection at the Nazareth synagogue (4:15-30)

(i) The anointing of Jesus in the house of Simon (7:36-50)

(j) The women who ministered financially to Christ (8:1-3)

(k) James and John desiring to call down fire on Samaritans (9:51-56)

(l) The sending out of the Seventy (10:1-12)

(m) Christ at the home of Mary and Martha (10:38-42)

(n) Christ entertained by a Pharisee (11:37-54)

(o) Discourse to a large crowd (12:1-53)

(p) Pilate's murder of some Galileans (13:1-5)

(q) Teaching on the number to be saved (13:22-30)

(r) Teaching on discipleship (14:25-35)

(s) Questions about the kingdom (17:20-37)

(t) Christ's conversation with Zacchaeus (19:1-10)

(u) Christ's warning to the disciples (22:31-38)

(v) Events in Gethsemane (22:43-44)

(w) Christ's trial before Herod (23:6-12)

(x) Christ's words to the women of Jerusalem (23:27-31)

(y) The repentant thief (23:39-43)

(z) Christ's appearance to the Emmaus disciples (24:13-35)

(aa) Details of His appearance to the eleven (24:37-49)

(bb) Christ's ascension (24:50-53)

SUMMARY OF LUKE

I. The Prologue of Luke's Gospel (1:1-4)

Luke directs his gospel to "most excellent Theophilus" (1:3). This title suggests that this Gentile friend of Luke was a man of high official position. Luke's purpose in writing to Theophilus was to give him (and all the readers of this gospel) the assurance that the faith he had embraced rested on a sure and solid historical foundation. The phrase "in consecutive order" (1:3) suggests that Luke's presentation would be done in a logical way, with the probability that the gospel would reveal an accurate chronological order as well.

Luke apparently used three sources in gathering material for his gospel. First, he studied many of the written documents that were available—documents written by many who had heard Christ's teachings and had seen His miracles (1:1). Second, Luke spoke with eyewitnesses of Christ's ministry (1:2). And third, he received information from the "servants of the Word" (1:2). Many Bible scholars believe that these individuals, with the approval of the apostles, functioned as tradition bearers; that is, they passed on in a fixed form truths about Christ during those years before the inspired gospel records were written.[7]

II. The Coming of Jesus the Son of Man (1:5–4:13)
   A. His Entrance into the World (1:5–2:52)

Luke records the breaking of the divine silence that had existed since the days of Malachi. When God sent the angel Gabriel to announce the births of John the Baptist and Jesus, the "four hundred silent years" ended.

Gabriel appeared in the Temple one day to tell an old priest by the name of Zacharias that he and his wife Elizabeth would have a son. This child would not be an ordinary child, for he was to be the prophesied forerunner of the long-awaited Messiah (Isa. 40:3; Mal. 3:1). The child would be instrumental in pointing many Israelites to God (1:15-17). When the child, John the Baptist, was born it became clear to many in Israel that God was indeed beginning to work again among His people.

In the sixth month of Elizabeth's pregnancy (1:24-26), Gabriel made his second appearance. He came to a young girl of Nazareth by the name of Mary and startled her with the news that she was to be the mother of the Messiah. Gabriel told Mary that the conception of the child would not be by means of normal sexual relations, but rather the creator God would generate life within her womb (1:35). Her child would not only be her physical son (truly man), but He would be the "Son of God" (truly deity). He was to be called Jesus ("the Lord is salvation"), which pictured His great work of redeeming mankind. Furthermore, He would

7. Paul N. Benware, *Luke* (Chicago: Moody, 1985), pp. 26-27.

reign on the throne of David over the nation of Israel, fulfilling the great Davidic Covenant (2 Sam. 7). These words of Gabriel regarding the glorious kingdom reign of Jesus the Messiah will be fulfilled someday when He comes a second time as King of kings and Lord of lords.

Several months after the birth of John the Baptist, Jesus was born. Luke informs his readers that God used a Roman decree to move Mary and her husband Joseph from Nazareth to Bethlehem, in order to fulfill the prophecy regarding the birthplace of the Messiah (Mic. 5:2). The birth of Jesus was announced by heavenly angels (2:9-11) to shepherds near the birthplace, and they became the first human announcers of Messiah's birth.

In the years that followed His birth, there was normal growth and development in Jesus. Jesus experienced normal development mentally, physically, spiritually, and socially (2:40-52). Evidently no one thought of Him as unusual or anything more than a common man. The people of His day certainly did not point to Him and exclaim, "There is God!"

B. His Presentation to Israel (3:1–4:13)

Because Jesus of Nazareth was apparently "ordinary," it was necessary to have the ministry of John the Baptist. John pointed out to Israel that Jesus was the Messiah. John's message was designed to prepare the nation of Israel spiritually for His appearance. In a relatively few months John's ministry and message affected the nation in a powerful way (3:1-20).

John baptized Jesus in the waters of the Jordan River (3:21-22). This act publicly identified and set apart Jesus as the Messiah of Israel. (See Matthew's account for greater detail.)

Jesus, after His baptism, went into the wilderness where He was tempted for an entire forty-day period by Satan, who sought in many ways to bring Jesus into sin (4:1-13). The temptation revealed that Jesus was morally and spiritually qualified to be the Messiah and the redeemer of mankind.

III. The Ministry of Jesus the Son of Man (4:14–9:50)

A. His Ministry Begins (4:14-30)

As Luke begins his record of the ministry of Jesus Christ, he gives two general verses about that ministry. Luke mentions the two major elements of Jesus' ministry, His teaching and His miracle working ("the power of the Spirit"). It is important to recognize that Luke's summary verses (4:14-15) are actually summarizing a full year of the Lord's ministry. (Only John's gospel gives information about the first year of Christ's ministry.) So when Luke begins his account of Christ's ministry, he actually is starting about one year after the events of the baptism and the temptation.

The first specific incident recorded by Luke was the teaching by Jesus in His hometown synagogue of Nazareth (4:16-30). Using Isaiah 61, Jesus declared that He fulfilled this messianic prophecy. Disbelief was the general response of the hearers, and Jesus confronted this unbelief. But this account revealed that Jesus would indeed experience opposition in His ministry, fulfilling the prophecy given when He was a baby (2:34-35).

B. His Authority Demonstrated (4:31–6:11)

The town of Capernaum, located on the northern shore of the Sea of Galilee, became the base of operations for the Lord Jesus' ministry for the next year. Because many men had come along claiming to be Messiah or some representative of God, it was necessary for Jesus to authenticate His claims. In order to do that, Jesus performed powerful miracles in the power of the Holy Spirit. This portion of Luke's gospel records a number of such demonstrations of power. Jesus demonstrated His authority over demons (4:31-37), over sickness and disease (4:38-44), over nature (5:1-11), over leprosy (5:12-13), and even over men and their traditions (5:13–6:11).

C. His Disciples Chosen (6:12-49)

Jesus had hundreds of disciples, and from this large group He selected twelve. These twelve He named apostles (ones "sent with authority"). This was a momentous decision, as Jesus would be spending much of His time and energies training these men for a future ministry of great significance.

D. His Multifaceted Ministry (7:1–9:50)

In this section Luke emphasizes both the words and the works of the Lord Jesus. But in doing so he reveals the amazingly wide spectrum of people that Jesus successfully ministered to. He ministered effectively to a grieving widow (7:11-17) and a repentant prostitute (7:36-50). He dealt with a Roman centurion (7:1-10) and fearful disciples (8:22-25). He instructed the great and the lowly (8:40-56). With insight He ministered to a man of God and a man of Satan (7:18-35; 8:26-39). No social status or rank hindered Jesus from effective ministry.

IV. The Ministry of Jesus the Son of Man in Times of Rejection (9:51–19:27)

A. His Final Journey to Jerusalem (9:51-62)

At this point in Luke's gospel the Lord Jesus left Galilee and headed for Jerusalem. On a number of occasions Luke specifically states that Jesus' objective was Jerusalem (9:51-53; 13:22, 33; 17:11; 18:31; 19:11, 28). The exact itinerary of the journey is not clear as Luke is not precise in many details of chronology and location. But Luke is clear that from the time Jesus left Galilee, the cross and His sufferings were central in His thinking. The extent of time from this point in Luke's gospel to the crucifixion is about three or four months.

This section is one of Luke's most significant contributions to our knowledge of the ministry of Christ. In this section, Luke deals largely with the teachings of Christ, just as he emphasized the works of Christ in the previous portion. Many parables and teachings of Christ are found here and nowhere else, such as those priceless stories of the Prodigal Son and the Good Samaritan.

The following chart illustrates something of the emphasis and contribution of Luke to our understanding of the life and ministry of Christ.

CHRONOLOGICAL EMPHASIS IN LUKE'S GOSPEL

Chapters in Luke	1:1—2:52	3:1—9:50	9:51—19:27	19:28—24-53
Time involved	About 30 years	3 years	3-4 months	8 days

B. His Instruction in View of His Rejection (10:1–19:27)

As the Lord's ministry rapidly drew to a close, there were still many towns and villages that He had not ministered in. As a result of this need, He sent out seventy of His disciples, in groups of two, to preach and to heal. Later, Jesus Himself would come, but this initial contact gave these places an opportunity to be prepared for the Lord's personal coming (10:1-24).

This three-month period was particularly used to instruct those who were already His followers, preparing them for the difficult days ahead. Many of the Lord's most notable teachings are found in this period, such as His instructions on prayer (11:1-13), discipleship (14:25-35), the lost (15:1-32), wealth (16:1-31), salvation (18:15-30), and the kingdom (19:11-27).

V. The Suffering and Sacrifice of Jesus the Son of Man (19:28–23:56)

A. His Triumphal Entry (19:28-44)

When Jesus entered Jerusalem riding on a donkey (fulfilling the Old Testament prophecy in Zech. 9:9), there were deep, but mixed, feelings about Him. Many loved Him and saw Him as the Messiah or at least as a prophet of God. But many others hated Him and desired to see Him dead. However Jesus knew that it was necessary for Him to have this "triumphal entry" so that He could present Himself publicly to Israel. Because the nation had already rejected Him, the primary purpose of this event was to fulfill prophecy.

B. His Debates with the Leaders (19:45–21:38)

Because the leaders did not have a solid case against Jesus, they attempted to ask Him questions or put Him in difficult situations in order to catch Him saying something offensive or heretical. However, when all the questioning was over, it was the religious leaders and not Jesus who looked bad.

C. His Betrayal and Arrest (22:1-53)

The Jewish authorities did not have much of a case against Jesus and were, therefore, quite happy when Judas Iscariot, one of Jesus' own followers, decided to betray Him for some money. The plot reached its fruition when Jesus was arrested by His enemies (with Judas leading the mob) in the Garden of Gethsemane.

D. His Trials (22:54–23:25)

Before He would finally be placed on the cross, Jesus would go through six trials (see chart on page 73). Three of them were before the Jewish authorities and three were before the Romans. Luke records five of them, omitting the first one before Annas. The trials were, of course, mockeries of true justice and should never have taken place. Nevertheless, Jesus was finally condemned and sentenced to death on a cross.

E. His Death (23:26-56)

Even while heading toward His own death on the cross, Jesus warned the nation of Israel of coming judgment. And even on the cross itself, Jesus' concern for others was seen as He spoke encouraging words to the repentant thief.

VI. The Final Authentication of Jesus the Son of Man (24:1-53)

A. His Empty Tomb (24:1-12)

There can be no doubt that the resurrection of Jesus Christ permeates the entire New Testament and is the foundation on which the Christian faith is built (1 Cor. 15:12-20). Perhaps one of the greatest evidences of the resurrection is seen in this chapter of Luke—the radical change that occurred in the lives of the disciples who went from depression to joy and from fear to boldness. This chapter also records several of the resurrection appearances of Christ. (See the chart on Christ's resurrection appearances on page 71.)

B. His Emmaus Disciples (24:13-35)

Only Luke tells the story of these two disciples who met the resurrected Christ on the Sunday evening of the day of resurrection. After coming to understand the Scriptures as never before because of His instruction and after coming to realize that Jesus was actually alive, they became two of the very first witnesses of the resurrection of Christ.

C. His Resurrection Appearances (24:36-49)

In this section Luke records several of Christ's appearances to the group of the disciples. He particularly focuses on His body—it was the same body, yet it was different. He could be touched and He could eat food, yet He was able to appear and disappear.

D. His Ascension into Heaven (24:50-53)

The Lord's earthly ministry was over. Now the Lord God, who had taken on the form of a man more than thirty years before was now returning to His rightful glory with the Father. His followers could not help but praise and worship Him.

Luke began and ended His gospel in the Temple, but what a change had taken place. The Old Covenant had been set aside, and the New Covenant with all its hope, power, and reality had been established.

8

JOHN

INTRODUCTION TO JOHN

A. AUTHORSHIP OF JOHN

No verse in this gospel records the name of the author. However, the traditional view that the author was John the apostle has very early support. Irenaeus (A.D. 120-202) and Theophilus of Antioch (A.D. 115-188) both testify that John was the author of this fourth gospel. Irenaeus' witness is particularly interesting since he claims to have received his information from Polycarp, a disciple of the apostle John himself.[1] Although a few have proposed alternate views of authorship, the evidence strongly supports John the apostle as the author.[2]

The evidence within the gospel itself confirms the idea that the apostle John wrote it. The author was clearly an eyewitness of the ministry of Christ. He states that he was an eyewitness of the glory of the Lord Jesus (1:14), he viewed the crucifixion (19:35) and, as a disciple, he wrote this gospel (21:24). Based on a normal rendering of John 21:20, the author is "the disciple whom Jesus loved," the one who leaned on Jesus' breast at the Last Supper. Of the three closest disciples who could possibly fit that description (Peter, James, and John), John is the choice. Peter is not possible, since he is distinguished from "the disciple whom

---

1. Homer Kent, Jr., *Light in the Darkness* (Grand Rapids: Baker, 1974), pp. 15-17.
2. Donald Guthrie, *New Testament Introduction* (London: Tyndale, 1966), pp. 216-43.

Jesus loved'' in the text itself. James cannot qualify because James died too early for the story to circulate that he would not die (as mentioned in 21:23).[3]

Other lines of evidence are also followed in order to demonstrate that the author was the apostle John. It is noted that the author was a Palestinian Jew who clearly possessed a knowledge of Jewish customs, Jewish history and Palestinian geography. It is also observed that the author gave the kind of detail that only an eyewitness could have made.[4]

With strong external and internal evidence pointing to the apostle John as the author, it is possible to say a number of things about the man himself. John was one of the sons of Zebedee. Along with their father and their partners, Peter and Andrew, they fished the Sea of Galilee (Mark 1:19-20; Luke 5:10). Apparently their fishing business was prosperous enough to have hired help (Mark 1:20). John's mother was Salome, who was probably a sister to Mary, the mother of Jesus (cf. Matt. 27:55-56; Mark 15:40; John 19:25).

Most likely John was a disciple of John the Baptist before he began to follow Christ (John 1:40). After following the Lord Jesus for over a year, he was selected along with eleven others to have a special relationship with the Lord Jesus as His apostles (Luke 6:12-16). He became part of Christ's ''inner circle'' and was allowed to witness the events of the Transfiguration (Luke 9:28), the raising of Jairus's daughter (Luke 8:51), and the private moments in the Garden of Gethsemane (Mark 14:33). He was the only apostle actually to witness the crucifixion (John 19:26). After the church began, John ministered alongside Peter on several occasions (Acts 3:1–4:22; 8:14-17) and became a significant part of the Jerusalem church (Gal. 2:9). As an old man he was exiled to the island of Patmos by the Roman government because of his testimony for Christ (Rev. 1:9). Here he wrote the book of Revelation, the final book of the New Testament.

3. Kent, *Light in the Darkness,* p. 18.
4. Guthrie, *New Testament Introduction,* pp. 224-28.

B.   PLACE AND DATE OF JOHN

As is the case with the other gospels, differing views exist as to the date and the place of composition. However, the best evidence points to a late date, near the end of the first century, perhaps around A.D. 85-95. It is noted by many that the content of John's gospel strongly suggests that John assumed that his readers were familiar with the synoptic gospels, thus placing John well after the synoptics. The fact that 92 percent of John's material is not found in the synoptics reveals that John consciously avoided repeating their material.

Certain details within the gospel of John point to a later date. (For example, it must have taken some time for the false story about John not dying to circulate around the church [21:23].) And, once again, the testimony of the church Fathers is valuable. For example, Irenaeus stated that John wrote the gospel while living in Ephesus, which mandates a later date because John did not go there until later on toward the end of the first century.

The place of the writing is generally thought to be Asia Minor, and most likely Ephesus. "It was apparently written in Gentile surroundings, for the feasts and usages of the Jews are explained for the benefit of those who were unfamiliar with them (John 2:13, 4:9, 19:31)."[5]

So it can be concluded that an aged apostle John, reflecting a mature viewpoint, wrote the fourth gospel late in the first century from Asia Minor.

C.   PURPOSE OF JOHN

John clearly states his purpose for writing this gospel (20:30-31). It was written to evangelize. John presents evidence so that people might come to the point where they believe in Jesus Christ with the result that they would receive eternal life.

---

5. Merrill C. Tenney, *New Testament Survey* (Grand Rapids: Eerdmans, 1961), p. 189.

D. BASIC OUTLINE OF JOHN

    I. Introduction (1:1-51)
        A. The Person of Jesus Christ (1:1-18)
        B. The Announcer of Jesus Christ (1:19-28)
        C. The Presentation of Jesus Christ (1:29-34)
        D. The Disciples of Jesus Christ (1:35-51)
    II. The Ministry of Presentation to the Nation (2:1–12:50)
        A. The Beginning (2:1-25)
        B. The Early Ministry (3:1–4:54)
        C. The Person (5:1-47)
        D. As the Bread of Life (6:1-71)
        E. As the Water of Life (7:1-53)
        F. As the Light of the World (8:1–9:41)
        G. As the Good Shepherd (10:1-42)
        H. As the Resurrection and the Life (11:1-57)
        I. The Final Presentation (12:1-50)
    III. The Ministry of Instruction to the Disciples (13:1–17:26)
        A. Concerning Service (13:1-38)
        B. Concerning Future Fellowship (14:1-31)
        C. Concerning Relationships (15:1–16:4)
        D. Concerning the Holy Spirit (16:5-33)
        E. Through Prayer (17:1-26)
    IV. The Ministry of Redemption to the World (18:1–19:42)
        A. The Humiliation and Suffering (18:1–19:16)
        B. The Crucifixion and Burial (19:17-42)
    V. The Ministry of Revelation to the Believers (20:1–21:25)
        A. The Revelation of Himself (20:1-31)
        B. The Revelation of His Power (21:1-25)

E. THEME OF JOHN

It has been noted already that each of the four gospel writers views the Lord Jesus Christ from a different perspective. John presents Jesus Christ as God. Throughout the gospel, he demonstrates the deity of Jesus Christ. The gospel begins with the declaration that Jesus is God (1:1) and ends with the climactic statement of Thomas proclaiming that Jesus is Lord and God (20:28).

Jesus Himself made claims about who He was, sometimes clearly stating His oneness with the Father and sometimes making it clear that He is greater than ordinary man, sustaining a relationship with the Father that is unique or doing things that only God does. (For examples, see 2:16; 3:13; 5:17-25; 6:35-38; 6:46 and 1:18; 8:18-19; 8:46-58; 9:35-37; 10:15; 10:18; 10:28-36; 11:25-26; 13:19; 14:1; 14:6; 14:7-11; 14:20; 15:23; 16:7; 16:15; 17:1-6; 17:21-23; 18:6; 19:7; 20:23.) Added to these are the miracles He performed that are designed to demonstrate that He is the Son of God.

F.   SPECIAL CONSIDERATIONS ON JOHN

1. Salvation in the gospel of John

Because the gospel of John was written to bring people to a saving knowledge of Jesus Christ, it has important truths to communicate regarding the doctrine of salvation.

(a) It is balanced. There is a wonderful balance in this gospel between God's work in man's salvation and man's need to respond. In twenty-one passages salvation is seen as an act of God as He is the one who selects and draws men to Himself (e.g. 5:21; 6:37; 6:44). In some twenty-five passages the emphasis is on man's need to respond and to believe (e.g., 1:12; 3:14-16; 5:24). John makes no attempt to blend these truths together. He simply states both to be true. Man may have a problem putting these truths together, but the all-wise God has no such difficulty.

(b) It is gracious. Salvation is presented as the free gift of God (e.g., 3:16; 4:10). Salvation is not something man works for, but it is something to be received. Jesus' work on the cross was totally sufficient to pay for all of man's sin (19:30). Man does not contribute to his salvation by works of any kind.

(c) It is available. John is clear that salvation comes to those who believe in Jesus Christ (20:31). The word *believe* (Greek: *pisteuo)* is used ninety-nine times in the gospel of John, usually in the phrase ''believe in'' or ''believe that.'' ''PISTEUO . . . to believe, also to be persuaded of, and hence, to place confidence in, to trust, signifies, in this sense of the word, reliance upon, not mere credence.''[6]

Saving faith, then, carries with it the idea of trust. It is that attitude of complete reliance on Christ and on Him alone for salvation. Saving faith is that which appropriates the gift of salvation. (For example, the woman at the well was to ''drink'' of the water of life, 4:14; and the people were to ''eat'' of the bread from heaven, 6:51.) The important point was to receive or appropriate what was being offered. Saving faith has three elements.

> (1) Faith has an intellectual element—certain facts must be known and believed (20:31).
> (2) Faith has a volitional element—a rational choice is made to trust in Christ as Savior.
> (3) Faith has an emotional element—the sense of the need of a Savior because of one's separation from God, one's ''lostness.'' For John, the basic sin that man must turn from is the sin of unbelief.

(d) It is efficacious. John emphasizes the fact that saving faith brings eternal life. (He speaks of eternal life some thirty-five times.) Eternal life is the present possession of the one who believes (5:24). Eternal life is not simply endless existence, since even the unsaved will experience that. Eternal life is a new and different quality of life—it is the life of God.

John, then, presents salvation as a free gift that comes to man through the one and only Savior, Jesus Christ (14:6). The God-man alone can give eternal life based on His totally sufficient work on the cross. For men to receive the gift of eternal life, they must ''believe in Him.''

2. John's unique contribution

It has been noted earlier that ninety-two percent of John's gospel is unique. The fact that John omits a number of significant events in Christ's life (such as the temptation and Transfiguration) and parallels the other three gospels only eight percent of the time, strongly suggests that John was quite familiar with the content of the synoptics. Such a large percentage of unique material

6. W. E. Vine, *An Expository Dictionary of New Testament Words* (London: Oliphants, 1963) 1:116.

makes it impossible, in this study, to detail all this distinctive material. But there are some areas that should be mentioned.

(a) Seven signs. John records a total of seven sign miracles that were meant to help bring a person to faith in Christ. Of these, five are found only in John.

(1) The water being changed into wine (2:1-11)
(2) Healing the nobleman's son (4:46-54)
(3) Healing the man by the pool (5:1-9)
(4) Healing the bind man (9:1-7)
(5) The raising of Lazarus from the dead (11:38-44)

(b) Feast days. John's gospel is uniquely helpful in establishing a chronology of the ministry of Christ. John's notation of the various feast days makes this possible.

CHRONOLOGY OF CHRIST'S MINISTRY

Reference	Feast	Time Before the Crucifixion
2:13	Passover	3 years
5:1	Passover (or the Feast of Tabernacles)	2 Years (or 1½ years)
6:4	Passover	1 year
7:2	Tabernacles	6 months
10:22	Dedication	3 months
12:1	Passover	Same day

(c) Christ's discourses. John's uniqueness is seen in the many discourses of Christ that he records. While he omits some, such as the Sermon on the Mount, he includes many not found in the synoptics.

(1) The new birth (3:3-21)
(2) The water of life (4:10-26)
(3) The Person and work of Christ (5:17-47)
(4) The bread of life (6:32-59)
(5) The light of the world (8:12-20)
(6) True faith (8:32-58)

(7) The good shepherd (10:1-18)
(8) His oneness with the Father (10:25-39)
(9) The Upper Room discourse (14:1–16:33)

SUMMARY OF JOHN

I. Introduction (1:1-51)

A. The Person of Jesus Christ (1:1-18)

In developing his theme that Jesus Christ is God, John immediately declares His deity (1:1). John proclaims three essential truths about Christ: (1) He is eternal (''In the beginning *was* the Word''), (2) He is distinct from God (the Word was *with* God), and (3) He is identical in essence with God (''Word *was* God''). John stated that Christ is the Creator of all things, which is a profound declaration of His deity (1:3 with Gen. 1:1). In discussing who Jesus Christ is, John spoke of a point in time when this eternal God became flesh—adding true humanity to deity (1:14). John presents Jesus Christ as the God-man.

B. The Announcer of Jesus Christ (1:19-28)

John leaves out any discussion of the birth and childhood of Jesus and begins his account of Christ's life with the ministry of John the Baptist. John the Baptist made a great impact on the nation of Israel, so much so that he was questioned by the religious leaders as to his person and his purposes. John made it clear that he was not the Christ, but simply the announcer of the Christ.

C. The Presentation of Jesus Christ (1:29-34)

In this paragraph, John recorded John the Baptist's recollections of the baptism of Jesus, that time when Jesus was identified as the Messiah and anointed as Israel's savior and king.

D. The Disciples of Jesus Christ (1:35-51)

It is probably with great fondness that John wrote this section, remembering his own first encounter with the Lord Jesus. In this account, there were five men who met Jesus for the first time. These five, who were disciples of John the Baptist, would later be part of the twelve apostles.

II. The Ministry of Presentation to the Nation (2:1–12:50)

John began his discussion of the ministry of Christ by relating those events which took place very soon after Christ's baptism and temptation. (Note that the synoptics do not discuss this first year of Christ's ministry.) Once Jesus was set apart as Israel's Messiah and anointed with the Holy Spirit (3:34), He worked His first miracle to begin to verify that He was indeed Messiah. The changing of the water into wine at the wedding in Cana was the first of His many miracles (2:1-11). In speaking of the miracles of Christ, John used the word *semeion*.

> *Semeion* . . . when applied to a miracle, usually implies that the deed is an indication of some power or meaning behind it to which it is secondary in importance. . . . John, then, presented the miracles not merely as supernatural deeds nor as manifestations of supernatural power, nor even as exceptions to the usual current of events, but definitely as material witnesses to underlying spiritual truth. . . . Furthermore, these deeds bespoke something unusual in Christ's personality, and were themselves signposts pointing in the direction of something new.[7]

When He began to work miracles (2:11), He was immediately noticed by the religious leaders. At first, most of these leaders seemed favorable toward Him (3:2), but that would rapidly change.

The first year of the Lord's ministry was highlighted by His first cleansing of the Temple, His interview with Nicodemus, and His discussion with the Samaritan woman (2:13–4:42).

Knowing that the synoptics recorded a great deal of Christ's activity during the second year of His ministry, John moves rather quickly through that time period. However, four out of the seven signs given in this gospel, as well as the very important discourses on Christ's Person and work, and the Bread of Life sermon were all parts of the second year of Christ's ministry. Although John does not include a great deal of material from this period, he does talk about the two strategic issues that generated a great hatred for Christ among the religious leaders: (1) His claims of deity and a special relationship with the Father, and (2) His working on the

7. Merrill C. Tenney, *John, the Gospel of Belief* (Grand Rapids: Eerdmans, 1976), pp. 29-30.

Sabbath day. The religious leaders believed that Jesus was guilty of blasphemy and on a number of occasions tried to kill Him for it. They also viewed Him as a law breaker, violating God's Sabbath law. (Jesus, of course, did not break God's laws, but did go against the traditions of the Pharisees.) These issues were major ones and would (from a human point of view) be the issues that put Jesus on the cross.

John's account of the third year of Christ's ministry revolved around His teachings, such as the Good Shepherd, the Light of the World, and the Resurrection and the Life (7:1–11:57). Not only are the messages themselves important, but the responses of the people to the messages are significant. John makes it clear that as Christ's ministry progressed, the opinion about Jesus of Nazareth increasingly became polarized. Fewer and fewer people stayed neutral about Him. Jesus was seen as being from God or He was thought to be an agent of Satan. The public ministry of Christ is summarized by John in 12:36-43.

III. The Ministry of Instruction to the Disciples (13:1–17:26)

The last week before the crucifixion was primarily spent with the disciples. The highlight of that week in John's gospel is the night before the crucifixion. That night was spent celebrating the Passover with the disciples. In those hours with His disciples Jesus revealed many new truths concerning the Holy Spirit, the church, and the disciples' relationship with Him. This section ends with Christ's great prayer (17:1-26). Jesus especially prayed for the unity, sanctification, and protection of His people.

IV. The Ministry of Redemption to the World (18:1–19:42)

After spending His final hours with His men, Jesus went to the Garden of Gethsemane. After spending time in prayer, His enemies came and arrested Him. Here and elsewhere in his gospel, John leaves no doubt that Jesus allowed Himself to be arrested and crucified. He knew ahead of time what was going to happen and was not a victim of circumstances. He was in charge and He voluntarily gave Himself for man's salvation. It is important to see the following texts: 2:4, 19; 3:14; 6:51, 64; 7:6, 8, 30; 8:20; 10:11, 15, 17, 18; 12:23, 27; 13:1, 3, 11; 14:2; 18:4, 11; 19:28,

30. These passages clearly point out that Jesus was not a helpless martyr, that He was not caught by surprise, and that men had no power against Him, except what He allowed them to have. (See the chart on pages 72-73 for the order of events during the Passion week and for John's contribution to that time period.)

V. The Ministry of Revelation to the Believers (20:1–21:25)

John includes four of the eleven known resurrection appearances of Christ. (See the chart on page 71 for the list of resurrection appearances.) The only one unique to John is the Lord's appearance to the seven disciples by the Sea of Galilee.

John concluded his gospel with information not recorded elsewhere (21:1-25). This epilogue to the gospel is intended to clarify the roles of the apostles and the relationship of Christ to His followers.

Part 3

The Acts:
The New Covenant Proclaimed

9

ACTS

INTRODUCTION TO ACTS

The book of Acts is the only historical record of the birth and the early days of the church. While some of the activities of the apostles and others who spread the gospel of Christ can be gleaned from the New Testament letters, the book of Acts is our primary source of information on what took place during those first thirty years of the church's existence.

A. AUTHORSHIP OF ACTS

Both internal evidence within Acts and the external evidence of church tradition declare Luke to be the author. It is the unanimous testimony of church tradition that Luke authored the book of Acts. "Certainly Clement of Alexandria, Tetullian, and Irenaeus, all speak of LUCAS or S. Luke as the author, as if there was no doubt upon the subject. The Muratorian Canon tells us that the acts of all the apostles were written in one book: Luke compiled them for the most excellent Theophilus because they severally took place in his presence."[1]

The book of Acts itself contains evidence that Luke was the author. It is clear that the author was a companion of the apostle Paul. This is seen in the "we" sections of Acts (16:10-17; 20:6–21:18; 27:1–28:16). In those sections the author uses the

1. Richard B. Rackham, *The Acts of the Apostles* (Grand Rapids: Baker, 1964), p. xvi.

first person plural indicating that he was with the apostle Paul, and was a participant in the events being recorded. In compiling a list of Paul's companions from the period of time covered by the "we" sections, a total of seventeen individuals is found. Through a process of elimination, the list is reduced to Luke. (For example, Timothy, Trophimus, Aristarchus, and others are listed in 20:4 as being distinct from the "we" of 20:6, eliminating them as possible authors of this book.)

The "we" sections of Acts are uniform in style and language with the rest of Acts, which indicates that one individual, Luke, wrote the entire book.[2]

If it is concluded that Luke wrote the third gospel, then it must be concluded that he wrote Acts as well. Both books were addressed to Theophilus; the latter refers to the former ("the former treatise"); and the terminology and style of the two works are similar.

> His familiarity with Greek and Greek literature is also shown by his vocabulary. He is very fond of using rare, very often classical and poetical words. In fact we can hardly take a single paragraph without coming across some striking or peculiar word. Thus in the Gospel and Acts there are about 750 words peculiar to S. Luke in the [New Testament], and of these 440 occur only in the Acts.[3]

Many of these words are found only in Acts and Luke and nowhere else in the New Testament.

The evidence is overwhelming for Lucan authorship. And this conclusion is verified by the medical terms found in Acts that a physician like Luke would use (1:3; 3:7ff.; 9:18, 33; 13:11; 28:1-10).[4] (For additional information on the man Luke, see *Introduction to Luke* in chapter 7.)

2. F. F. Bruce, *The Book of Acts* (Grand Rapids: Eerdmans, 1966), p. 328.
3. Rackham, *The Acts of the Apostles,* p. xix.
4. Charles C. Ryrie, *The Acts of the Apostles* (Chicago: Moody, 1961), p. 9.

B.   PLACE AND DATE OF ACTS

The book of Acts ends with the apostle Paul's imprisonment in Rome. Paul came to Rome around A.D. 61 and stayed there for two years (28:30). Therefore, the story of Acts ends in A.D. 63 and this is the probable date for the writing of the book. This date seems reasonable since Acts makes no reference to the open persecution of Christians which erupted under Emperor Nero in A.D. 64, or to the martyrdom of Paul in the late sixties, or to the destruction of Jerusalem in A.D. 70.

Since Luke was with Paul in Rome at the time, it is reasonable that Rome was the place of writing.

C.   PURPOSE OF ACTS

Luke apparently had a number of reasons for writing Acts. In considering the purposes of Acts it is absolutely necessary to review Luke's stated purpose for writing his gospel (Luke 1:1-4). Since the gospel of Luke and the book of Acts are two parts of one literary whole, we do not have to guess concerning Luke's purpose. Clearly, Luke's primary purpose in writing his two volumes was to give an accurate and orderly account of the development of Christianity.

In volume one (Luke), Luke related to Theophilus the words and works of Jesus Christ, and in volume two (Acts) he told the story of the words and works of Christ that were done through His apostles. Acts is the record of the apostles' witness to the resurrected Lord Jesus Christ. The first thirty years of Christianity are chronicled as Luke recorded the spread of the gospel of Christ from Jerusalem to Rome.

A second purpose in writing Acts was to give a written defense of Christianity. There is a clear apologetic emphasis in this book. Luke was concerned about the perceptions that people had about the church of Jesus Christ. Wherever Christianity went it seemed to be accompanied by trouble and disorder. In Acts, Luke attempted to remove this false perception that the church caused trouble by setting forth a clear and accurate account of what happened, particularly noting the role played by the antagonistic Jewish leaders.

A third purpose in writing Acts was to provide stability to the new faith. Luke wanted his readers to know that this movement was not merely the result of the efforts of zealous men. Therefore, he placed a great emphasis on the workings of the Holy Spirit, noting how His ministries were experienced in the lives of the Christians, and His power was evidenced in supernatural manifestations.

D. BASIC OUTLINE OF ACTS

There can be little doubt that the key to the book is Acts 1:8. This verse provides the inspired structure for the book, as Luke developed his history of the spread of Christianity from Jerusalem to Rome.

I. Introduction (1:1–2:4)
   A. The Prologue (1:1-5)
   B. The Ascension of Christ (1:6-11)
   C. The Preparation for the Witness (1:12–2:4)
II. The Witness in Jerusalem (2:5–8:3)
   A. At Pentecost (2:5-47)
   B. Of Peter and John (3:1–4:31)
   C. Of the Apostles (4:32–5:42)
   D. Of Stephen (6:1–8:3)
III. The Witness in Judea and Samaria (8:4–12:25)
   A. Of Philip (8:4-40)
   B. Of Saul (Paul) (9:1-31)
   C. Of Peter (9:32–11:18)
   D. Of the Church (11:19–12:25)
IV. The Witness to the Uttermost Part of the Earth (13:1–28:31)
   A. The First Missionary Journey (13:1–14:28)
   B. The Jerusalem Council (15:1-35)
   C. The Second Missionary Journey (15:36–18:22)
   D. The Third Missionary Journey (18:23–21:16)
   E. The Journey to Rome (21:17–28:31)

E.   THEME OF ACTS

Acts 1:8 is a key to this book, as it reveals the Great Commission given to Christians. Christians are to be witnesses for Jesus Christ, spreading the good news that He died and rose again in order to redeem mankind. The evangelization of the world is the great theme of this book.

F.   SPECIAL CONSIDERATIONS ON ACTS

1. Some important background Scriptures

As Luke wrote the book of Acts there were certain truths that he apparently assumed that his readers fully understood. Several Scriptures summarize these important background truths. Matthew 16:18 records Christ's prophecy of the coming church. The church (which was not in existence at the time Christ made this statement) would be ''built,'' and would be victorious over Satan. Acts would record the beginning and the building of this new entity known as the church.

In Matthew 12:38-40, Christ told the religious leaders that only one more sign would be given to Israel—His resurrection. The death and resurrection of Christ is the background and basis of the book of Acts.

Luke 21:23-24 gives the Lord's statement that the city of Jerusalem would be destroyed. That generation of Israelites was under divine judgment for the national sin of rejecting its Messiah. There was an urgency in the apostles' message to the Jews. They were to save themselves from that perverse generation (Acts 2:40). And Matthew 21:43 declares that the kingdom was taken from Israel (that generation) and given to another people (the Gentiles/the church). While God would still fulfill His covenant promises to Abraham and David in the future, that generation which had been given the opportunity to receive the kingdom had lost its opportunity to experience the fulfillment of those covenant promises. As Acts opens, these truths are assumed, not argued.

2. Interpreting Acts

When Christ died and rose again the New Covenant was instituted. The outworking of the New Covenant began in full force on the Day of Pentecost when the Holy Spirit came in His fullness and the church began. The Old Covenant, with all its laws and regulations, was set aside. While a sharp line of distinction can be drawn between the end of the old and the beginning of the new, it must also be remembered that it takes time for such a change to take place in human experience. Acts is the book that records this transition from the Old to the New Covenant.

Acts records the decline of the old system and the rise of the new. When interpreting Acts it is important to remember this. It is essential to note who the individual is that is being described and how much he knew. For example, well into the church age (the New Covenant era) there were Jews who had genuine faith in the Lord God of Israel but had no knowledge of Jesus Christ. There were others who had responded positively to the ministry of John the Baptist, but who knew almost nothing about the One he had announced. It is important, therefore, to observe carefully who the text is focusing on in order to properly interpret that text. Acts is uniquely a book of transition.

3. Signs and miracles in Acts

Very infrequently in the Bible we find God setting aside His natural laws and working miracles through some chosen individual. But Acts records many such miraculous events, as the Holy Spirit worked powerfully through certain men. Why were these miraculous works employed in the days that Acts records? There are probably two primary reasons for this outpouring of the supernatural.

First, these miracles authenticated the new message that was being preached by the apostles. With so many religious ideas around and with so many claiming to be sent from God, the claims of the apostles would be seen as simply another to be added to the long list. But miracles set this new faith apart, demonstrating powerfully that it was indeed from God. (Note how Peter carefully integrated the miraculous events with his sermons in 2:15, 33; 3:12; 4:16.) Miracles verified that these men were giving a message from God. It should be noted that God authenticated the Old Covenant through miracles at Mt. Sinai. The message and the messenger (Moses) were clearly seen as being from God. If, therefore, God was giving a New Covenant, it was reasonable to expect that it would be authenticated through miracles also. God did so.

Second, miracles were used to keep the new movement together. The church would easily have divided along lines of race and prejudice if miracles had not been employed to make it clear to Jews, Samaritans, and Gentiles that the church was to be one. Miracles were used by God to convince the new believers that all were equal in the church. All needed to know that no one was superior in the New Covenant. The Jews, who were primary in the Old Covenant, particularly needed to understand this equality.

SUMMARY OF ACTS

I. Introduction (1:1–2:4)

    A. The Prologue (1:1-5)

Luke begins his second volume, like he did his first, with a long introductory sentence. In the earlier one he had summed up his gospel, and also gave what turned out to be three themes of the second volume that was yet to be written. First, a second volume would be an accounting of the words and works of Christ which followed His ascension back to heaven. Second, that future ministry would be carried on through the apostles—those men that He had chosen to represent Him and preach the gospel. And third, that future ministry would be done through the Holy Spirit who would empower the apostles and others for service.

Luke also relates Christ's two main objectives that were accomplished during the forty days between His resurrection and ascension. First, during those days the Lord Jesus gave many proofs that He was alive and had been raised bodily from the tomb. This, of course, was the basis of the message of the apostles; it was the validity of the Christian faith (cf. 1 Cor. 15:12-20). If there was no resurrection then there was no Christian faith.

Second, the other accomplishment of those post-resurrection days was Christ's instruction of the apostles. There were many truths that they could not understand until they had experienced the events of Christ's death and resurrection. However, once they fully understood these necessities of the faith they were able to grasp so much more. Many of Christ's earlier teachings made sense, many of the predictions of the Old Testament prophets were understandable for the first time, and they were able to comprehend the doctrines related to the New Covenant.

The forty days which preceded the ascension of Christ were crucial days for the apostles and for the church that would soon be formed.

B. The Ascension of Christ (1:6-11)

Christ's ascension took place near Bethany on the eastern side of the Mount of Olives (Luke 24:50). Just before His departure into heaven, the Lord was asked if He was going to restore the kingdom to Israel at that time. Christ, in reply, did not deny the future establishing of the kingdom, but rather informed them that the timing was God's decision. The Lord instead gave them a command to go throughout the world preaching His gospel. He encouraged them with the truth that they would be able to do so because of the power of the Holy Spirit. When He had made their work sufficiently plain, He left them and returned to the Father. The ascension reveals the approval of the Father on the work of the Son. After the Lord disappeared from sight the apostles continued to look heavenward. Their meditation was interrupted by two angels who spoke of the "blessed hope," that one day the Lord Jesus will return again.

C. The Preparation for the Witness (1:12–2:4)

The first duty of the apostles was clear. They were to return to Jerusalem and wait. Much time was spent in prayer with other believers who gathered with them (1:14). During these days they also dealt with the practical issue of a replacement for Judas Iscariot. Most likely this was something that the Lord Jesus told them to do. Peter took the leadership and saw this as a situation foretold in Old Testament prophecy (Ps. 69:25; 109:8). There were two essential qualifications for Judas' replacement: (1) he had to be a witness of Christ's resurrection, and (2) he had to be a witness of Christ's ministry from the days of John the Baptist until the ascension. Two men fit these requirements. The apostles left the final decision to God, and Matthias became part of the Twelve. (Perhaps a twelfth man was needed because of rulership in the future kingdom [cf. Matt. 19:28].)

It seems as though the apostles were expecting something to happen on the feast day of Pentecost. Jesus had promised that not many days would go by after His ascension before He would send the Holy Spirit (1:5). The Spirit came on the Day of Pentecost. Since the Spirit is invisible, it would be impossible to know when He came unless some evidence was given. To verify His coming, the believers heard the sound of a violent, rushing wind. (The wind was used to symbolize the Spirit's working. Cf. Ezek. 37:9, 14; John 3:8.) Also, they saw tongues as of fire resting on each believer. (Fire oftentimes speaks of divine presence in the Scriptures. Cf. Ex. 3:2; 40:34-38.) Also, as the Spirit came upon them they were able to speak in tongues. The speaking in tongues would be used by God to give an opening for the preaching of the gospel. (See appendix, *Note D: The Gift of Tongues.*)

  II. The Witness in Jerusalem (2:5–8:3)
    A. At Pentecost (2:5-47)

The Jews who were dispersed over the world would come in great numbers to Jerusalem to celebrate the key Jewish feasts. They would probably know Greek, Aramaic, and then their own dialect as well. These pilgrims were amazed to hear a small band of Galileans speaking (praising God) in their own unique dialects (2:6-8). This sensation caused great interest and confusion among the Jews; they desired to know how these things could be.

Peter, speaking for the apostles, immediately took his hearers to the prophet Joel. Peter used Joel to communicate two points: (1) God does pour forth His Spirit on man, and (2) anyone who will call on the Lord will be saved. Peter then reminded the people about the recent past, pointing out that Israel had put Jesus of Nazareth to death. But Jesus had been authenticated by God through signs and miracles and finally by His resurrection from the dead. Peter then expounded on the words of King David, noting that he looked forward to this day of resurrection. Peter, again speaking of the reality of Jesus' resurrection, observed that the tongues-speaking was proof of the fact that the resurrected Jesus was at the Father's right hand pouring out the Holy Spirit on people (2:33). The climax of Peter's message (2:36) is that Jesus, whom you crucified, is Lord and Christ.

Peter's message made a deep impression as the magnitude of Israel's guilt in murdering their own Messiah dawned on these people. With a feeling of helplessness and hopelessness they cried out, "What shall we do?" (2:37). Peter told them that they needed to change their minds concerning Jesus of Nazareth, and to change their public identification (2:38). The national decision, which led to Christ's crucifixion, was that He was a blasphemer and an agent of the devil himself. They must change their view and acknowledge Him as the Messiah. And, they were to identify with Him publicly through water baptism. Some three thousand responded favorably to Peter and were added to the church.

When these people believed, they cut themselves off from much of Jewish social and religious life. The church now became the center of these things for these new believers. During the next months much time was spent together in being taught the doctrines of the New Covenant, worshiping, praying, and ministering (2:42-47). The miracles worked by the apostles, the wonderful unity among these believers, and the real love for one another attracted many whom the Lord kept adding to the church.

B. Of Peter and John (3:1–4:31)

Luke stated that the apostles worked many signs (2:43). He now records one such sign. It illustrates the fact that the apostolic miracles authenticated the message and the messenger, and gave openings for the preaching of the gospel. The Temple was used by the apostles as a place of teaching and evangelism, following the example of the Lord Jesus. In the Temple area Peter and John healed a man who had been lame for about forty years (cf. 4:22). This genuine miracle brought about a reaction of amazement, and it also gave Peter an opportunity to preach again about the resurrection of Jesus Christ (3:11-26). The response was great, increasing the number in the Jerusalem church to five thousand (4:4). But this incident also gave the apostles their first taste of persecution from the religious leaders. When questioned by the leaders, Peter responded with a message that contained the same basic elements as the previous two—that his hearers were guilty of killing the Messiah, that God approved of Jesus as evidenced by His resurrection from the dead, and that they must come to Him as the only way of salvation (4:8-12). The rulers were amazed at their boldness and use of the Scriptures and could not deny the validity of the miracle. But nevertheless they issued an order that there was to be no more preaching in the name of Jesus of Nazareth (4:18). Peter and John voiced their decision to ignore such a decree (4:19-20). They returned to the other believers to pray about the matter, asking God for boldness (4:23-31).

C. Of the Apostles (4:32–5:42)

Unity, love, power, and growth characterized the church in the days that followed (4:32-35). The gates of hell were under attack. Satan's counterattack on the church not only included external strategy (persecution by the rulers), but also internal tactics (attempts to destroy unity and purity by sin within the assembly). The story of Ananias and Sapphira is the story of one such attempt (5:1-11). This married couple purposely deceived and lied, and they immediately paid for their sin with their lives. God's severe and dramatic judgment of these two believers loudly proclaimed His desire for purity in His church (a lesson that the modern church seems to have forgotten). The result was that great fear came upon everyone who heard about this incident.

Following the deaths of those two, there was another surge forward in the life of the church; many came to faith in Christ (5:12-16). With the apostles working many miracles and preaching effectively in the Temple, the Jewish leaders once again arrested the apostles. This arrest showed a greater feeling and determination by the religious leaders. Once again Peter confronted them with the message that although they had murdered their own Messiah, God raised Him from the dead. In response, there was a desire among some leaders to kill the apostles (5:33), but the advice of Gamaliel, one of the great teachers of that day, kept this from happening. They flogged the apostles, hoping that such a beating would quiet them. But such was not the case; the apostles continued their preaching (5:42).

D. Of Stephen (6:1–8:3)

Stephen is now introduced to Luke's readers as the story of the spread of Christianity continues. As a result of a financial problem involving the care of widows, Stephen enters the story.

He was a man of excellent character and spiritual wisdom (6:3). He not only dealt successfully with the financial problem (along with the other men who were selected), but he also ministered the Word of God and performed miracles. His ministry took him to the Synagogue of the Freedmen (6:9) where he discussed and debated the claims of Jesus. He was so filled with the Spirit and the knowledge of Scripture that the unbelievers were unable to answer him effectively. He was falsely charged with blasphemy and brought before the Great Sanhedrin. In his defense (7:2-53), Stephen skillfully refuted his accusers, and concluded his message with a severe denunciation of the rulers. This bold speech led to his death when the enraged leaders took Stephen out of the council chambers and stoned him to death. The church had its first martyr. The death of Stephen was the beginning of a great general persecution of the church (8:2). This persecution was led by a man named Saul (8:3).

III. The Witness in Judea and Samaria (8:4–12:25)

    A. Of Philip (8:4-40)

For the first time the church leaves the confines of the Jerusalem area and spreads to other localities. The persecution of the church had the beneficial effect of the gospel spreading to other people. The story focuses on Philip, who was one of those chosen to deal with the financial problem (Acts 6). Philip went to the area of Samaria preaching the gospel and working miracles. The result of his ministry was the remarkable conversion of multitudes of people. When the apostles heard of the evangelism among the Samaritans, they sent Peter and John to verify what was happening. Through apostolic miracles the Lord showed that the Samaritans were genuinely saved, and that they were equals in the church. This unique experience at Samaria was necessary to keep the movement together and ensure the unity of the church.

    B. Of Saul (Paul) (9:1-31)

Luke now picks up from 8:3, continuing his narrative about the religious leader Saul. Not being content with local persecution in Jerusalem, Saul requested and received extradition papers on Christians found in other places. He had probably received information that a sizeable group of Christians was at Damascus.

Therefore he headed for that city. As Saul and his group approached Damascus, he saw the glorified, risen Christ. Although the other individuals in the group knew that something was happening, only Saul saw and heard Jesus Christ. Saul came to faith in the One he had been persecuting. Saul was temporarily blinded and had to be led into the city of Damascus. He was there helped by a man named Ananias, who encouraged Saul in his new-found faith. Saul then spent some time in Arabia, and later returned again to Damascus (cf. Gal. 1:15-17). Saul (better known as Paul) began to preach that Jesus of Nazareth is the Messiah. His preaching caused great distress among the unbelieving Jews. They desired to kill him. The great persecutor had become a powerful preacher of the faith he once tried to destroy. The Lord revealed to Paul (Saul) that He had a special ministry for him among the Gentiles. (Note Acts 22:3-21 and 26:6-23 for additional information on the conversion experience of Paul.) Paul fled from Damascus, went to Jerusalem, and then journeyed to Tarsus (9:26-30).

C. Of Peter (9:32–11:18)

Peter ministered in a number of cities, but it was the incident at Caesarea that was particularly noteworthy. There a number of Gentiles (who were not proselytes to Judaism) came to faith in Jesus Christ. After they responded to Peter's message, the Holy Spirit confirmed the validity of their faith through supernatural signs—the same kind as had occurred to the Jews at Pentecost. This made it clear to the Jewish believers that God had brought Gentiles into the church as equals with the Jews. (This lesson would have to be relearned a number of times in the years that would follow.)

D. Of the church (11:19–12:25)

A new phase of evangelism begins to enter the life of the church as the gospel goes to the city of Antioch of Syria. Paul now becomes an important part of Gentile evangelism (11:19-26). The church at Antioch became the first church to be predominantly Gentile in its make-up. It is at Antioch that Paul and Barnabas first ministered extensively together to the Gentiles.

At this time another wave of persecution hit the Jerusalem church. This persecution, led by Herod Agrippa I (a grandson of

Herod the Great), apparently was carried out in order to find favor with the Jews. The first apostle to be martyred (James) was killed, and Peter was thrown into prison. These were dark days for the church, but God was still working mightily. The gospel still continued to spread (12:24).

IV. The Witness to the Uttermost Part of the Earth (13:1–28:31)
    A. The First Missionary Journey (13:1–14:28)

    In the timing of God the moment had arrived for the gospel to spread out to the world as it had never been done before. While praying and fasting the believers at Antioch learned what the will

PAUL'S FIRST AND SECOND JOURNEYS

of God was. Perhaps through one who had the gift of prophecy, Paul and Barnabas were selected for a special work. This ministry would take them into new areas with the gospel.

The missionaries' first stop was the island of Cyprus where they evangelized in the two cities of Salamis and Paphos. They then sailed to the shores of Asia Minor, proceeding inland to the cities of Antioch (of Pisidia), Iconium, Lystra, and Derbe. In each city they evangelized and started churches. But they also experienced the hatred and persecution of the Jews. The two missionaries returned to their home base of Antioch (of Syria) and reported all the wonderful things that God had done.

B. The Jerusalem Council (15:1-35)

While teaching again at Antioch, Paul and Barnabas were confronted by Jews from Judea. These Jews were teaching that in order to be saved, people (Gentiles included) had to be circumcised and keep the law of Moses. Paul and Barnabas disagreed with them and heated debates followed. The problem was of such magnitude that it was decided to go to Jerusalem and there, with the apostles, work out the solution. This event was very serious and extremely important in the history of the church. This theological wedge could split the church in two. If the rites of Judaism were attached to the New Covenant, then there probably would have been division.

After discussing the issue and listening to the testimonies of Peter, Paul, and Barnabas, it was decided that Gentiles did not have to keep the law to be saved. However, Gentile Christians were encouraged to respect the feelings and thinking of the Jewish Christians and not purposely offend them.

C. The Second Missionary Journey (15:36-18:22)

Paul realized that he needed to check up on the new churches that were started on the first missionary journey. When his companion Barnabas wished to take his nephew John Mark along, Paul refused to allow it. (Mark had failed to continue with them on the first journey, but instead had left the missionary group.) This caused a division between the two men, resulting in a parting of company. Barnabas took Mark and revisited Cyprus. Paul chose Silas to go with him. Paul and Silas confirmed the churches of Asia Minor that had been started on the first journey. Also in Asia Minor, Timothy joined the missionary group. After being kept by the Holy Spirit from entering certain provinces (16:6-7), the missionary party arrived at Troas.

Here Luke joined them, and Paul saw the ''Macedonian Vision'' in which a man requested the gospel for that territory. They went to the cities of Philippi, Thessalonica, Berea, Athens, and Corinth. Where there was a synagogue in these cities, Paul would go there first and preach Jesus. Paul would speak there until he was forced to leave. Often his attention was shifted next to the Gentiles, with whom he usually had a better response. Paul remained in the city of Corinth for a year and a half, which was the longest stay in any city on the second journey. In most of these cities churches were started.

D. The Third Missionary Journey (18:23–21:16)

After spending a period of time in Antioch of Syria, Paul returned to his missionary activity. After journeying through the regions of Galatia and Phrygia, he went to Ephesus where he ministered for about three years, longer than any other place on the third journey. His ministry there was extremely effective (19:20). He then returned to the cities of Macedonia and Greece to see that the churches there were doing well. Following this he went to Troas on his way to Jerusalem where his journey ended. All along on this trip to Jerusalem Paul had been warned that trouble awaited him there. Paul was arrested in Jerusalem and this began about four years of imprisonment.

E. The Journey to Rome (21:17–28:31)

Paul gave a number of defenses before Jewish and Roman authorities. His life was very much in danger in Jerusalem and he was able to be moved to the Roman dominated city of Caesarea. After giving defenses before Festus, Felix, and Agrippa, Paul demanded to be tried as a Roman citizen in Rome. Since this was his right, Paul was transported to Rome. The apostle's ship left late in the year, which was not a weather-wise time for sailing on the Mediterranean. The ship was caught in a terrible storm and driven some 435 miles to wreck on the island of Miletus. Here, after a stay of three months, Paul was taken to Rome (27:1–28:16).

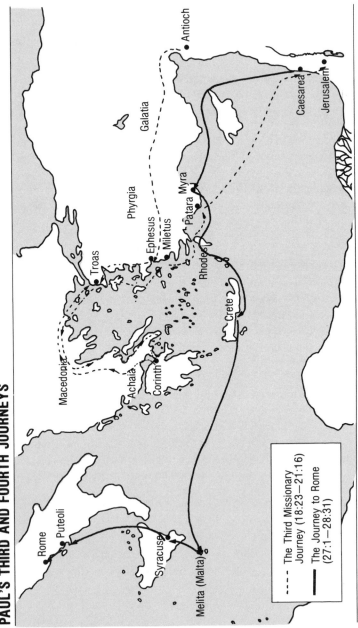

PAUL'S THIRD AND FOURTH JOURNEYS

Antioch

Caesarea

Jerusalem

Galatia

Phyrgia

Myra

Patara

Ephesus

Miletus

Rhodes

Troas

Crete

Macedonia

Achaia

Corinth

Rome

Puteoli

Syracuse

Melita (Malta)

- - - - The Third Missionary
Journey (18:23—21:16)

———— The Journey to Rome
(27:1—28:31)

CHRONOLOGY OF ACTS AND THE EPISTLES

	A.D. 33 – 47	47 – 48	48 – 50	50 – 53	53 – 57	57 – 58	58 – 60	60 – 62	62 – 64	64 – 100
Peter and Paul	Peter's Ministry; Paul's Conversion	Paul's 1st Journey	Jerusalem Council: Peter and Paul	Paul's 2nd Journey	Paul's 3rd Journey	Paul's Arrest: Jerusalem	Paul in Prison: Caesarea	Paul in Prison: Rome	Paul's Final Travels, Martyrdom	Nothing
New Testament Epistles	James	Galatians	None	1 Thessalonians 2 Thessalonians	1 Corinthians 2 Corinthians Romans	None	None	Ephesians Colossians Philemon Philippians	1 Timothy Titus 2 Timothy	Written before A.D. 70: 1 Peter 2 Peter Hebrews Written after A.D. 70: Jude 1, 2, 3 John Revelation
Chapters in Acts	1-12	13-14	15	15-18	18-21	21-24	24-26	27-28	None	None

Paul was under house arrest at Rome, but did have the freedom to preach the gospel to those who came to visit him. Most likely, Paul was freed after his two years at Rome and continued his missionary activity. But with the coming of the gospel to Rome, Luke's purpose in writing Acts had been accomplished.

THE APOSTLE PAUL

It would be safe to say that no human being has impacted the Christian church as forcefully as the apostle Paul. His missionary activity spread the gospel across the world of his day. His letters provided much of the theological base on which the church of Jesus Christ rests. This man was carefully prepared by God for his role as the apostle to the Gentiles. Paul's conversion on the Damascus Road was spectacular and supernatural, but it was not the starting point in his preparation as God's apostle to the Gentiles.

> The choice of [Paul] himself was the final execution of a design which had been long maturing in the purpose of God, and which was worked out step by step in the process of events. Already before his birth Paul had been chosen and set apart as the apostle of the Gentiles; and, when the proper moment had arrived, the revelation took place, and the design of God was made consciously present in the mind and heart of the man. It was not a sudden and incalculable choice of a human instrument. It was the consummation of a process of selection and preparation which had begun before the man was born, but of which he had at first been wholly unconscious—so unconscious that he had spent his energy in fighting vainly against its compelling power.[5]

Since the apostle Paul is such a dominant figure in the early church and in the literature of the New Testament, it is appropriate to discuss briefly something of his life and back-

---

5. William M. Ramsay, *The Cities of St. Paul* (Grand Rapids: Baker, 1960), p. 86.

ground. Charles Ryrie provides a fine outline that we will basically follow.[6]

A.   THE INFLUENCE OF JUDAISM ON PAUL

1. Paul was a Hebrew patriot

Although he was sent to the Gentiles, Paul always had a deep love for his own people Israel (e.g., Rom. 3:1; 9:1-3). Paul's early training in the law and his learning of a trade (tentmaking) reveal that he came from a family who lived by true Israelite ideology.

2. Paul was a Pharisee

Paul's father was a Pharisee (Acts 23:6) and Paul himself was a zealous Pharisee (Phil. 3:5). He outstripped his contemporaries in his advancement in Pharisaism with its emphasis on knowledge of the Scriptures, external righteousness, fasting, and tithing. (See *The Religious Background to the New Testament* in chapter 3, pages 31-34, for a discussion of the Pharisees.) "Pharisaism gave Paul habits of discipline for his life as a Christian, and Christianity gave him freedom from the legality of his life as a Pharisee."[7]

3. Paul was a student of the Old Testament

In the synagogue at Tarsus, Paul would have learned the Hebrew Scriptures. Up until the age of 12 he would have learned to write the Hebrew characters, studied the Law and the Prophets, and mastered Jewish history. At the age of 13 he was probably sent to Jerusalem to advance his education under the master teacher Gamaliel (Acts 22:3).

> During the next five or six years he sat at the feet of Gamaliel. . . . Paul learned to dissect a text until scores of possible meanings were disclosed. . . . Paul learned to debate in the question-and-answer style known to the ancient world as the "diatribe" and to expound, for a rabbi was part

6. Charles C. Ryrie, *Biblical Theology of the New Testament* (Chicago: Moody, 1959), pp. 154-63.
7. Ibid., p. 155.

lawyer who prosecuted or defended those who broke the sacred Law, and part preacher.[8]

4. Paul was a missionary

As a pupil of Gamaliel, Paul would have known the goal of one proselyte per year for every Jew. The idea of spreading God's truth to others was instilled in him from his youth. This idea would be sanctified and used by the risen Christ in the propagation of the gospel during the adult years of Paul.

B. THE INFLUENCE OF HELLENISM ON PAUL

1. The city of Tarsus

Paul was born and reared in Tarsus, the capital of the Roman province of Cilicia. Tarsus was founded as a Greek city-state in 171 B.C. by Antiochus Epiphanes. Evidence points to the fact that Jews settled in Tarsus from the founding of the city and were given rights as citizens.[9] Paul clearly claimed to be a Roman citizen (e.g., Acts 21:39) and it could be that this citizenship had long been a part of Paul's family. "The rights of citizenship could only be got by inheritance from a citizen father, apart from exceptional cases in which it was bestowed by a formal law on an individual as a reward for services rendered to the city; but such cases were comparatively few in any one city, for the right was jealously guarded."[10] Paul's Roman citizenship proved valuable as he traveled the Roman world preaching the gospel.

Tarsus was also a seat of learning, having a university there. Although it was probably not a key university, it was a place where philosophy was taught and debated. Paul may or may not have been a formal part of that situation, but he certainly became exposed to Greek thinking in a way that a Palestinian Jew would not (e.g. Titus 1:12). Tarsus was valuable in preparing Paul to be the apostle to the Gentiles.

8. John Pollock, *The Man Who Shook the World* (Wheaton, Ill.: Victor, 1972), pp. 6-7.

9. Ramsay, *The Cities of St. Paul*, pp. 180-86.

10. Ibid., p. 174.

2. The mystery religions

Paul must have been well acquainted with these religions which promised a special relationship with the gods. (See *The Religious Background to the New Testament* in chapter 3, pages 29-30, for a discussion of the mystery religions.) "Though Paul may show acquaintance with mystery terminology and even though Paul may have used some of those terms in a deliberate attempt to interest Greek readers in the Gospel of God's salvation, this by no means proves that Paul's theology was in any way derived from or dependent upon the theology of those cults."[11] There are significant differences between Paul's theology and the teachings of the mystery religions.

C. PAUL'S PERSONAL LIFE

It was common for an individual to be known by several names in the Roman world of Paul's day. Paul was his Latin name and Saul was his Hebrew name. He always had these names and they are unrelated to his conversion; that is, his name was not changed to Paul after his conversion.

It is the opinion of a number of scholars that Paul was married at one time but that his wife died or perhaps left him when he became a believer in Christ. While this falls into the realm of speculation, Paul's teachings on marriage and his presence in the Jewish Sanhedrin strongly suggests that he had been married.

D. PAUL'S CONVERSION

Paul's conversion was brought about suddenly when he met the risen Christ on the Damascus road. However, there were issues that had been bothering Saul of Tarsus before that momentous event. Jesus Himself had reminded Saul that it was hard "to kick against the goads" (Acts 26:14). These goads that prodded the mind and heart of Saul probably included the witness and the martyrdom of Stephen, the godly lives of the

11. Ryrie, *Biblical Theology,* pp. 157-58.

Christians that he was persecuting, and his knowledge of the miracles and teachings of the Lord Jesus. When the voice from heaven said, "I am Jesus whom you are persecuting" (Acts 9:5), the inner struggle ended and Paul became a Christian.

The conversion of Saul of Tarsus is one of the great apologetics of the Christian faith. There is no adequate explanation (except the biblical one) for the dramatic change that occurred in the man. Unbelief has not been able to satisfactorily answer the biblical claim that this one who hated believers in Christ would suddenly become one himself, and the greatest preacher of the faith in Jesus Christ.

A CHRONOLOGY OF PAUL'S LIFE

Date (A.D.)	Events
1	Birth of the apostle Paul
14	Paul sent to Jerusalem to study under Gamaliel
34	Paul's conversion (Acts 9)
44	Paul's ministry at Antioch
47	Paul's first missionary journey
49	The Jerusalem Council
50	Paul's second missionary journey
54	Paul's third missionary journey
58	Paul imprisoned at Caesarea
60	Paul's first Roman imprisonment
62	Paul released from his Roman imprisonment
64	Paul's second Roman imprisonment; his death

Part 4

The Epistles:
The New Covenant Explained

10

PERSPECTIVES ON THE EPISTLES

THE NEED FOR THE EPISTLES

As the church grew beyond the confines of Jerusalem and began to spread across the world, it became absolutely necessary for the truth that guided the church to be written down in a permanent form. Letters of instruction were written to churches and to individuals. These twenty one-letters, which have been preserved in our New Testament, were written almost exclusively by apostles. They grounded the church in its faith and guaranteed an authoritative, consistent body of truth for the church to live by.

THE ADVANTAGES OF THE EPISTLES

These letters are commonly called ''epistles,'' which is simply a less common name for a letter. An epistle, as a form of communication, had certain advantages.

> A letter affords a writer more freedom, both in subject and expression, than does a formal treatise. A letter is usually occasional, that is, it is written in consequence of some circumstance which requires it to be dealt with promptly. The style of a letter depends largely on the occasion that calls it forth. . . . Paul frequently used the letter form for the purpose of conveying instruction and counsel.[1]

1. C. F. Hogg and W. E. Vine, *The Epistles to the Thessalonians* (Fincastle, Va.: Scripture Truth, 1959), p. 5.

The Length of the Epistles

The New Testament epistles were much longer than the average letter that was written in those days. Literary letters written by such men as Cicero the statesman and Seneca the philosopher averaged about 200 words in length, whereas the average letter written by Paul was about 1,300 words with Romans containing some 7,100 words.[2]

The Study of the Epistles

In this study, our approach will be to look first at the thirteen epistles written by the apostle Paul and then to survey the eight general letters written by several other authors. Our approach to the letters of Paul will be chronological, studying them as they appeared in history and also dividing them into four groups. The eight general epistles will also be studied in chronological order.

---

2. Robert H. Gundry, *A Survey of the New Testament,* rev. ed. (Grand Rapids: Zondervan, 1981), p. 245.

THE PAULINE EPISTLES:
GROUP ONE

PAUL'S EARLY EPISTLES

Letter	Date (A.D.)	Written from
Galatians	48	Antioch of Syria
1 Thessalonians	51	Corinth
2 Thessalonians	51	Corinth

11

GALATIANS

Introduction to Galatians

A. AUTHORSHIP OF GALATIANS

The apostle Paul identifies himself as the author in the opening verse of this letter.

B. PLACE AND DATE OF GALATIANS

There is a great variety of opinion among scholars concerning the date and the place of the writing of Galatians. Opinions range from A.D. 48 (from Antioch of Syria) to 60 (from Rome). One's view on this matter is largely determined by the interpretation of the term *Galatia*. (See later section *Special Considerations on Galatians*.) There are several possible meanings of the term *Galatia*, and the meaning selected by an individual will dictate the date and place of writing.

In this study, Galatians is viewed as the earliest of Paul's writings, being penned shortly after Paul's first missionary journey. This would give the book a date of late 48 or early 49. The place of writing would be Antioch of Syria.

C. PURPOSE OF GALATIANS

The need for this letter is clearly stated in the first chapter of the book. Judaizers had infiltrated the Galatian churches. They were in the process of perverting the gospel of Christ, and they were attacking the authority and credibility of the apostle Paul. In response to this situation, Galatians was written. Several reasons for writing can be observed. First, Paul wrote this letter to defend his apostolic authority. He declared that he was a genuine apostle, selected by Christ Himself. Second, he wrote to reaffirm the truth that salvation is by faith alone. People are saved by faith (justification) and are to live by faith (sanctification). Third, he penned this epistle to correct the errors of legalism and thus defend the concept of Christian liberty.

D. BASIC OUTLINE OF GALATIANS

    I. Introduction (1:1-9)
      A. Salutation (1:1-5)
      B. Occasion (1:6-9)
    II. Personal: Paul's Defense of His Apostolic Authority (1:10–2:21)
      A. Paul's Reception of Direct Divine Revelation (1:10-17)
      B. Paul's Apostleship Acknowledged (1:18-24)
      C. Paul's Teaching Recognized as True (2:1-10)
      D. Paul's Authority Displayed (2:11-21)
    III. Doctrinal: The Exposition of Justification by Faith (3:1–4:31)
      A. The Explanation of Justification by Faith (3:1–4:7)
      B. The Exhortation to Forsake Legalism (4:8-31)
    IV. Practical: The Life of Christian Liberty (5:1–6:18)
      A. The Call to Christian Liberty (5:1)
      B. The Peril to Christian Liberty (5:2-12)
      C. The Holy Spirit and Christian Liberty (5:13-26)
      D. Service and Christian Liberty (6:1-10)
    V. Conclusion (6:11-18)

E. THEME OF GALATIANS

The theme of this book is Christian liberty. The concept of Christian liberty is built squarely on the doctrine of justification by faith. Those who have received Jesus Christ as personal Savior have been set free. A proper understanding of Christian liberty frees believers from legalism and allows them to live by faith, enjoying spiritual freedom.

F.   SPECIAL CONSIDERATIONS ON GALATIANS

1. The Galatian people

In the third century B.C. a large number of Gauls crossed into Asia Minor from areas in the west. They occupied the north central area of Asia Minor and rapidly gained mastery over the native population of the Phrygians. These Gauls (also called Galatae, or Galatians) dominated the region for some time until they were finally subdued by the Romans in 189 B.C. The Gallic rulers were able to stay in favor with Rome and until 25 B.C. were considered a separate kingdom, an ally of Rome. However, in 25 B.C. the area was made into the Roman province of Galatia after some additional territory was added to it. During those years the Gauls amalgamated with other racial groups.[1] By the time of the first century the territory contained Gauls, Phrygians, and Romans as well as Greeks and Jews.

2. The recipients of the Galatian letter

Whom did Paul have in mind when he wrote this epistle to "the churches of Galatia" (Gal. 1:2)? The problem revolves around the meaning of the term "Galatia." In Paul's day the term had two meanings: (1) the small area in north central Asia Minor that was dominated by the Gauls or (2) the much larger Roman province of Galatia. If Paul is referring to the smaller area, then Galatians would be addressed to some churches founded by Paul on his second missionary journey. (This is called the *north Galatian theory.*) If the larger area of the Roman province is being referred to, then the book of Galatians would be addressed to churches founded by Paul on his first missionary trip. (This is called the *south Galatian theory.*)

According to the *north Galatian theory*, Paul visited the ethnic area of Galatia on his second journey on his way to Troas and established churches there (Acts 16:6-8). It is believed by advocates of this theory that Luke used territorial names in Acts and

1. William Hendriksen, *New Testament Commentary: Exposition of Galatians* (Grand Rapids: Baker, 1974), pp. 4-5.

not the political titles. It is noted that Paul, too, often used territorial names. (Thus "Galatia" would not be the Roman province of Galatia). This view had been the traditional view of the church until more recent times. Numerous other points are made in support of this view, which cannot be dealt with in this study. Others have detailed the support for this view.[2] If this view is correct, Paul would have gone on the first missionary journey, attended the Jerusalem Council, gone on his second journey, and then wrote Galatians, thus giving Galatians a later date.

According to the *south Galatian theory* the churches of Galatia were founded on Paul's first missionary journey. "Galatia," in this case, refers to the large Roman province. It is clear that Paul did found churches in this area. (It is not clear that he ever founded churches in northern Galatia.) Advocates of this view note that in Galatians Paul makes no reference to the Jerusalem Council's decision, which was an important decision about the place of the law in Christianity—the very subject Paul deals with in Galatians. The reasoning is that the book of Galatians must have been written prior to the council meeting, since its decision would have made a powerful point in Paul's discussion. Numerous other arguments are made in support of the south Galatian theory.[3] If this view is correct, then Paul would have gone on his first missionary journey to the province of Galatia, returned and wrote Galatians, and then attended the Jerusalem Council. If this view is correct, this would make Galatians the earliest of Paul's writings. Although both views make some excellent points, the south Galatian theory seems to be the better view.

SUMMARY OF GALATIANS

I. Introduction (1:1-9)
   A. Salutation (1:1-5)

The apostle Paul had learned that there were both theological and practical problems among his new converts of Galatia. Of pri-

---

2. J. B. Lightfoot, *The Epistle of St. Paul to the Galatians* (Grand Rapids: Zondervan, 1967), pp. 18-35.
3. Merrill C. Tenney, *Galatians, the Charter of Christian Liberty* (Grand Rapids: Eerdmans, 1961), p. 46-55.

mary importance were the issues being raised by some false teachers who were Jews. These Judaizers were exerting influence in the new churches and were making a twofold attack: first, they were discrediting Paul's apostleship, and, second, they were distorting Paul's message of grace.

Paul immediately faced the issue of his apostleship. He asserted that he was appointed by God and that no group of men appointed him or voted him in as an apostle. He also declared that his message was from God (1:3-5). This message included deliverance—that believing men are rescued from the bondage of sin and set free. It included the fact of substitution—that Christ died in our place. It also included the grace of God—that salvation is a gift of God, totally apart from man's works.

B. Occasion (1:6-9)

Paul was amazed at the sudden and impulsive defection of the churches from the message of grace. The apostle spoke of their "desertion" that was at that time going on. He pointed out that they were not only abandoning the truth but the God of that truth. And then, in one of the severest statements in the New Testament, he warned that those who pollute the gospel of grace are in grave spiritual danger, setting themselves apart for judgment. After forcefully setting forth the issues at hand, Paul launched into a defense of himself and the message that he preached.

II. Personal: Paul's Defense of His Apostolic Authority (1:10–2:21)

A. Paul's Reception of Direct Divine Revelation (1:10-17)

In defending himself and his message, Paul demonstrated that nothing from his past could be the origin of the message that he preached. No man taught him the gospel of grace, and Judaism, with its emphasis on works, did not produce it either. He reminded his readers that he once was zealous in his persecution of the church and in his observance of Judaism. (Judaism is not a reference to the scriptural observance of the Old Testament, but rather the Jew's religion with its man-made traditions. See Matt. 15:1-6 and Mark 7:7, 13.) The only legitimate explanation for his message and his apostleship was that he was confronted by the risen Christ and set apart by Him (1:15-17).

B. Paul's Apostleship Acknowledged (1:18-24)

Paul next traced his early history as a Christian in order to establish two points: first, his theology was not formed by any contact with other men (particularly the twelve apostles), and, second, his doctrinal system was developed before his public ministry began. In combining his statements in Galatians with those of Luke in the book of Acts, the following chronology is revealed. (This chronology assumes the correctness of the south Galatian theory.)

1. Saul of Tarsus met the risen Christ on the Damascus Road (Gal. 1:15; Acts 9:3-5).

2. After a few days in Damascus, He spent several years in Arabia (Gal. 1:17-18).

3. After returning from Arabia, Paul preached in Damascus for a short time (Gal. 1:17; Acts 9:19-25)

4. Forced to leave Damascus, he went to Jerusalem, but spent only spent fifteen days visiting Peter and James, as well as preaching (Gal. 1:18-19; Acts 9:26-30).

5. Because of a plot on his life, Paul fled to Tarsus, where he spent some seven years (Gal. 1:21; Acts 9:30).

6. He was brought to Antioch of Syria by Barnabas to help teach the Word of God to the church there (Acts 11:19-30).

7. He, along with Barnabas, brought gifts to help the church at Jerusalem in a time of famine. They also met privately with the apostles (Gal. 2:1-10; Acts 11:30).

8. He went to Galatia on the first missionary journey (Acts 13:1).

C. Paul's Teaching Recognized as True (2:1-10)

In chapter 1 Paul defends the *source* of his message (that he got it directly from Christ), and in chapter 2 he begins to defend the *content* of his message.

The trip to Jerusalem (2:1-10) was crucial because the oneness of Jew and Gentile was hanging in the balance. Paul came to the apostles to lay before them the truth that law-keeping was not necessary for salvation (or even for sanctification). Paul, in this private meeting with some of the leaders of the church, was not there to find out if his gospel was true and accurate but rather wanted them to acknowledge that circumcision was not necessary for salvation.

Note that circumcision was the sign of the Abrahamic Covenant, which had been integrated into the law of Moses. It was the "door" by which Judaism was entered, and it came to stand for the entire system of law-keeping. If the leaders disagreed with Paul, then a barrier would immediately be erected between Jew and Gentile in the church. The leaders, however, approved both the message of Paul and his ministry to the Gentiles.

This meeting demonstrated that Paul was recognized as an apostle on equal footing with Peter and the others and that his message was the same as theirs. The results of this meeting would forcefully contradict what the Judaizers were telling the Galatian believers about Paul.

D. Paul's Authority Displayed (2:11-21)

Paul recounted this incident when he confronted Peter to show that he was an equal with him. Peter's hypocrisy, on that occasion, not only led other believers into hypocrisy but also raised the possibility of splitting the church. Paul's fearless rebuke not only saved the situation but also demonstrated his apostolic authority.

The next section (2:15-21) is best viewed as an explanation to the Galatians and not as part of the rebuke of Peter. In it Paul begins his marvelous discussion of justification by faith. This passage has a number of difficult phrases. But the main thrust of the passage is that law-keeping of any variety has no place in a person's salvation (2:16). Furthermore, Paul states that Christ lives in the believing individual, making it possible for him to live righteously day by day (2:20). So then, believers are not only justified by faith, but are sanctified by faith as well. (Sanctification is our being set apart from sin and unto God.) Living daily with confidence in Christ who has set us free makes living according to legalistic restrictions unnecessary and wrong. One is not saved by faith and sanctified by law.

JUSTIFICATION BY FAITH

The doctrine of justification by faith is a cornerstone truth of the New Testament Scriptures. To justify means to "declare righteous." It is a courtroom word; the judge pronounces his verdict of "not guilty," thus acquitting the prisoner. However, in this case, the prisoner is not only set free but is declared to be righteous because the righteousness of Jesus Christ is imputed to him.

> Justification, as a judicial act of God, rests not on human works (Rom. 3:20, 28; Gal. 3:11; 5:4), not even on faith as a work of man (Eph. 2:8), but solely on God's sovereign grace in Jesus Christ. It is His accomplished mediatorial work that furnishes the legal basis upon which man's justification becomes both possible and actual. Christ fully satisfied the demands of God's law: He both paid our debt and also rendered the obedience that we owed (Matt. 20:28; Rom. 3:24; 2 Cor. 5:21; Gal. 3:24; Eph. 1:7; Titus 3:7).[4]

God does not arbitrarily declare people to be righteous but rather does so on the objective reality of Christ's finished work on the cross. "But any righteousness the sinner has must be actual, not fictitious; real, not imagined; acceptable by God's standards, and not a whit short. If this could be accomplished, then, and only then, can He justify. . . . He changes sinners into righteous people. How? By making us the righteousness of God in Christ (2 Cor. 5:21)."[5]

Law-keeping or works of any kind do not contribute to God's pronouncement. Since man cannot earn his salvation, it is given as a free gift. Man receives this great salvation by faith. The object of this faith is the completed work of the God-man, Jesus Christ. When a man acknowledges his sinfulness and his inability to save himself and reaches out to accept the free gift of salvation, he is justified.

4. Hendriksen, *Exposition of Galatians,* p. 98.
5. Charles C. Ryrie, *Basic Theology* (Wheaton, Ill.: Victor, 1988), p. 299.

III. Doctrinal: The Exposition of Justification by Faith (3:1–4:31)
    A. The Explanation of Justification by Faith (3:1–4:7)

Paul defended the principle of justification by faith by reminding the Galatians of their own experience in the recent past (3:1-5). He asked them, "How were you saved—by faith or law-keeping?" The answer, of course, was by faith. He then noted that human effort did not bring salvation and it does not bring sanctification either. He reminded them that the Old Testament method was also that of justification by faith, and he used Abraham as an example (3:6-9).

Then, because the Galatians were in the act of making a choice to live under the law, he warned them that the law had a curse attached to it and this curse would come on anyone who broke the law—even one point of it (3:10-14). But in His death Christ took the curse of the law and anyone who identifies with Him can be saved and avoid the curse of the law (which was present alienation from God as well as eternal separation from Him). Paul noted that in the Abrahamic Covenant (see p. 18). God promised to bring salvation to men (which is "by faith" as Paul has shown). This promise of God was not set aside by the giving of the law of Moses (3:15-18).

A question would naturally arise at this point. "If the law has no place in salvation, then why did God bother giving it?" There are several answers to this question (3:19– 4:7). First, the law was given to carefully define sin (cf. Rom. 3:20).

Second, the law revealed the righteous requirements of God. Paul used an illustration from Roman society to get his point across on the purpose of the law. The pedagogue (tutor) in Roman society was an adult (often a well educated slave) who taught, disciplined, and protected a child until the child reached the age when he was declared to be an adult by his father. At that point in the child's life, the pedagogue lost his authority and jurisdiction over the child. Paul stated that the law was designed by God to be temporary until Christ came. The law functioned as a pedagogue, protecting and teaching Israel. But now that God has declared believers *adult* sons of His (4:1-5), the law no longer has jurisdiction over the believer.

B. The Exhortation to Forsake Legalism (4:8-31)

In light of the believer's position as an adult child of God, ''Why,'' asked Paul, ''do you want to put yourself back under the authority of the pedagogue (the law)?'' He begged them to forsake Jewish legalism and to enjoy their new-found freedom in Christ (4:31).

IV. Practical: The Life of Christian Liberty (5:1–6:18)

A. The Call to Christian Liberty (5:1)

This verse is a great summary of what the apostle Paul has been discussing and it is also an introduction to what is ahead in his letter. Clearly, law and grace are mutually exclusive.

B. The Peril to Christian Liberty (5:2-12)

Christian liberty is in danger when adherence to the law is required. By placing themselves under the law system, the Galatians were removing themselves from the sphere of the spiritual life where Christ works (5:4). Christ saves and sanctifies by faith. Paul warned that unless they rid themselves of the Judaizers they would cease making progress in the Christian life.

C. The Holy Spirit and Christian Liberty (5:13-26)

The Christian has been set free from law-keeping as a rule of life. There is, however, another danger for the believer at this point. Some will be tempted to interpret freedom as ''doing whatever I want.'' This is false liberty. Paul emphasizes that believers have been set free in order to serve one another. This way of life can take place by ''walking by means of the Holy Spirit.'' The power of the Holy Spirit is available to believers to enable them to live quality, God-pleasing lives. However, there will always be a struggle between the Spirit and our sinful, fleshly nature. (This nature remains with us until death or the rapture.) This struggle is inevitable and continual.

How do we know which of these two forces is dominating our lives? Paul gives two objective lists by which we can measure ourselves. The first list is the deeds of the flesh (5:19-21). If these are dominant, then the flesh is in control. However, if the ''fruit of the Spirit'' (5:22-23) is increasingly characterizing our lives, then we know that the Holy Spirit is successfully working. (The ''fruit of the Spirit'' is a good, objective description of Christlikeness—which is God's goal for all believers.) In the lives of most Christians the battle rages on numerous fronts between the flesh and the Spirit, with some territory being won by the Spirit while some remains in the possession of the flesh.

D. Service and Christian Liberty (6:1-10)

For the first time in life, a person who knows Christ can live unselfishly and seek what is best for others. Believers who walk by means of the Spirit will serve one another. This service will be seen in such areas as restoring sinning believers, bearing the burdens of one another, and by giving material resources to aid one another.

V. Conclusion (6:11-18)

As he closed his letter to these Galatian Christians who were in real spiritual danger, the apostle reminded them that he had paid a high personal price to deliver this marvelous message of salvation by grace. He told them that peace will be the lot of those who live by faith.

12

1 THESSALONIANS

INTRODUCTION TO 1 THESSALONIANS

A. AUTHORSHIP OF 1 THESSALONIANS

There is no serious question about the authorship of this book. The apostle Paul wrote it. This is stated in the opening verse and is verified by internal evidence.[1] Paul included Timothy and Silas in the opening statement as those who participated in the ministry with him.

B. PLACE AND DATE OF 1 THESSALONIANS

On his second missionary journey Paul came to Thessalonica and preached the gospel of Christ (Acts 17:1-10). Although a church was founded then, Paul was forced out of the city by enemies of the gospel. Eventually he journeyed to the city of Corinth where he ministered for about eighteen months. It was at Corinth that he wrote 1 Thessalonians.

Paul probably arrived in Corinth in late A.D. 50 or in early 51. He apparently wrote 1 Thessalonians shortly after his arrival there. This would mean a date of 51 for the writing of this letter.[2]

---

1. Donald Guthrie, *New Testament Introduction* (Downers Grove, Ill.: InterVarsity, 1970), pp. 567-68.
2. D. Edmond Hiebert, *The Thessalonian Epistles* (Chicago: Moody, 1971). pp. 23-25. .

C.   PURPOSE OF 1 THESSALONIANS

Since Paul was forced to leave Thessalonica and was unable to do all that he wanted to there, he had a deep concern for the well-being of his new church. Therefore, he sent Timothy back to Thessalonica to minister and to observe the situation. It was Timothy's return to Paul with news of the church that prompted Paul to write (Acts 18:5; 1 Thess. 3:5-7). Timothy's report was basically positive, but it also revealed that the church had some concerns and needs.

First, Paul wrote to defend his own ministry there. Certain detractors were saying that Paul was just another self-centered, wandering religious teacher. He had no real interest in the Thessalonian believers but taught for personal gain. They apparently were saying that if he cared about them, why didn't he return? Although Paul did not like focusing on himself, it was important in this case to deal with these accusations. "For the Thessalonians to believe these charges would be fatal to the work of the gospel in Macedonia. They must be refuted. But Paul's answer to these charges . . . was not evoked by a feeling of wounded personal pride; he was motivated by a passionate concern to safeguard the faith of his converts."[3]

So Paul wrote to assure the Thessalonian believers of his love and concern for them.

A second purpose in writing was to clarify the truth about the Lord's return for His church. There were some doctrinal and practical errors that were beginning to emerge because of their misunderstanding about the Lord's return.

And third, Paul wrote to encourage them to live lives that were holy and pleasing to the Lord. He was grateful for their progress in the Christian life but wanted them to excel still more.

3. Ibid., p. 22.

D. BASIC OUTLINE OF 1 THESSALONIANS

I. The Past Ministry Among the Thessalonians (1:1–2:16)
   A. The Past Ministry of the Word in Their Lives (1:1-10)
   B. The Past Ministry of Paul in Their Lives (2:1-12)
   C. The Past Ministry Brought Response in Their Lives (2:13-16)
II. The Present Ministry to the Thessalonians (2:17–5:11)
   A. The Ministry of Encouragement (2:17–3:13)
   B. The Ministry of Edification and Exhortation (4:1–5:11)
III. The Future Ministry by the Thessalonians (5:12-28)
   A. Their Obligations in Christian Living (5:12-22)
   B. Their Obligations to Paul and Others (5:23-28)

E. THEME OF 1 THESSALONIANS

The main theme of this letter is the return of Jesus Christ. Although a number of other matters are dealt with (such as the gospel ministry), the primary thrust of the letter is the believer's life and thinking in light of Jesus Christ's return. This coming of Christ was to motivate and encourage them.

F. SPECIAL CONSIDERATIONS ON 1 THESSALONIANS

1. The city of Thessalonica

Thessalonica was located in the region of Macedonia and was its chief city. It was located some 100 miles west of the city of Philippi on the Egnatian Way (the major east-west highway that led to Rome itself). Geographically, it was located at the mouth of the Gulf of Therma. The seaport had been developed, and as a result Thessalonica was a commercially oriented city. The city was a loyal Roman city, having been declared a free city in 42 B.C. (A free city meant it was ruled by its own local rulers.) In New Testament times the city's population was about 200,000. Its size and strategic location made it a prime target for the church planting ministry of Paul. The city had a fairly large Jewish population but was predominantly Greek. Nearby was Mt. Olympus (the mythical mountain of the gods), and this accounted for the city's devotion to the gods of the Greek pantheon.

2. The composition of the Thessalonian church

Paul had the custom of going to the Jewish synagogue when he came to a new field of ministry This was true in Thessalonica, and as a result the "charter members" of the church were Jews (Acts 17:4). In the first weeks of preaching, Gentiles who had adhered to the synagogue and a number of "chief women" were converted as well. Jewish resistance to the gospel came quickly with the result that Jewish converts were effectively cut off. Apparently the church's majority became those who had been saved out of paganism (1 Thess. 1:9).

SUMMARY OF 1 THESSALONIANS

I. The Past Ministry Among the Thessalonians (1:1–2:16)

    A. The Past Ministry of the Word in Their Lives (1:1-10)

The good report from Timothy caused Paul to rejoice. The Word of God had been received and was at work in their lives. He was thankful for their good works and their excellent testimony. It had become obvious to all that they had turned from their idolatry to the true God (1:3-9). These new believers lived in anticipation of Christ's return and their own deliverance from the wrath to come (1:10).

The apostle Paul was teaching these believers that Jesus would rescue them out of *the* coming wrath. Paul speaks here of a future aspect of divine wrath commonly referred to as the Tribulation. He knew that Christians suffer persecution at the hands of men, but he made a distinction between persecution from men and wrath from God. They differ in kind as well as intensity. When the term *wrath of God* is used in a future sense, it usually has the judgments of the Tribulation in view.[4]

    B. The Past Ministry of Paul in Their Lives (2:1-12)

In this section the apostle defended himself against the charges that were being leveled against him. He did this by re-

---

4. C. F. Hogg and W. E. Vine, *The Epistles to the Thessalonians* (Fincastle, Va.: Scripture Truth, 1959), p. 49.

minding the Thessalonians of his past ministry among them. He stated that he was not guilty of teaching error, speaking in deceitful or manipulative ways, or being motivated by greed and self-glory (2:1-3, 5-6). On the other hand his ministry was characterized by his plain teaching of God's Word, his hard work, and his deep love for them. He reminded them that he was like a mother and a father to them (2:4; 7-12).

C. The Past Ministry Brought Response in Their Lives (2:13-16)

Paul's ministry had been received for what it really was—a word from God. They had responded in a positive way in spite of persecution from the unbelieving Jews.

II. The Present Ministry to the Thessalonians (2:17–5:11)

A. The Ministry of Encouragement (2:17–3:13)

Paul encouraged these believers by assuring them of his strong desire to be with them (2:17-20), by sending Timothy to them to minister to them (3:1 8), and by his consistent praying for them (3:9-13)

B. The Ministry of Edification and Exhortation (4:1–5:11)

Paul had learned that certain issues and problems were present in the church, and the apostle now addressed them. First, he exhorted them to correct moral problems (4:1-8). He stated that sexual immorality is not God's will. He warned that involvement in immorality will bring a believer into the severe discipline of God (cf. Heb. 13:4). Paul then encouraged them to excel in genuine love, seeking to do what is best for others (4:9-12).

When Paul was in Thessalonica, he had taught them that one day Jesus would return and suddenly take all believers to heaven. (This event is commonly called the "rapture.") He apparently taught them that the rapture could occur at any moment with no events necessarily preceding it. When, therefore, some Christians died, the church was distressed that these would miss out on the rapture. Paul wrote to comfort them (4:18) by assuring them that all believers in Christ will be taken in this event. In fact, the ones who have died will go first and will be followed immediately by the living Christians. (In 1 Cor. 15:51-53, Paul explains that all

Christians will receive their resurrection bodies at the rapture, with the dead being raised and the living being changed instantly.)

Paul continued his discussion of future things in the next section (5:1-11), but changed subjects from the rapture to the "day of the Lord." (The "day of the Lord" is an Old Testament term that refers to the Tribulation period, when the context is about judgment.)[5] Paul emphatically assures believers that they will not experience the "day of the Lord" (5:9). Apparently some at Thessalonica thought that the persecution they were enduring was the Tribulation.

III. The Future Ministry by the Thessalonians (5:12-28)

A. Their Obligations in Christian Living (5:12-22)

Paul had urged these believers to live concerned, balanced lives in view of future events. He gave instructions for positive relationships in the church (5:12-14) and instructions for positive, godly living (5:15-22).

B. Their Obligations to Paul and Others (5:23-28)

As Paul concluded this epistle, he encouraged them to be praying for him and to be gracious and open to other believers.

5. Paul N. Benware, *Survey of the Old Testament* (Chicago: Moody, 1988), p. 183.

13

2 THESSALONIANS

INTRODUCTION TO 2 THESSALONIANS

A. AUTHORSHIP OF 2 THESSALONIANS

This letter was written by the apostle Paul. Twice he mentions his own name (1:1; 3:17). The evidence within the letter itself and the evidence from the early church Fathers leave no doubt that Paul wrote it.

B. PLACE AND DATE OF 2 THESSALONIANS

The second letter written to the Thessalonian Christians was probably written shortly after the first. Therefore, it too was written from Corinth about A.D. 51.

C. PURPOSE OF 2 THESSALONIANS

The main reason for writing this letter was to deal with error in the church at Thessalonica. First, Paul needed to correct the doctrinal error that the ''day of the Lord'' (the Tribulation) had already come. Second, he found it necessary to talk about the discipline of problem believers.

---

1. D. Edmond Hiebert, *An Introduction to the Pauline Epistles* (Chicago: Moody, 1971), pp. 55-59.

D. BASIC OUTLINE OF 2 THESSALONIANS

    I. Instructions Concerning Future Things (1:1–2:12)
        A. An Explanation About Present Persecution (1:1-12)
        B. Reasonings About the Day of the Lord (2:1-12)
    II. Instructions Concerning Present Responsibilities (2:13–3:17)
        A. The Encouragement to Continue (2:13-17)
        B. The Exhortation to Pray (3:1-5)
        C. The Exhortation to Correct Problems (3:6-15)
    III. Conclusion (3:16-18)

E. THEME OF 2 THESSALONIANS

Paul learned that the believers were still not clear on what he had taught concerning future events This letter is a fuller explanation of the Lord's return and the "day of the Lord." Paul demonstrated that they were not in the Tribulation (in spite of their persecution and the teaching of some).

F. SPECIAL CONSIDERATIONS ON 2 THESSALONIANS

This epistle contains important information on the Antichrist. The Antichrist is a man who will become a great political leader in the last days, being the dominant human figure in the Tribulation. Although he is a political leader prior to the Tribulation, it is his signing of a treaty with the nation of Israel that marks him out as the Antichrist and begins the Tribulation itself. He will be a man of great natural abilities but also one who is empowered by Satan. He will be aggressively opposed to God and will be responsible for the deaths of millions of God's people. Powerful and deceptive miracles will characterize his life and rule, resulting in the worship of him by multitudes. He will be Satan's attempt to give the world a messiah before the Messiah, Jesus Christ, comes to reign on the earth (cf. Daniel 7:20-26; 9:24-27; Matt. 24:15-24; Rev. 13:1-18; 17:12-17).

SUMMARY OF 2 THESSALONIANS

I. Instructions Concerning Future Things (1:1–2:12)

A. An Explanation About Present Persecution (1:1-12)

Even though this second letter is less personal than the first, Paul still gave a word of thanksgiving, expressing gratitude for their growing faith (1:1-4). He then encouraged these believers in their time of severe persecution, explaining that God knew their situation and would repay with judgment those who were persecuting them. Their enemies, who did not know God or the gospel, will pay the penalty of eternal ruin. This judgment will take place at the second coming of Christ to the earth (1:5-12).

B. Reasonings About the Day of the Lord (2:1-12)

The Thessalonian believers were shocked by the idea that the Tribulation had already begun. Apparently some were using Paul himself as their source for this idea (2:2). But Paul declared that they were not in the ''day of the Lord.'' Three events, he stated, must take place before this time can come.

1. The arrival of *the* apostasy

There will be a massive departure from the true faith in those days.

2. The appearance of the Antichrist

The one signing a treaty with Israel will be Antichrist.

3. The removal of the Holy Spirit's restraining ministry

Note that the Spirit, who is omnipresent, does not leave the world, but rather His ministry of restraining sin is removed. Since the Spirit does use the true church of Jesus Christ as a means of restraining evil in the world, this could well indicate that the church is removed prior to the beginning of the Tribulation period.[2] None of these events had yet occurred.

Paul then revealed more truth about the Antichrist (''the man of sin,'' ''the lawless one''), emphasizing the deceptive nature of the signs and wonders that will be performed. These miracles will cause many to believe ''the lie,'' which is probably the idea that the Antichrist is the Messiah.

2. J. Dwight Pentecost, *Things to Come* (Grand Rapids: Dunham, 1964), pp. 259-74.

II. Instructions Concerning Present Responsibilities (2:13–3:17)

A. The Encouragement to Continue (2:13-17)

Paul again gave thanks for their salvation and encouraged them to continue in their faithfulness to the Lord, looking forward to a glorious future.

B. The Exhortation to Pray (3:1-5)

Paul was deeply convinced of the power of prayer and requested that these believers support him by their prayers. Specifically he wanted them to pray for the advancement of the gospel and for the safety of those who proclaim it.

C. The Exhortation to Correct Problems (3:6-15)

The church is responsible to maintain its own purity. Paul, therefore, commanded the church to admonish those who were out of step with the truth. If believers do not respond, then they must be dealt with more severely.

III. Conclusion (3:16-18)

THE PAULINE EPISTLES:
GROUP TWO

PAUL'S MAJOR EPISTLES

Letter	Date (A.D.)	Written from
1 Corinthians	54/55	Ephesus
2 Corinthians	55/56	Macedonia
Romans	55/56	Corinth

14

1 CORINTHIANS

A. AUTHORSHIP OF 1 CORINTHIANS

The apostle Paul was the author of this letter. No serious question is raised concerning the Pauline authorship of 1 Corinthians, as the author identifies himself as Paul (1:1; 16:21) and refers to Apollos (3:5) and Timothy (4:17) as his associates. Both men were closely associated with Paul in Acts. The author claims to have founded the Corinthian church, which was founded by Paul on his second missionary journey (3:10 with Acts 18:1-17). This internal evidence, coupled with the testimonies of Polycarp, Irenaeus, Clement of Rome, and Tetullian, who refer to 1 Corinthians as being of Pauline authorship, make a strong case for the apostle Paul.

B. PLACE AND DATE OF 1 CORINTHIANS

The letter was written from Ephesus during the third missionary journey of Paul (1 Cor. 16:8, 19). The date of writing was probably late A.D. 54 or in early 55.

C. PURPOSE OF 1 CORINTHIANS

Information had come to the apostle from several sources concerning ''serious problems'' that were gripping the Corinthian assembly. Also a letter had arrived from Corinth with a series of questions that needed some apostolic insight. Paul's purpose in writing 1 Corinthians was twofold: (1) to deal with those severe problems in the church, and (2) to answer the questions from the church.

D.   BASIC OUTLINE OF 1 CORINTHIANS

I.   Introduction (1:1-9)
II. Divisions in the Church (1:1–4:21)
   A. Paul's Declaration on Division (1:10-17)
   B. Paul's Condemnation of Division (1:18–4:21)
III. Sins in the Church (5:1–6:20)
   A. Loose Morals and a Lack of Discipline (5:1-13)
   B. Lawsuits in the Church (6:1-11)
   C. Immorality in the Church (6:12-20)
IV. Problems of the Church (7:1–15:58)
   A. The Matter of Marriage (7:1-40)
   B. The Matter of Doubtful Things (8:1–11:1)
   C. The Matter of Worship and Ministry (11:2–14:40)
   D. The Matter of Resurrection (15:1-58)
V.   Conclusion (16:1-24)

E.   THEME OF 1 CORINTHIANS

Although there are a great variety of subjects that are dealt with in this letter, the main underlying theme is sanctification. Now that these people were saved by faith in Christ, Paul wanted their lives to accurately reflect their position as children of God. *Sanctification* means to be set apart. As believers in Christ, we are to be in the process of being set apart unto God and as a result set apart from sin. This was Paul's desire for the Corinthian believers.

F.   SPECIAL CONSIDERATIONS ON 1 CORINTHIANS

1. The City of Corinth

The isthmus of Corinth was the land bridge between northern and southern Greece. The city of Corinth was located in a strategic place on that land bridge with a gulf on either side. This gave Corinth several important harbors, thus placing it on significant trade routes. The city was also important politically as the capital of the province of Achaia.

The dominant minority in Corinth was the Romans, many of whom were veterans of war. Two other groups were influential, namely the Greeks and the Jews. The city also had a large slave population. Some estimate that the slaves constituted about 60 percent of the population. Added to these residents were the unusually large number of travelers and traders that could be found there at any given time.

Corinth was known as a prosperous but corrupt city. ''To live like a Corinthian'' became synonymous with a life of luxury and licentiousness. The city was known throughout the Roman world for its vice and immorality. One of the major influences on that degenerate moral climate was the degrading worship of the goddess Aphrodite (the goddess of love). Her temple was located on the top of the Acrocorinthus (the ''high Corinth'' on a rock plateau rising perpendicularly 1,800 feet above the city of Corinth). This temple housed some 1,000 prostitutes who were there to aid in the ''worship'' of Aphrodite. Many other temples were found in the city, and these simply added to its moral corruption. It is not suprising, therefore, that the church at Corinth had a major problem with immorality. It is also interesting to note that Paul wrote his letter to the Romans from Corinth, a letter in which he discusses the terrible depravity of man.

2. The Church at Corinth

This church was started by Paul on his second missionary journey and received more attention from him on that journey than any other church. The church itself was made up of both Jews and Gentiles. (Believers' names in 1 Corinthians are both Jewish and Greek.) Although the New Testament contains two letters of Paul to the church at Corinth, he actually wrote more than two letters to them. It is also clear that he visited Corinth more than the two times recorded in Acts. From Acts and from 1 and 2 Corinthians something of the apostle's relationship with this church can be determined.

Paul's relationship with the Corinthian believers is probably an excellent illustration of the apostle's constant care and concern for those churches that he founded. He did not simply start churches and then leave them to try to survive on their own.

SUMMARY OF 1 CORINTHIANS

I. Introduction (1:1-9)

As Paul begins the letter he expresses his gratitude for the good things that God had done at Corinth. While fully aware of their sins and failures, he focuses first on some positive elements in their lives. The apostle gives thanks that they had been saved by Christ (1:2-4), that they had an understanding of the Scriptures, that they were fully gifted with spiritual gifts (1:5-7), and that they were waiting for the Lord to come back. About a dozen times he refers to Christ in this section, emphasizing the truth that Jesus is Lord of the church. He concludes his opening remarks by reminding them that they have been called by God to the most important relationship in the universe—to live in fellowship with Jesus Christ (1:9 and 1 John 1:3, 6-7).

II. Divisions in the Church (1:1–4:21)

A. Paul's Declaration on Division (1:10-17)

Paul is greatly concerned about the lack of unity in the church, and he deals with that problem first, realizing that many other problems flow out of disunity. (The church, the Body of Christ, is incapable of division without destruction taking place.) This church had divided into four groups, behind four personalities. Paul condemns their exclusiveness, pointing out that only Christ can save people and only Christ is worthy of having disciples. Men do have good and legitimate ministries, but believers are to identify with Christ and not a particular man.

B. Paul's Condemnation of Division (1:18–4:21)

The basic problem of the Corinthians was that they were viewing matters as unsaved people would view them. They were operating according to the wisdom of the world. They lacked God's wisdom, and this was the fundamental reason that they were divided and were experiencing so many problems. God's wisdom makes it possible to view life from God's perspective. According to Paul, the core of God's wisdom is the cross of

Christ. It alone shows the real situation of mankind (that he is sinful and helplessly lost), and the only solution to this situation (God's power to save and sanctify). Once a person sees these basic issues (of God's holiness, man's sinfulness, and God's power to save through the death of Christ), then and only then can he possibly deal correctly with the issues of life (1:18-25).

Paul reminds them that most Christians do not come from the ranks of the rich, powerful, or wise of this world (1:26-31). Yet Christians, as the "lesser" occupants of this planet, can live successfully and wisely, thus bringing great glory to God since it is obvious that His wisdom and not our resources are accomplishing this. (See James 3:13-18 for contrasts between the wisdom of God and man.)

Paul then reminds them that when he first came to them he just preached "Jesus Christ and Him crucified" (2:2), which is the foundation of God's wisdom. He did not try to overpower them with his intellect or with clever arguments (2:1-5). But even though the gospel is simple, it does have great wisdom (2:6-13). Its truths do not pass away (they are eternal); its truths bring a person to glory (sin is gone and replaced by eternal life); and its truths are so deep that the Holy Spirit is needed to understand them.

Paul points out that the manner in which a person responds to the Word (the wisdom of God) determines his ability to live wisely and determines his spiritual health. The Word must be understood and applied to life (2:14–3:4). Wisdom appropriated brings a person to spiritual maturity, whereas perpetual infancy is the result of wisdom ignored.

After sharing these truths about the need for wisdom, the apostle touches on the ministries of different men at Corinth—men that the Corinthians were dividing up behind. He wanted the Corinthians to be wise and understanding about those who ministered in their midst. Using himself and Apollos as examples, he notes that both ministries were important. But though each had his role, ultimately God is the One who brings spiritual life and growth to the church (3:4-7). Paul informs them that all believers are servants of God and are, therefore, accountable to Him.

This leads into the most extensive discussion in the New Testament on the evaluation and rewarding of believers (3:11–4:5). The apostle notes that the Lord will not only be reviewing what we have done in this life, but will base much of our rewarding on our faithfulness as stewards of that which He has given to us, and on our motives. Paul insists that he was telling them these things and warning them because, like a parent, he was deeply concerned for the welfare of his children (4:6-21).

III. Sins in the Church (5:1–6:20)
    A. Loose Morals and a Lack of Discipline (5:1-13)

The apostle was upset that immorality existed in the church. (The word *immorality,* or *fornication,* is a comprehensive term that includes all forms of wrong sexual behavior.) The particular sin focused on here was that of incest. The church knew of the situation and tolerated it. (Worldly wisdom is always broadminded about sin.) The Corinthian church was in danger of being badly affected by it. Paul rebukes them for their prideful tolerance. He declares that they were responsible for the purity of the church. He had told them in a previous letter not to tolerate immorality (5:9). They were commanded to deal with the sin and to remove the offending member from the church (5:12-13).

    B. Lawsuits in the Church (6:1-11)

Their lack of wisdom is also seen in their inability to solve disputes among themselves. Instead they would go to the secular law courts and have unbelievers settle their cases. Paul rebukes them for doing this and tells them to find wise leaders in the church to resolve these matters. Better than that, he tells them, simply surrender your "rights" and suffer wrong. They were focusing on their rights, whereas Paul focused on their attitudes.

    C. Immorality in the Church (6:12-20)

Immorality had been a way of life for many at Corinth. Paul exhorts these believers to flee immorality because their bodies had been purchased by Christ. Also he instructs them that their bodies are indwelt by the Holy Spirit and would someday be resurrected. Their bodies are important to God and are not to be involved in immorality.

IV. Problems of the Church (7:1–15:58)

At this point the letter changes. Paul begins to answer the questions that the believers at Corinth had asked him.

A. The Matter of Marriage (7:1-40)

The terribly immoral climate of Corinth raised questions regarding sex, marriage, divorce, and singleness. Being surrounded by depraved sexual behavior, the Corinthian Christians wondered if celibacy or abstinence was best, even in marriage. Paul says that sexual desires are a legitimate part of our lives, and within marriage bring satisfaction and fulfillment. Both partners bear a responsibility to the other in this matter. An unhappy sex life within the marriage relationship will open a person to sexual sin (7:1-9).

Since marriage was not sacred in the Roman world, divorce was accepted as a part of life. Paul discusses the matter of divorce next, first dealing with the situation when both partners are believers (7:10-11) and then looking at the marriage where one partner is an unbeliever. He declares that Christians are not to be divorced. (Note that "departing" or "leaving" means divorce and not some sort of legal separation.) If Christian couples do divorce, they are not to remarry. (This probably assumes that immorality is not the issue. If Matthew 19:9 makes immorality the exception, then a Christian could divorce an immoral Christian spouse with the possibility of remarriage.) If the marriage has an unbeliever as part of it, that does not give the believer a right to divorce the unbeliever. If the unbeliever, however, initiates the breakup of the marriage, the believer is not under obligation to that marriage and is free to remarry.

In dealing with the matter of singleness, the apostle points out some of the advantages of being unmarried. He notes that greater dedication to Christ is possible, since the single person does not have the obligations toward other family members that take time, energy, and resources. But Paul is not against marriage. His counsel must be interpreted in light of his statement that the present difficult times made singleness the better option (7:26). The circumstances of persecution and difficulty for Christians were the backdrop for his advice.

B. The Matter of Doubtful Things (8:1–11:1)

A "doubtful thing" is something (often having to do with an activity or one's adornment) about which the Bible has no specific commands and concerning which sincere Christians differ. At Corinth, one such doubtful thing had to do with eating meat that previously had been sacrificed to idols. Although Paul does not take sides on the issue, he does give some principles to apply to such situations. (See Romans 14 as well.)

First, Paul says, believers are to make decisions on the basis of knowledge. There ought to be a biblical basis for the choice made. Second, they are to act on the basis of love. They should be willing to suppress their liberties for the sake of weaker Christians. Paul modeled this truth in his own life, giving up his own personal rights in order to benefit other believers.

C. The Matter of Worship and Ministry (11:2–14:40)

There were several matters having to do with the public meeting of the church that needed apostolic insight. First, he addresses the issue of women in the public assembly (11:2-16). He teaches them that a woman could pray and prophesy as long as it was clear that she was under the authority of men (11:3). This was not a cultural issue at Corinth, but something taught in all the churches (11:16, and 1 Timothy 2:11-15).

Second, Paul instructs them to treat with reverence the ordinance of the Lord's Supper. He rebukes them for their sacrilege (11:17-22), reminds them of the significance of the ordinance (11:23-26), and warns them of additional chastening from the Lord (11:27-34).

A third matter in the public worship of the church had to do with spiritual gifts. (A spiritual gift is a God-given ability to serve the Lord effectively in some particular way.) Paul informed the church that spiritual gifts were given to believers so that they might bring strength to the other believers in the church (12:1-11). He reminded them that the church is like a body and that just as the various parts of the physical body depend on one another for health and strength, so also do the members in the Body of Christ (the church). The Body is one (12:12-13), has diverse parts (12:14-20), but these parts are interdependent (12:21-27 and Eph. 4:7-

14). Since spiritual gifts are for the common good (12:7) of all believers, they are not to be used selfishly. They are to be used in love (13:1-13).

Paul then wrapped up his discussion of gifts by dealing with a problem that existed at Corinth in relationship to the gift of tongues (14:1-40). The basic point of this section is that the gift of prophecy is greater than the gift of tongues. (See appendix, *Note D: The Gift of Tongues.*)

D. The Matter of Resurrection (15:1-58)

Apparently someone at Corinth was teaching the false idea that there is no resurrection from the dead (15:12). Paul declared that the resurrection of Jesus Christ is the cornerstone of the Christian faith. If Jesus was not raised bodily from the grave, then there is no valid Christian faith, sin has not been conquered, and there is no hope for the future (15:12-20). But since Jesus was the "firstfruits" of the resurrection, this is the guarantee that believers too will be raised from the dead, receiving new bodies and experiencing victory over death (15:50-58).

V. Conclusion (16:1-24)

Paul concluded this letter by encouraging them to abound in the work of the Lord by giving of their money. They were to give regularly according to the degree that the Lord had prospered them. He also told them that he did intend to come to see them, and he sent greetings from other believers.

15

2 CORINTHIANS

INTRODUCTION TO 2 CORINTHIANS

A. AUTHORSHIP OF 2 CORINTHIANS

The apostle Paul was the author, but once again he includes Timothy in the letter's introduction.

B. PLACE AND DATE OF 2 CORINTHIANS

Second Corinthians was probably written shortly after 1 Corinthians, perhaps in A.D. 55 or 56. It was written from Macedonia, where Paul had gone seeking Titus, his co-worker (2 Cor. 2:12-13; 7:4-16). Tradition states that he wrote it from the Macedonian city of Philippi.

C. PURPOSE OF 2 CORINTHIANS

As trouble continued to fester in the Corinthian church, Paul sent his capable associate Titus to Corinth to deal with the situation. Later on, Paul himself left Ephesus and travelled to Troas where opportunity was favorable for him to minister (2:12-13). However, Paul was so deeply concerned about conditions at Corinth, and was so very anxious to hear from Titus, he journeyed to Macedonia hoping to meet Titus there.

Finally, Titus did arrive in Macedonia and reported that things at Corinth were generally positive. But, he told Paul, there was still an aggressive minority that was still opposed to Paul.

Paul, therefore, wrote 2 Corinthians to reinforce his authority as an apostle of Jesus Christ. It was absolutely necessary for him to do this in order to preserve the health of the church. He also wrote to give thanks for the favorable response toward him and his ministry that was now being exhibited by the majority. Furthermore, he felt he needed to remind them about giving to the poor saints of Judea and to instruct them about the proper attitude toward one who repents.

D.   BASIC OUTLINE OF 2 CORINTHIANS

     I. Introduction (1:1-11)
    II. Paul's Personal Testimony (1:12–2:13)
   III. Paul's Teachings About the True Ministry of Christ (2:14–6:10)
   IV. Paul's Exhortations to the Corinthians (6:11–7:16)
    V. Paul's Instructions About Giving (8:1–9:15)
   VI. Paul's Defense of His Apostolic Ministry (10:1–13:10)
  VII. Conclusion (13:11-14)

E.   THEME OF 2 CORINTHIANS

Because of the negative attitudes toward him at Corinth, Paul found it necessary to defend his ministry and to vindicate his apostolic authority. In the process of defending himself and his ministry, the apostle reveals a great deal about the nature of the gospel ministry. This is the theme of this letter. This is the most significant letter in the New Testament regarding a genuine ministry for the Lord Jesus Christ. It has, therefore, a special place in the lives of those who desire to serve Christ effectively.

F.   SPECIAL CONSIDERATIONS ON 2 CORINTHIANS

This letter was written in the midst of turmoil and conflict with certain ones in the Corinthian church, but at the same time reflects Paul's great joy and his love for others there. The letter reveals the deep emotions of the apostle Paul as no other epistle does. It is the least systematic of Paul's writings, but the one that reveals the most about the man himself. '' Erasmus compares this epistle to a river which sometimes flows in a gentle stream, sometimes rushes down as a torrent bearing all before it, sometimes spreading out like a placid lake, sometimes losing itself, as it were, in the sand, and breaking out in its fullness in some unexpected place.''[1] The letter reflects Paul's intense emotional stress. There are broken constructions, mixed metaphors, rapid shift in content, and a wide variety of emotions.[2] The unique style of this letter makes it more difficult to interpret in a logical, systematic way.

SUMMARY OF 2 CORINTHIANS

I. Introduction (1:1-11)

Paul opens this letter with a word of praise to God. Paul had experienced some severe trials but he also experienced the comfort of God (cf. 11:23-28).

II. Paul's Personal Testimony (1:12–2:13)

As the apostle enters into the subject of his relationship with the church, he is candid with them. He is able to say that he had a clear conscience in the matter of his relationship with them. Some apparently had accused Paul of being fickle and unreliable, pointing out that he said he would come and then he did not arrive (1:12-17). But Paul reminds them that he had always been open and honest with them, never manipulating them. He tells them that he is convinced by the Spirit that he should not adhere to his original intention to come to them. The reason for this is that they might be given time to act and minister on their own. Paul's presence at that time would cause unnecessary pain and dependence on him (1:18–2:4).

At this point, he gives instructions about restoring the believer who was under church discipline (2:5-11). He says that a genuinely repentant believer needed to receive comfort and encouragement or else Satan could well destroy him with guilt and

---

1. Charles Hodge, *Commentary on the Second Epistle to the Corinthians* (Grand Rapids: Eerdmans, n.d.). p. 2.
2. D. Edmond Hiebert, *The Thessalonian Epistles* (Chicago: Moody, 1971). pp. 149-51.

grief. Paul concludes this section by sharing with them how deeply he had been affected by the situation at Corinth (2:12-13).

III. Paul's Teachings About the True Ministry of Christ (2:14–6:10)

One of the great contributions of 2 Corinthians is found in this section as Paul reveals the true nature of the gospel ministry. Paul believed in the ultimate triumph of Christ no matter what feelings of failure, frustration, or anxiety he may have had (2:14-17). Paul does not have a utopian view of the ministry. He understands that while there was indeed joy in being a bondslave of Christ, there is no getting away from trials, heartaches, and pressures. Some apparently doubted that Paul's ministry was genuinely of God, and they were saying so. But Paul responds by pointing out that the Corinthian church itself is proof that his ministry is valid (3:1-3).

He further notes that it was not his ability that brought results, but rather the transforming power of the New Covenant—that salvation provided by the work of Jesus Christ (3:4-18). He then goes on in the letter to tell them that as a minister of the New Covenant he does not get discouraged when people do not believe (4:1-6). He understands Satan's activity of blinding people to the gospel message. He also understands that God's power, not human gimmicks, will bring people to Christ. Our personal insufficiency serves to manifest more clearly the power of God (4:8-18).

As Paul thinks about the afflictions of this life, he is encouraged by the truth that someday he will be with the Lord. The earthly physical body which is subject to decay will be transformed. But whether he is on the earth or with the Lord, he wants to please Him. Paul pleases Him now by ministering for Him (5:1-10). Our ministry is one of reconciliation. (Reconciliation means to remove enmity between individuals, or to make friendly again.) When Christ died on the cross, He fully satisfied God's righteous demands. The sin issue was settled once and for ever, and now God waits for men to turn back to Him. Man must be reconciled to God, and this is the ministry of believers today (5:11-21).

IV. Paul's Exhortations to the Corinthians (6:11–7:16)

In this section Paul encourages them to be open to him (6:11-13) and to be separate from the world (6:14–7:1). Also, he wants them to understand the nature of true repentance (7:2-16).

V. Paul's Instructions About Giving (8:1–9:15)

Sometime in the past the Corinthian believers had committed themselves to give financial aid to needy believers. Paul now reminds them of their commitment and encourages them to be generous. He tells them that it is essential to have a proper attitude when giving (9:6-9). He uses the Macedonian Christians as well as the Lord Jesus as examples of excellence in giving (8:1-9). He also makes it clear that financial matters are sensitive issues. Care must be exercised to give no appearance of wrongdoing (8:16-24).

VI. Paul's Defense of His Apostolic Ministry (10:1–13:10)

There is a dramatic change in the tone of the letter at this point. He now faces those who challenge his apostolic authority. There are probably no more severe statements in all of Paul's writings than those found in this section. Paul understands several facts about his authority.

First, he realizes that he has been given authority by Christ Himself. Second, this authority is given to be a blessing to Christians as he builds them up in their faith. Third, he knows that this authority could be used to discipline them severely if necessary. He is reluctant to use his authority in discipline, but would if he had to. His opponents are not to count on his restraint, or assume that he has no real power. A fourth fact is that God has placed the Corinthians under his authority since he founded the church. Paul does not attempt to usurp the authority of other apostles or to enter into their realm of jurisdiction (10:1-18).

Paul hated to commend himself, but because his detractors at Corinth had undermined the people's confidence in Paul, he is forced to do so for the good of the church. He reminds them of his personal conduct among them (11:1-15), and of his personal sufferings as Christ's apostle (11:16-33). Paul was clearly not in the ministry for pleasure or gain. He told them of his visions and of his "thorn in the flesh" (12:1-10). He reminds them that he has been accredited as an apostle through signs and miracles (12:11-13).

He issues a final warning to those who resist him and his ministry (12:14–13:10). They have no more time. They either must repent or face the full exercise of his apostolic authority. He will discipline when he comes.

VII. Conclusion (13:11-14)

16

ROMANS

INTRODUCTION TO ROMANS

A. AUTHORSHIP OF ROMANS

There is no real question that the apostle Paul wrote this letter. The letter claims to be from his pen and the internal evidence strongly supports that claim. "So conclusive is the argument for Pauline authorship of this epistle that no serious scholar doubts it comes from the noted apostle to the Gentiles."[1]

B. PLACE AND DATE OF ROMANS

By combining the historical data found in the book of Acts with statements made in the Corinthian letters and Romans, it becomes clear that Romans was written from Corinth on the third missionary journey. Paul spent about three months at Corinth at the end of his third journey (Acts 20:2-3). At this time, he received a collection for the poor saints in Jerusalem and was headed there in order to deliver it (cf. Acts 24:17; Rom. 15:25-26; 1 Cor. 16:1-4; 2 Cor. 8:1–9:15). This would place the writing of this letter about A.D. 56.

---

1. Alan Johnson, *Romans: The Freedom Letter,* rev. ed. (Chicago: Moody, 1984), 1:10.

C.   PURPOSE OF ROMANS

Twice in the letter the apostle Paul gives the reason for writing Romans (1:10-13; 15:22-25). He tells them that he really wants to come to see them, but circumstances have kept him from coming time and again. He, therefore, is writing this letter. He hopes to come to them eventually, but probably realizes that he might not ever arrive at Rome, considering the trouble that he expected at Jerusalem and realizing that many sought his death.

To our knowledge the church at Rome did not have any major doctrinal or practical problems that needed apostolic attention. It is not for such reasons that Paul wrote Romans. However, he probably did have a number of reasons for writing. Paul wrote to enlist the help of the church at Rome for his missionary efforts to the west, including Spain. He wrote to emphasize the universality of the gospel of Christ—it is for Jews and Gentiles. He wrote to give to the church of Jesus Christ a clear and comprehensive presentation of the doctrine of salvation by faith. And he wrote for some personal reasons, including seeking prayer support for himself and hoping to have some spiritual fruit among them (1:11-13; 15:30-33).[2]

D.   BASIC OUTLINE OF ROMANS

   I. Introduction (1:1-17)
     A. Paul's Greeting (1:1-7)
     B. Personal Matters (1:8-13)
     C. Theme Statement (1:14-17)
  II. The Sinfulness and Condemnation of All Men (1:18–3:20)
     A. The Guilt of the Gentiles (1:18-32)
     B. The Guilt of the Jews (2:1–3:8)
     C. The Guilt of All Men (3:9-20)
 III. The Justification of Believing Sinners (3:2l–5:2l)
     A. The Basis of Justification (3:21-26)
     B. Justification and the Law (3:27-31)

2. D. Edmond Hiebert, *An Introduction to the Pauline Epistles* (Chicago: Moody, 1971), pp. 178-81.

E.   THEME OF ROMANS

The theme of Romans is righteousness. This letter discusses in detail the righteousness that God provides for sinful mankind. This is the only kind of righteousness that God approves. The epistle also discusses the kind of righteous living that ought to characterize those who are believers in Christ.

F.   SPECIAL CONSIDERATIONS ON ROMANS

1. The City of Rome

By the time of Paul Rome was the most influential city in the world. Paul was a citizen of the Roman Empire, and it was his great desire to preach the gospel of Christ in the imperial city. When Paul wrote to the saints at Rome he was writing at a time of peace, prosperity, and order. Although the infamous Nero was ruling at this time (A.D. 54-68), it was basically a good era because Nero had chosen able men to govern. Rome was a well ordered society. It is estimated that the city may have had a population as large as four million.[3] With this huge population, the typical characteristics of a big city could be found.

> Luxury and squalor, wealth and want existed side by side. The institution of slavery cast its baneful influence over the whole. Physical toil was despised and deemed fit only for slaves. Manufacturing and trade were considered the business of the slave and the foreigner. Only somewhat over half of the population were free citizens. Of these a comparatively small number were wealthy, while the vast majority were poor and lived on public or private charity. These pauper citizens were proud of their Roman citizenship and disdained the degradation of manual labor. . . . In the city might be found elements of almost every nationality, and each group brought its train of vices with it.[4]

It was in this atmosphere that the church was founded and was growing. For a period of time the peace of Rome allowed this development to go on. But that ended when Nero began his diabolical persecution of Christians.

2. The Church at Rome

The church at Rome was not founded by any apostle in general (Rom. 15:20), nor Peter or Paul in particular. Most likely the church was started by those who came to faith in Christ elsewhere and brought their faith to Rome with them. Some Jews may have

3. Ibid., p. 165.
4. Ibid.

come to Rome after being saved on the Day of Pentecost (Acts 2:10). However, the church at Rome apparently was basically Gentile (although there was a sizable Jewish element as well) and it is doubtful that Jews would have founded a Gentile church. "The door to the heathen was not opened until years after the descent of the Spirit. It would be a much better guess to say that some from the household of Cornelius (Acts 10) carried to Rome the news of a Savior for the Gentiles."[5] These may well have been the founders of the church. But it is also likely that some of Paul's converts from other places had gone there also, as is suggested by the many names listed in Romans 16.

There were Jews in the church since Paul seems to be arguing with them (e.g. 4:1; 7:1-10). There was a Gentile element as well (e.g., 11:13, 18, 25; 15:16, 18, 27). The church contained both groups, but the majority were Gentile.

SUMMARY OF ROMANS

I. Introduction (1:1-17)

Since most at Rome had not directly been under Paul's ministry, he gives his credentials (1:1). He tells them that the gospel entrusted to him was that gospel which had brought the Romans to Christ (1:2-7). He observed that in a matter of about ten years their faith in Christ had become known everywhere. It was his desire to develop and nurture that faith along (1:8-13).

Paul begins an entirely new thought in 1:14 when he states that he is a debtor. Up to that time he had had no transactions with the Romans that caused him to be a debtor to them. Rather he had had dealings with Christ Jesus that made him a debtor. The grace of Christ toward him, and his possession of the universal gospel made Paul a debtor to all people. This gospel alone can save men, and, therefore, he was not at all ashamed of it. ("Salvation" is used here in its complete sense as both an act and a process. Believers are saved from the penalty and the power of sin.)

Paul further declares his great theme that righteousness is a gift based on faith. ("Righteousness" is that condition where one

---

5. James Stifler, *The Epistle to the Romans* (Chicago: Moody, 1960), p. 12.

is not guilty of violating any laws of God. This, of course, is not at all possible for man; it must be done for him by God. This righteousness that fully satisfies God is provided for man—it is imputed to him.)

II. The Sinfulness and Condemnation of All Men (1:18–3:20)

This portion discusses why mankind needs this gospel of Christ. All men need it because all men are guilty of sin and are unable to save themselves.

A. The Guilt of the Gentiles (1:18-32)

Paul's main point in this passage is that when a man rejects the truth of God he degenerates doctrinally (in his beliefs) and morally (in his living) and experiences God's judgment (1:18). The Gentiles had a revelation of God in nature that told them that God exists, and He is powerful. They chose not to pursue this revelation. Because they turned from it, they cannot claim ignorance; they rightly stand guilty before God. (Note that if a man responds to revelation in nature and seeks more about God, then God will reveal more truth to such a one.)

B. The Guilt of the Jews (2:1–3:8)

The Jews also stand guilty before God. They had far more of God's truth and knew His standards. Yet, in spite of knowing the difference between right and wrong, they actually did the same things as the Gentiles (e.g., 2:17-24). They too will experience the wrath of God.

C. The Guilt of All Men (3:9-20)

At this point, Paul looks back over his entire argument noting that he has charged both Jew and Gentile with being guilty before God. He now demonstrates the validity of his position with a series of quotations from the Old Testament. The conclusion is that all people are sinful and unable to save themselves.

III. The Justification of Believing Sinners (3:21–5:21)

A. The Basis of Justification (3:21-26)

At this point Paul ceases discussing the sinfulness of man and now begins to discuss the solution to this terrible situation of mankind. Since all have sinned, all need righteousness. This righteousness has its source in God Himself and does not come by human effort. It comes by faith (3:21-22). Paul uses several key words in this section. (See *Justification by Faith* in chapter 11, pages 163-66, for a more detailed discussion.)

1. Justification. This is an act of God whereby He declares a believing sinner to be righteous. This declaration is based on the death of Christ. It includes the removal of sin's penalty as well as the addition of Christ's righteousness to the believer's account.

2. Redemption. This is deliverance that is brought about by the payment of a ransom. Christ is seen as the One who sets people free from sin by the payment made on the cross.

3. Propitiation. This means to appease or satisfy. The death of Christ has fully satisfied God's righteous demands. God's holiness and justice are satisfied and God is now able to save men.

B. Justification and the Law (3:27-31)

Paul now shows how law (works) fits into the matter of man's salvation. He points out that salvation by faith excludes law (works) and man's boasting that results from works. We are saved by faith, not works (3:27-28). He further points out that there is one God, and as a result only one method of justification. That method is by faith (3:29-30). The law is not a means of justification, but rather a revealer of sin.

C. Justification and the Place of Faith (4:1-25)

Using Abraham and David, the apostle shows that men have always been justified by faith. Abraham was declared righteous long before he did the work of circumcision. And David, who was guilty of murder and adultery, and had no provision in the law to take care of these sins, experienced God's mercy and grace. He was declared righteous.

D. The Certainty of Justification by Faith (5:1-11)

Justification is an accomplished fact (not an ongoing process) in the life of one who believes. Believers are guaranteed that they will not experience God's wrath. God who saved us when we were His enemies will surely keep us safe now that we're His children. Believers are secure in Him. Furthermore, Paul declares, we have peace with God, access to Him, hope, joy, and the presence of the Holy Spirit.

E. The Reign of Sin and the Reign of Grace (5:12-21)

In this section Paul contrasts Adam with Christ, teaching that Adam brought death to mankind while Christ brings life to mankind. Sin entered the world through Adam's one act of sinful disobedience and that sin affected all of his descendants. Adam's sin is imputed to all men and so all are guilty. But Christ's one act (His death on the cross) makes life and righteousness available to all. Great is the grace of God.

IV. The Sanctification of Believing Sinners (6:1–8:39)

Up to this point in the book of Romans, the apostle Paul had been stressing the fact that man is under the penalty of sin. This penalty (eternal separation from God) has been cared for by Christ's death. Now (in chapters 6-8), he will emphasize the point that Christ's work on the cross has delivered believers from the oppressive power of sin.

A. Union with Christ (6:1-14)

Paul had stated (5:20-21) that God's grace abounded where sin increased. So a question is now raised: "Shall we sin more so that God's grace can be displayed even more?" (This question indicates that Paul preached an absolutely free salvation.) His answer is an emphatic "No." He also makes the point that we Christians have died to sin, and we have been placed into union with Christ.

Our new position as believers is that we have been united with Christ by means of Holy Spirit baptism (cf. 1 Cor. 12:13). This union makes it possible to live victoriously over sin. In his writings Paul is clear that sin remains as an alien power within the believer, always trying to dominate him. This "old self" (which is the whole unregenerated nature) works through the "body of sin." (The physical body is not sinful but is the place where sin manifests itself.) This "old self" lost its jurisdiction and power over us when Christ died and rose again. Our relationship with Christ is seen as so vital that when He died, we died. And when He rose victoriously over sin, so did we. This is our position.

Positionally the "old self" is dead. (If we died physically right now, we would shed the old self.) Since the "old self" has been rendered powerless by Christ (not annihilated), we no longer have to be slaves to sin (6:6). In light of Christ's work, we are to do two things. First, consider this as true (6:11). Spiritual victory over sin is built squarely on the fact that sin has lost its authority over us. Believers can now say "no" to sinful practices, since power from Christ is available. Second, believers are to present themselves to God and, in a practical way, draw on His power.

B. Enslavement to Sin or to Righteousness (6:15-23)

Even though sin has lost its authority over the believer it still tries to regain mastery over us. Paul points out that Christians can be slaves to sin or slaves of righteousness. The choice belongs to the believer. He has no other than these two options. If sin is the master, then believers will experience shame, guilt, and death. (Death means separation. Believers who stay in sin and do not confess their sins experience a separation from God in their walk with Him. Paul is not talking about physical death or eternal separation from God.)

C. Freedom from the Law (7:1-25)

Though believers are saved from the penalty of sin, they still have to deal with the reality of the power of sin in their lives. Does the law help with the sin problem? In one sense, the law does help in that it defines the sin problem. But in another sense the law does not help because it gives no power to overcome sin (7:1-12). Paul used his own experience to illustrate this point (7:13-25). Paul describes the ongoing experience of believers, not just a once for all experience. (Note the use of the present tense.)

Giving oneself to law-keeping (legalism) in the Christian life will not free a Christian from sin's power. Trying our best will not keep us from failure as time and again the principle of evil (7:21) overwhelms us. Paul knows that our wills (the choices we make) are important, but "will power" is not enough. The believer needs outside help in his struggle against sin. Paul rejoices that provision for victory, success, and freedom have been made (7:25).

D. Righteous Living Through the Holy Spirit (8:1-17)

The new power for living comes from the Holy Spirit who indwells every believer. (The Holy Spirit is mentioned 19 times in this passage.) The Holy Spirit indwells these bodies that have yet to be redeemed. At the time of the resurrection, the body will be redeemed eliminating the "flesh," that principle of evil. However, until that time the struggle between the flesh and the Spirit will go on (8:1-11). Since the Spirit deals with our sinful appetites, we do not have to sin like we once did before our salvation (8:12-13). Victory is possible for the Christian.

E. After Sufferings Come Glory (8:18-39)

Believers may well experience severe trouble now in this life, but Paul declares that marvelous things are in store for them. In fact, he sets forth the truth that present sufferings do not begin to compare with the glory that is to come. He particularly focuses on the return of Christ which will bring about immortality of the body and also tremendous changes in nature (8:18-27).

As Paul reflects back on the truths which he has shared with the Christians at Rome (chapters 1-8), he can do nothing else than give praise to God. As he thinks about this God-given salvation, he declares that God will bring to a final conclusion our salvation. We shall be glorified and we can be assured of the fact that there is nothing in this universe that can break the union between Christ and the believer (8:28-39).

V. The Place of Israel in the Plans of God (9:1–11:36)

A question would naturally come into the mind of the Jew who was closely following Paul's line of thinking. The Jew would ask, "What now happens to the nation of Israel?" "What about God's covenant promises to Israel?" The Jew would feel that either Paul's gospel is true with the result that God's promises to Israel are set aside, or that Paul's gospel is false and God's promises remain true. The answer from Paul is that it is the Mosaic law (covenant) that is done away with, not the Abrahamic Covenant. (See chart entitled *God's Covenants with Israel* in chapter 2, page 19.) He declares that Israel still has a future, and God's promises will yet be fulfilled.

A. The Unbelief and Rejection of Israel (9:1-33)

Israel was sovereignly chosen by God in the past to be a special people with a special relationship to God. This choice by God was not based on anything that Israel did, but simply on His mercy (9:11, 15). But even though Israel had this special relationship with God, they had to come to God by faith. Israel had to be saved by faith and not by works (9:30-33).

B. The Explanation of Israel's Rejection (10:1-21)

Paul was personally grieved over Israel's unbelief, but notes that their present rejection is their own fault. They insisted on being saved in their own way (by works) rather than God's way (by faith). This accounts for their present alienation from God and their lost condition (10:1-11). Presently (in this church age) Israel has the same standing as the Gentiles and like the Gentiles they must hear and believe the gospel in order to be saved (10:9-21). Any Jew who calls on the Lord for salvation will be saved.

C. Israel's Rejection Is Neither Complete Nor Final (11:1-32)

In light of Israel's disobedience (10:21), has God cast them aside? The answer is an emphatic "No." Israel is stubborn, disobedient, and undeserving. However, the promises God made in the Abrahamic Covenant were eternal and unconditional. Israel's present spiritual blindness is limited in extent (it is "partial," 11:25) and duration (it is "until," 11:25). Someday God will fulfill His promises to Israel and "graft" Israel as a nation back into the Abrahamic Covenant experientially (11:23-25). They will finally be redeemed as a nation, partaking for the first time of the New Covenant.

VI. The Righteousness of God in Practical Living (12:1–15:13)

A climax to the epistle is reached in 12:1-2 when Paul pleads with the Roman Christians to give themselves totally to the Lord. In light of all that God has done for them, he encourages them to present themselves, once for all, to God as a living sacrifice. He tells them to stop being conformed to the world system, and to be transforming their minds. The process of transformation comes by conditioning the mind by the Word of God. The purpose of transformation is to know the personal will of God.

Following this exhortation is a series of matters where righteous living should be exhibited. He briefly discusses spiritual gifts and our ministry to other believers (12:3-13). He gives instructions concerning the believer's relationship to those who are not Christians (12:14-21). Continuing with his thought about the Christian's relationship with those who are not Christians, he speaks about human government. Paul certainly was aware of the abuses and evils that often abound in human government. Yet, he instructs believers to submit to those who are in authority, recognizing that government has been established by God and those in authority have been placed there by God (13:1-7).

He then devotes a great deal of space to the subject of doubtful things (14:1–15:13). Every church in every age will have to deal with issues about which the Scriptures do not specially speak. Paul gave the Roman Christians some guidelines to help them determine what was best for them.

First, he notes that they must think matters through until they have come to biblically based conclusions. As individuals they must come to know what is right for themselves. Second, they are to be considerate of other believers who are weaker in the faith. If they determine that certain things are right for them to do, this does not automatically give them liberty to do them. Love for others must dictate. Third, Paul reminds them of the judgment seat of Christ. They are ultimately accountable to Jesus Christ for their choices and the way they live.

VII. Conclusion (15:14–16:27)

As Paul brings this lengthy letter to a close, he once again shares his reason for writing (15:14-21). He tells them of his desire to minister in the region of Spain later on. He hopes to see them on his way there (15:22-33).

The final chapter has no formal arrangement as he gives numerous greetings to believers (35 people are mentioned by name), interspersing commands and warnings.

THE PAULINE EPISTLES:
GROUP THREE

PAUL'S PRISON EPISTLES

Letter	Date (A.D.)	Written from
Ephesians	61	Rome
Colossians	61	Rome
Philemon	61	Rome
Philippians	62	Rome

THE PRISON EPISTLES

The "prison epistles" received this title simply because Paul wrote them during a time when he was imprisoned by his enemies. Each of the letters mention his current confinement (Eph. 3:1; 4:1; 6:20; Phil. 1:7, 13, 14, 17; Col. 1:24; 4:3, 10, 18; Philem. 1:1, 10, 13, 23).

THE ORIGIN OF THESE EPISTLES

The place of Paul's imprisonment has generated some discussion with Ephesus, Caesarea, and Rome being set forth as possibilities.[1] Ephesus is the least likely as the place of composition because there is no clear reference to any imprisonment of Paul at Ephesus. Also, Acts 20:31 suggests strongly an unbroken ministry at Ephesus.

Paul did experience imprisonment at Caesarea (Acts 23:33–26:32). But statements within the letters point to Rome, not Caesarea. For example, the references to the "praetorian guard" and "Caesar's household" (Phil. 1:13; 4:22) fit well with Rome but are forced and strained when applied to Caesarea.

Paul was imprisoned in Rome (Acts 28:30-31). While under house arrest he was able to continue to preach the gospel (Acts 28:30-31 with Phil. 1:12-18). Church tradition has favored Rome as the place of composition for these four letters of Paul.

THE DATES OF THESE EPISTLES

Ephesians, Colossians, and Philemon were written at the same time and together were sent by Paul to their destinations. These three letters were carried by Onesimus (the runaway slave of Philemon) and Tychicus (cf. Eph. 6:21-22; Col. 4:7-9;

---

1. Donald Guthrie, *New Testament Introduction* (Downers Grove, Ill.: Inter-Varsity, 1970), pp. 472-78; D. Edmond Hiebert, *TheThessalonian Epistles* (Chicago: Moody, 1971). pp. 205-11.

Philem. 1:10-12). A date of about A.D. 61 is assigned to these three letters.

Philippians was probably the latest written of these prison epistles. This is seen in the fact that Paul's confinement seems to have been of some length already (1:14-17). Furthermore, if written early in the imprisonment, there would not be enough time allowed for the several journeys that are implied in the letter. (First, news from Rome reached Philippi that Paul had been imprisoned. Then a collection was taken and sent to Rome carried by Epaphroditus. Later Epaphroditus became very ill and news of his illness went back to Philippi. The resulting concern of the church there was relayed to Rome. All this took time.)

Also, the letter seems to indicate that the moment of crisis had come regarding Paul's imprisonment. His fate would be decided shortly (Phil. 1:23; 2:23-24). And finally, both Luke and Aristarchus have left Paul in Rome, yet both did send greetings in Colossians and Philemon (Acts 27:2; Phil. 2:20; Col. 4:10, 14; Philem. 1:24). All these facts point to a time later than the other prison epistles. Therefore, a date of A.D. 62 is given for Philippians.

THE THEME OF THESE EPISTLES

If any one theme could be given to these letters, it would be the Person and work of Jesus Christ. Many commentators classify these letters as the ''Christological epistles.''

17

EPHESIANS

A. AUTHORSHIP OF EPHESIANS

The letter was written by the apostle Paul.

B. PLACE AND DATE OF EPHESIANS

Paul wrote this letter from Rome about A.D. 61.

C. PURPOSE OF EPHESIANS

Unlike many of Paul's other letters, Ephesians was not written to deal with any particular problem or controversy. Paul wrote the letter to instruct the Christians of Asia Minor concerning the privileges and responsibilities of those who were part of the church, the Body of Christ.

D. BASIC OUTLINE OF EPHESIANS

    I. The Calling of the Church (1:1–3:21)
       A. Praise for God's Redemptive Work (1:1-14)
       B. Prayer for an Understanding of God's Grace (1:15-23)
       C. Salvation Because of God's Grace (2:1-10)
       D. Jew and Gentile Reconciled Because of God's Grace (2:11-22)

E.   THEME OF EPHESIANS

The basic theme of Ephesians is the church, the Body of Christ. Christ is the Head and the Body is made up of believing Jews and Gentiles. The church is a new community purchased by Christ to carry out the purposes of God in this world.

F.   SPECIAL CONSIDERATIONS ON EPHESIANS

By comparing Ephesians 6:21 with Colossians 4:7, it is clear that both letters were carried by Tychicus, with Colossians going to the church at Colossae. However, the other letter ("Ephesians") is less clear, since the phrase "at Ephesus" is not found in many manuscripts. "The words 'in Ephesus' (1:1) are absent from some of our oldest and best MSS, and several of the Greek Fathers make it clear that they did not find them in all copies. Indeed it is almost certain that they do not come from St. Paul himself."[2]

Apparently this letter was designed to be a circular letter. It was intended for a number of churches in the region of Asia Minor. "The most acceptable view, having regard to the general character of the letter, is that it was intended for all the churches

---

2. J. Armitage Robinson, *St. Paul's Epistle to the Ephesians* (London: James Clark, n.d.), p. 11.

of the province of Asia, some of which were personally known to Paul, while others were not."[3]

There is evidence within the letter that it had a wider audience than just Ephesus. For example, there are no personal references in the letter, no details about his ministry among them, no mention of greetings to particular individuals and no warnings about any unique dangers or problems that they faced. It is inconceivable that Paul, who had spent three years with them, would be so absolutely impersonal. Only a circular letter could account for such a phenomenon.

The recipients of this letter were, therefore, the many believers of Asia Minor. The title of "Ephesians" was probably attached to it later on. "The capital of the Roman province of Asia was Ephesus. To Ephesus such a letter would naturally go first of all; and when, in later times, a title was sought for it, to correspond with the titles of other epistles, no name would offer itself so readily and so reasonably as the name of Ephesus."[4]

In light of the circular character of this letter, it is quite likely that the letter that was coming to Colossae from Laodicea (Col. 4:16) was this letter that we call "Ephesians."

SUMMARY OF EPHESIANS

I. The Calling of the Church (1:1–3:21)
    A. Praise for God's Redemptive Work (1:1-14)

The church came into being because of God's great work of salvation. Paul said that each person of the Godhead was active in the redemption of mankind. God the Father sovereignly selected us out of the mass of humanity for Himself (1:3-6). This He did on the basis of His love and for His glory. God's unmerited favor was extended to us. But the blessing of salvation could not come merely because God made a decree that people could be saved. Divine justice had to be satisfied. Therefore, God the Son paid for this salvation by the shedding of His own blood, removing sin, and setting men free (1:7-12). God the Spirit secures this salvation

---

3. F. F. Bruce, *The Epistle to the Ephesians* (London: Pickering and Inglis, 1961), p. 13.
4. Robinson, *Epistle to the Ephesians*, p. 11.

in our lives by "sealing us." This work of sealing indicates His ownership of us, our absolute security, and salvation is a finished transaction (1:3-14). The primary purpose for this great work of salvation was the glory of God (1:6, 12, 14).

B. Prayer for an Understanding of God's Grace (1:15-23)

Paul was not simply content to describe their blessings in Christ, but he desired that they enter into the riches of it. Therefore, he prayed that they might really understand the hope of their calling, the fact that they are God's inheritance, and that there was power available to them for living. This great power of God, that is available to believers, was exhibited when Christ was raised from the dead and established as the Head of all creation and Head of the church.

C. Salvation Because of God's Grace (2:1-10)

Sometimes it is healthy to remember what we were like before God saved us. The apostle succinctly describes our past condition as death (corrupt and separated from God). Into that hopeless situation the grace of God came bringing salvation. Paul reminds these believers that works do not save. Salvation is a gift of God (2:8-9). Good works are a part of God's purpose for our lives, but not as contributions to our salvation (2:10).

D. Jew and Gentile Reconciled Because of God's Grace (2:11-22)

Because of this work of God in salvation, Jews and Gentiles can both be reconciled to God (2:16-18). Also, these two groups who used to be separated from one another can be reconciled to each other (2:14-15). In the church, the Body of Christ, there is no longer a distinction made between Jews and Gentiles. This unity of all believers in the church is emphasized through the imagery of being fellow citizens of a community, part of God's family, and part of the one temple building that is under construction (2:19-22).

E. Paul, A Steward of the Gospel of God's Grace (3:1-13)

At this point in the letter, Paul refers to a mystery (a truth not previously revealed). The mystery is that Jews and Gentiles were both equal in the Body of Christ (3:3, 6). Paul was the main revealer of this truth, as the apostle to the Gentiles.

F.   Prayer for Power and Understanding (3:14-21)

This section of the letter is Paul's prayer for the believers. He prays for enablement in their Christian lives and that they might experience God's love and power.

II.   The Conduct of the Church (4:1–6:24)

A.   In Unity (4:1-16)

Paul tells them that unity has been provided by the Spirit, but they must be diligent in preserving that unity. Unity, however, does not mean sameness. Believers are different. Each one has received spiritual gifts to help others mature in Christ. This interdependency strengthens the unity of the church.

B.   In Righteousness (4:17–5:14)

Believers are to live godly lives, ridding themselves of sinful habits. This progressive sanctification is accomplished by renewing of the mind. (The Word of God alone helps us think more as God thinks, thus seeing clearly what is good and evil.) The mind is the key in "putting off" the old and "putting on" the new (4:22-24). Paul then gives numerous practical examples of his point (4:25–5:14).

C.   In the Spirit's Control (5:15-21)

The Holy Spirit provides power for righteous living. The Spirit desires to fill (control) believers (5:18). This is an ongoing activity of the Spirit. As Christians come to understand God's truth regarding some area of life, and then submit to the Lord in that area, the Spirit controls them in that area.

D.   In Marriage (5:22-33)

One major area that needs the Spirit's control is the marriage relationship. Paul gives instruction about God's order of home government. The husband is the head of the family and is to provide loving leadership. The wife, recognizing God's order, is to submit with respect to her husband's leadership.

E.   In His Household (6:1-9)

In the larger family unit, children are to obey their parents and parents are not to misuse their authority. Servants are not to rebel but to submit to their human authorities.

F. In Spiritual Warfare (6:10-20)

Paul concludes this epistle by reminding Christians that they are in a spiritual war with a powerful, highly organized enemy. In this war, some times are worse than others (''the evil day,'' 6:13). But whatever the situation, God has provided all the armor necessary to ensure victory. Believers, however, must put that armor on and keep it on. Prayer is important in that process.

III. Conclusion (6:21-24)

18

COLOSSIANS

Introduction to Colossians

A. AUTHORSHIP OF COLOSSIANS

The letter was written by the apostle Paul.

B. PLACE AND DATE OF COLOSSIANS

Paul wrote this letter from Rome about A.D. 61.

C. PURPOSE OF COLOSSIANS

The letter was written primarily to stabilize this church doctrinally. The church was being affected by heretical teaching and Paul wrote to combat this subtle, but dangerous teaching.

D. BASIC OUTLINE OF COLOSSIANS

   I. Introduction (1:1-14)
      A. Thanksgiving (1:1-8)
      B. Prayer (1:9-14)
  II. The Doctrine of Jesus Christ (1:15-23)
      A. His Divine Person (1:15-18)
      B. His Saving Work (1:19-23)
 III. The Ministry of the Apostle Paul (1:24–2:7)
      A. Paul's Ministry to the Global Church (1:24-29)
      B. Paul's Concern for the Colossian Church (2:1-7)

E. THEME OF COLOSSIANS

The theme of Colossians is the deity and the all-sufficiency of Jesus Christ. In this letter, the apostle is showing the Colossian Christians that they were complete in Jesus Christ. They did not need anything else, in spite of the claims of the false teacher who was telling them that faith in Christ was not enough.

F. SPECIAL CONSIDERATIONS ON COLOSSIANS

1. The City of Colossae

The city was located in the Lycus valley about 100 miles east of Ephesus. Laodicea and Hieropolis (4:13) were located nearby. The city did not have any political significance under Roman rule. The church was not founded by Paul, but rather by Epaphras (1:7). Epaphras was probably a convert of Paul from the city of Ephesus who, perhaps, was sent to evangelize Colossae. The church was primarily Gentile in its membership, but with a Jewish element there as well.

2. The Colossian Heresy

The heretical teaching at Colossae seems to be a mixture of asceticism, Jewish legalism, and some kind of philosophic mysticism. The chief passage relevant to the problem is 2:8-23. In this passage various elements are mentioned or implied. Angel worship, ritualism, and some form of gnosticism seem to be present. (The basis of gnosticism is the idea that spirit is good but matter is evil. Thus, if Christ took on a material body, He had some evil.)

Paul shows the Colossians that they need none of these elements. Christ is all they need. Since Paul combats a heretical teaching in this letter, it is more philosophical in tone than most other Pauline epistles.

SUMMARY OF COLOSSIANS

I. Introduction (1:1-14)

The apostle Paul had had no personal contact with this church, but he had heard about their progress in the faith. Even though he had never been with them, he prayed for them. He thanked God for them and prayed that they would grow in real knowledge and wisdom.

II. The Doctrine of Jesus Christ (1:15-23)

In discussing the deity of Jesus Christ, Paul makes the point that Christ is the visible representation of the invisible God. The two words "image" and "firstborn" are particularly important in his discussion. Jesus is the "image" of God, meaning that He is the exact reproduction of deity, lacking nothing. In other words, He is an exact manifestation of the unseen God. Paul also says that Jesus is the "firstborn of all creation."

> The Greek word implied two things, *priority* to all creation and *sovereignty* over all creation. In the first meaning we see the absolute pre-existence of the Logos. Since our Lord existed before all created things, He must be uncreated. . . . In the second meaning we see that He is the natural ruler, the acknowledged head of God's household . . . He is Lord of creation.[1]

All the powers and attributes of deity are at home in Christ. He lacks none. Yet, He had a "fleshly body" which died in order to reconcile man (1:22). He made peace through "the blood of His cross" (1:20). Paul makes it clear that their faith is built upon the firm foundation of the deity of Christ and His totally sufficient

1. Kenneth S. Wuest, *Wuest's Word Studies: Ephesians and Colossians* (Grand Rapids: Eerdmans, 1953), p. 183.

death on the cross. His statements are a direct rebuttal of the false teaching that was being propagated at Colossae.

III. The Ministry of the Apostle Paul (1:24–2:7)

Paul's message everywhere was that people are made complete in Christ. It is in the Person of Jesus Christ that true wisdom is found, not in the philosophies of man. Paul was concerned for the Colossian Christians that they not fall into false teaching but that they continue as they had begun—in the true faith.

IV. The Discussion of False Philosophy (2:8–3:4)

After warning them about man's philosophies, Paul again declares that God's essential nature is found in Christ (2:9). He notes that all needed power and grace are found in Christ. We have been given life, forgiveness, deliverance, and victory in Jesus Christ. Since we have it all in Christ, why get involved in the legalism and ritualism of men? Since Christ has liberated us from all these things, why do you want to put yourself back under them again?

V. The Life of Practical Christians (3:5–4:6)

Paul has spoken of the believer's exalted position in Christ and now he challenges them to live a life that conforms to that position. In this section he points out that there are certain sinful actions and attitudes that they were to remove from their lives (3:5-9), but there were also certain virtues that were to become a part of their living (3:10-17). As he did in the Ephesian epistle, the apostle also exhorts them to godly living in their families. Their relationships in the home are to reflect their position in Christ (3:18–4:1). He concludes this section by encouraging them to be disciplined in their prayer lives.

VI. Conclusion (4:7-18)

People were very much a part of Paul's life and ministry. A large number of individuals are mentioned at the end of this letter. Some were known to the Colossian church while others apparently were not too familiar to them. Such a list does reveal something of the contact that existed between the churches in the first century.

19

PHILEMON

INTRODUCTION TO PHILEMON

A. AUTHORSHIP OF PHILEMON

The letter was written by the apostle Paul.

B. PLACE AND DATE OF PHILEMON

Paul wrote this letter from Rome about A.D. 61.

C. PURPOSE OF PHILEMON

Paul writes this personal letter to his friend Philemon in order to intercede for the slave Onesimus. Onesimus apparently had stolen from his master, Philemon, and then fled to Rome. At Rome he was converted under the apostle's ministry and was now returning to his master. Paul writes as a mediator for the slave.

D. BASIC OUTLINE OF PHILEMON

I. Salutation (vv. 1-3)
II. Thanksgiving and Prayer (vv. 4-7)
III. Request (vv. 8-21)
IV. Conclusion (vv. 22-25)

E. THEME OF PHILEMON

Since this is a personal letter, there is really no theme as such. The letter was designed to persuade Philemon to forgive and reinstate Onesimus, and even to receive him as a new brother in Christ.

F. SPECIAL CONSIDERATIONS ON PHILEMON

The letter is unique among the letters of Paul in the New Testament because it is the only one that contains no doctrinal teaching. The letter does reveal something of the persuasive powers of Paul as well as his love, courtesy, and tactfulness in handling a difficult (and probably emotional) matter.

SUMMARY OF PHILEMON

I. Salutation (vv. 1-3)

Paul always viewed himself as simply the bondslave of Christ, with the result that there was no bitterness or rebellion because of his confinement. He addresses the letter to his friends, Philemon, Apphia, and Archippus.

II. Thanksgiving and Prayer (vv. 4-7)

Whether Philemon will receive his slave back again depends a great deal on the character of this man. Paul's confidence that he will receive Onesimus back is based on Philemon's godly character. Something of it is revealed in these verses. His generosity, love, and faith are well known and Paul thanks the Lord for that.

III. Request (vv. 8-21)

When necessary Paul did issue orders and commands for believers to engage in right conduct. He could appeal to his apostolic authority in this case, but he did not want to force Philemon to do what was correct. Instead he appealed to him, reminding him that Onesimus is now a profitable (or useful) believer. He knew that although he wanted to keep Onesimus at Rome with him, legally and ethically he could not. Onesimus was still the slave of Philemon. So Paul was sending him back to Philemon.

The heart of Paul's request is that Philemon would receive Onesimus, just as he would receive Paul if he came (verse 17). Paul is aware that theft had been involved and that Philemon had lost financially because of this slave. Paul said that Philemon should charge that to Paul and he would repay it. This is a beautiful illustration of imputation. Paul signs the letter with his own hand as a guarantee that he will repay it. He then reminds Philemon of a parallel situation of far greater weight. Philemon once had been burdened with great spiritual debt. That was entirely paid by Jesus in his redemptive death. Personal relief from that debt came for Philemon through Paul's preaching of the gospel. In that sense Philemon owes far more to Paul than Onesimus owes to Philemon.

IV. Conclusion (vv. 22-25)

Paul is hoping to be set free and when he is free he will be returning to Asia Minor. At that time he intends to stop in and see Philemon and enjoy his hospitality. Paul's hope was not in the Roman judicial system, however, but in the prayers of God's people.

20

PHILIPPIANS

A. AUTHORSHIP OF PHILIPPIANS

The letter was written by the apostle Paul.

B. PLACE AND DATE OF PHILIPPIANS

Paul wrote this letter from Rome about A.D. 62.

C. PURPOSE OF PHILIPPIANS

Paul wrote this letter to thank the believers at Philippi for sending him a financial gift. They had done this in the past as well. He also wrote to let them know that even though he was a prisoner, the gospel of Christ was still being preached. He may have written also to tell them that he intended to visit them if and when he was released.

D. BASIC OUTLINE OF PHILIPPIANS

    I. Introduction (1:1-11)
       A. Greetings and Thanksgiving (1:1-8)
       B. Petitions for Philippian Believers (1:9-11)
    II. Paul's Personal Circumstances at Rome (1:12-26)
       A. His Ministry (1:12-14)
       B. His Joy (1:15-18)
       C. His Commitment (1:19-26)

E.   THEME OF PHILIPPIANS

This is a very personal letter from Paul to a church that has cared for him. It is a letter filled with joy and thankfulness. "The leading thought of the Letter, which is cordial and sincere, is: joy and gratitude . . . The word 'rejoice' or other words of similar meaning, appears sixteen times in the short Letter. Even the imprisonment or malicious action of opponents could not extinguish his joy in the Lord (cf. 1:18; 2:2; 3:1; 4:1; 4:4)."[1]

In the letter there are also some important doctrinal points made as well, such as Paul's discussion of the Person of Christ in His humiliation.

F.   SPECIAL CONSIDERATIONS ON PHILIPPIANS

The city of Philippi was located eleven miles inland from the Aegean Sea on the Egnatian Way—a strategic Roman highway. Philippi was important to the Roman military, since it was a key in the defense against northern invasions. The political structure and culture of Philippi was the same as that of Rome, and the city was said to be "a miniature likeness of Rome." Paul founded the church at Philippi on his second journey and visited again some five years later on his third journey. This letter was written some ten years after the founding of the church.

---

1. Jack J. Muller, *The Epistle of Paul to the Philippians and to Philemon* (Grand Rapids: Eerdmans, 1970), p. 21.

SUMMARY OF PHILIPPIANS

I. Introduction (1:1-11)

The church at Philippi had brought great joy and comfort to the apostle Paul. This letter is basically a "thank you" note to these believers for their contributions to his life and ministry. Paul was pleased with them because they had begun well and were continuing to serve Christ faithfully. Paul's prayer for them was that their love might continue to flourish, that they would have the ability to discern which things in life were most important, and that their lives might be pure and blameless (1:9-11).

II. Paul's Personal Circumstances at Rome (1:12-26)

A. His Ministry (1:12-14)

Apparently the Philippian believers assumed that the gospel was no longer being proclaimed since Paul was imprisoned. But Paul assured them that the opposite was true. Not only was Paul himself preaching effectively while under house arrest, but many others, encouraged by Paul's example, were having a greater witness than before.

B. His Joy (1:15-18)

After reporting that many were now witnessing and ministering, Paul informed his friends at Philippi that not everyone's motives were pure. Some opposed Paul and seemed to be motivated by self-glory. Although Paul did not rejoice in that, he did rejoice that the gospel was nevertheless being proclaimed.

C. His Commitment (1:19-26)

Paul seemed to be anticipating his release from imprisonment, but his hope was based on prayer and not on the Roman judicial system. Paul shared his double desire—he longed to be with Jesus Christ, and yet he desired to be with the church of Christ. His preference was to be with Christ, but he realized that he still had a ministry to the believers. (It is important to note that grammatically Paul leaves no doubt that death brings a believer immediately and consciously into the presence of Christ. Departure at death means to be in Christ's presence. There is no "soul sleep" or purgatory allowed for here.)[2]

III. Paul's Practical Exhortation to the Philippians (1:27–2:18)
    A. Admonitions for Unity and Humility (1:27–2:11)

Paul was concerned that the church at Philippi be characterized by unity. Apparently there was some problem of disunity there (cf. 4:1-3). He encouraged them to abandon all self-centeredness and to concentrate on others (2:1-3). As he spoke of selfless living, he could think of no greater example than the Lord Jesus Christ (2:5-11). Paul reminded them that Christ was (is) God and yet He was willing to set aside the external manifestation of His deity ("form of God") temporarily in order to become a man. When Christ added true humanity to His deity, He voluntarily limited the independent use of some of His attributes. He did this in order to die on the cross for the benefit of others. Paul told these believers to follow Christ's example. (See appendix, *Note A: The Person of Jesus Christ.*)

    B. Call to Correct Conduct (2:12-18)

Believers are to live lives in keeping with their faith. They are to translate ("work out," 2:12) their faith into godly living. This can be accomplished by the power of God within. Certain attitudes, such as complaining, are not to be part of life since they hurt a credible testimony before the world.

    C. Co-workers of Paul (2:19-30)

Paul was appreciative of his fellow workers Timothy and Epaphroditus. Both were excellent servants of Christ and were fine helpers of the apostle. Both of them would be coming to Philippi and would be with the believers there.

IV. Paul's Past and the Present Need (3:1-21)

This portion of the letter contains some statements about Paul's personal life. He recalled his life in Judaism. He had been a man of privilege and also a man who worked hard at being righteous. Yet, when he met Christ he abandoned it all for the superior relationship with the Lord. He now owed everything to Christ

---

2. Paul N. Benware, *Ambassadors of Armstrongism* (Fort Washington, Pa.: Christian Literature Crusade, 1985), pp. 116-25.

and had the single-minded goal of knowing Him and serving Him. From his own experience he warned the Philippians about the Judaizers, who were enemies of the true gospel and who would lead them astray.

V. Paul's Principles for Joyful Living (4:1-9)

Paul's rejoicing was not based on the circumstances of life, but rather came from seeing life from God's perspective. Paul encouraged these believers to stop being anxious about things and to learn to give them to the Lord with a thankful spirit. The Lord in turn would give them peace. Paul pointed out that when the mind is occupied with thoughts that are good it will not be occupied with anxious thoughts.

VI. Paul's Praise for the Meeting of His Needs (4:10-23)

Paul concludes by thanking them for their gift. He did appreciate it. He had learned to be content in all of life's circumstances—plenty or poverty.

THE PAULINE EPISTLES:
GROUP FOUR

PAUL'S PASTORAL EPISTLES

Letter	Date (A.D.)	Written from
1 Timothy	62	Macedonia
Titus	63	Ephesus
2 Timothy	64	Rome

THE PASTORAL EPISTLES

Three letters compose the pastoral epistles—1 and 2 Timothy and Titus. These letters are so designated because they deal with church order and discipline and because they were written to men who had the care of local churches committed to them.

THE AUTHORSHIP OF THESE EPISTLES

The first verse of each letter identifies Paul as the author. Some have objected to the Pauline authorship of these letters, but conservative scholars have answered these objections.[1] Evidence within the letters as well as a strong church tradition supports Pauline authorship.

THE CIRCUMSTANCES OF THESE EPISTLES

The time and place of writing depends on whether or not Paul was imprisoned twice. The book of Acts closes with Paul under house arrest in Rome. But there is good evidence that Paul was released and spent several years traveling. Putting a number of Scripture references together, a possible itinerary of Paul after his release is suggested.

Upon leaving Rome, Paul headed east to Ephesus and Colossae, while sending Timothy to Philippi (Phil. 1:23-26; 2:23; Philem. 22). On his way to Asia, Paul stopped on the island of Crete and founded the church. Paul arrived at Ephesus and was joined by Timothy some time later. Timothy updated Paul on the Philippian church. Paul then left for Macedonia to visit Philippi and other places, writing 1 Timothy while there.

After his Macedonian visit, Paul returned to Ephesus and then departed for Spain, possibly taking Titus with him (Rom. 15:24). On his return from Spain he journeyed to Crete where

---

1. D. Edmond Hiebert, *An Introduction to the Pauline Epistles* (Chicago: Moody, 1971), pp. 308-19; Everett F. Harrison, *Introduction to the New Testament* (Grand Rapids: Eerdmans, 1964), pp. 330-42.

he left Titus. Paul then returned to Ephesus and wrote the epistle of Titus. Paul soon left Asia Minor, going to Troas where he encountered serious opposition. He then went through Corinth to Nicopolis, where he was arrested and taken to Rome (1 Tim. 3:14-15; Tim. 4:13-20). From Rome he wrote 2 Timothy shortly before his death.

21

1 TIMOTHY

INTRODUCTION TO 1 TIMOTHY

A. AUTHORSHIP OF 1 TIMOTHY

This letter was written by the apostle Paul to his co-worker Timothy.

B. PLACE AND DATE OF 1 TIMOTHY

Paul wrote this letter in A.D. 62 while visiting churches in Macedonia.

C. PURPOSE OF 1 TIMOTHY

Probably because he knew that it would be a while before he saw Timothy, Paul wrote to assist Timothy in his oversight of the church. As Paul's apostolic representative, Timothy was reminded of his authority and of his ministry responsibilities. Paul also wrote this letter to instruct those in the church about their responsibilities in the local assembly (cf. 1:3; 3:14-15; 4:6, 11-16; 5:1, 21; 6:11-15,17).

D. BASIC OUTLINE OF 1 TIMOTHY

    I. Salutation (1:1-2)
   II. The Instructions Concerning Teachers in the Church (1:3-20)
      A. The Nature of the Instructions (1:3-4)
      B. The Goal of the Instructions (1:5)

E.   THEME OF 1 TIMOTHY

The emphasis of this letter is the proper ministry and administration of the local church. A variety of subjects are dealt with in order to assure that the church would be all that it should be.

F.   SPECIAL CONSIDERATIONS ON 1 TIMOTHY

The man Timothy is mentioned more than twenty times by name in the New Testament. Aside from Luke, he was probably the closest of all Paul's companions.

Timothy was probably converted on Paul's first missionary journey when Paul and Barnabas preached in the cities of Lystra and Derbe. On the second missionary journey, as Paul was going through the area again, checking on the situation of the new churches, Timothy joined the group.

According to Acts 16, Timothy had a Greek father and a Jewish mother, who instructed him in the Scriptures. Timothy spent a number of years with the apostle Paul, and the two became very close (cf. Acts 16:1; Rom. 16:21; 1 Cor. 4:17; 16:10; Phil. 1:1; 2:19-24; Col. 1:1; 1 Thess. 3:1-2; 1 Tim. 4:12; 5:23; 2 Tim. 1:7-8; 2:1, 3, 22).

SUMMARY OF 1 TIMOTHY

I. Salutation (1:1-2)

II. The Instructions Concerning Teachers in the Church (1:3-20)

From the earliest years the church had to face the infiltration of false teachers into its ranks. In this letter, Paul exhorted Timothy to confront Jewish false teachers who were teaching Jewish legends and who were basing doctrines on the allegorization of the Old Testament genealogical lists (1:3-4). Paul told Timothy that the law (and these creative teachings from the law) could not save, and he used himself as a powerful example of one who diligently attempted to please God through law-keeping, but was unable to do so (1:8-16). Paul then reminded Timothy that the main antidote to false teaching is the teaching of sound doctrine (1:18-20; cf. 4:6-7, 16; 2 Tim. 2:24-26).

III. The Instructions Concerning Life in the Church (2:1–3:16)

God who created the church has also given the principles for its operation. Paul sets forth some of these principles in this next section. First, he wished to exhort and instruct regarding prayer in the public assembly. Men are to take the lead in public prayer (2:8) and are to pray for the salvation of people and for peace so that conditions might be favorable for the spread of the gospel.

The apostle then spoke concerning the women's role in the public assembly (2:11-15). First, she is to dress in good taste and avoid excesses in personal adornment. Apparently such excesses had occurred and these had been destructive in the public worship. Second, she is to be a willing learner, but not to be *the* authoritative teacher of doctrine in the church. (In the New Testament, a teacher was seen as one with a unique authority. She is prohibited from being *the* teacher who establishes the doctrine of the church and who, then, has authority over others.) Paul noted that a woman's sphere of influence is generally greatest in the home environment, and this in turn gives the greatest satisfaction to her.

Continuing on with his discussion of life and order in the church, Paul addressed the matter of leadership. The two offices in the local church (that of elder and deacon) must have qualified men in order that the church will receive godly direction and avoid numerous problems that come with bad or inept leaders. Paul listed the needed qualifications that are related to the present life of a man (not his past life, or no one could qualify). In the list, Paul did not indicate that any one qualification is more significant than another. Although no man will ever perfectly fulfill all of these, they remain as God's standard in evaluating those who would be leaders.

IV. The Instructions Concerning Apostasy in the Church (4:1-16)

Paul revealed the truth that some who know the truth of God will purposely, knowingly, turn away from it (''apostasy''). These who defect from the truth then enter into false teaching from Satan (4:1-5). The truth is always the antidote to error, and Timothy was to teach and live the truth (4:6-16). He was told that godly discipline is the key to successful service.

V. The Instructions Concerning Groups in the Church (5:1–6:2)

Paul first exhorted Timothy to avoid treating people harshly (5:1-2). He then gave instructions concerning the widows, who were a special group in the church. Not all widows qualify for church support, but some do. Widows who are more than sixty and who have no families to support them may be eligible for financial support. However, they must also be women who are known for their godliness and service (5:3-16).

Another group in the church are the elders. Elders who teach are to be properly appreciated by showing respect and by the giving of financial support. Elders who sin (and do not repent) are to be disciplined.

Another group in the church were the slaves. (There was a very large number of slaves in the Roman Empire.) Slaves are reminded that salvation did not change their social status. They are still slaves and are to respect their masters.

VI. Conclusion (6:3-21)

After giving yet another word about false teachers (6:3-5), Paul gave instructions to those who are wealthy. These are to look for opportunities to use their material wealth for righteousness. They are not to depend on their money, and they must always remember that wealth brings constant temptation with it.

Paul concluded his letter to Timothy by exhorting him to guard the truth of God. It was his sacred responsibility.

22

TITUS

INTRODUCTION TO TITUS

A. AUTHORSHIP OF TITUS

This letter was written by the apostle Paul to his co-worker Titus.

B. PLACE AND DATE OF TITUS

Paul wrote this letter in A.D. 63 while at Ephesus. (Some place it later at about A.D. 66.)

C. PURPOSE OF TITUS

Paul wrote this letter to remind Titus to complete the needed organizational matters in the church on the island of Crete. He also encouraged him to teach the doctrines of the faith and in so doing refute the false teachers. Paul believed that it was important as well to encourage Titus in his ministry and to tell him to come to him at Nicopolis.

D. BASIC OUTLINE OF TITUS

    I. Introduction (1:1-4)
   II. The Importance of Godly Leadership in the Church (1:5-16)
      A. Appointing Qualified Leaders (1:5-9)
      B. Managing False Teachers (1:10-16)

III. The Importance of Godly Living in the Church (2:1-15)
    A. Church Leaders (2:1, 15)
    B. Various Groups (2:2-10)
    C. All Believers (2:11-14)
IV. The Importance of Godly Living Outside the Church (3:1-9)
V. Conclusion (3:10-15)

E.   THEME OF TITUS

The emphasis of Titus is similar to 1 Timothy, namely, the importance of proper administration and ministry in the local church.

F.   SPECIAL CONSIDERATIONS ON TITUS

The man Titus is mentioned numerous times in the New Testament, though never in the book of Acts (Titus 1:4; Gal. 2:1-3; 2 Cor. 2:13; 7:5-7, 13-15; 8:6, 16-19, 23-24; 12:18; 2 Tim. 4:10). He apparently was saved under Paul's ministry and became an important assistant to Paul in his ministry to the Gentiles.

Titus was at the heart of the law controversy in the early days of the church, being Paul's proof that Gentiles can be saved apart from the law (Gal. 2:1-3). From Paul's statements in 2 Corinthians, Titus seems to have been a man who was spiritually strong, able to handle problems and minister effectively. His presence and ministry were a comfort and strength to the apostle.

SUMMARY OF TITUS

I. Introduction (1:1-4)

Paul began this letter to a co-worker by emphasizing the fact that God's secret purposes in salvation were now being clearly proclaimed by the apostle Paul.

II. The Importance of Godly Leadership in the Church (1:5-16)
    A. Appointing Qualified Leaders (1:5-9)

Titus had the responsibility of establishing elders in the church at Crete, since they were essential to operating the church

effectively. But Paul reminded Titus that men must be well qualified to handle this important task of guiding the local church. A
list, similar to that in 1 Timothy 3, is given.

B. Managing False Teachers (1:10-16)

One of the major responsibilities of leadership is to guard the
flock from those who would hurt it with false teaching. Titus was
encouraged to actively deal with such individuals.

III. The Importance of Godly Living in the Church (2:1-15)

A. Church Leaders (2:1, 15)

Leaders are to constantly be teaching the truth of God. The
truth must be taught with authority because knowing the truth is
critical to correct living.

B. Various Groups (2:2-10)

A series of exhortation is given. Older men are exhorted to be
disciplined and dependable. Older women are encouraged to be
examples, using their tongues to instruct younger women, and not
to gossip. Younger women are to focus on their home responsibilities and by so doing bring honor to God. Younger men are to
demonstrate self-discipline and excellence in their lives. Slaves
are to subject themselves willingly to their masters.

C. All Believers (2:11-14)

As those who possess this great salvation, our lives are to reflect our position in Christ. Christ came the first time bringing salvation (vs. 11), and He will come the second time in power and
glory (vs. 13). Between these two events, believers are to live
godly lives (vs. 12).

IV. The Importance of Godly Living Outside the Church (3:1-9)

Believers are told not to speak reproachfully of unbelievers
or to be quarrelsome with them. Believers need to remember that
they once behaved like these people. They have been changed by
Jesus Christ, cleansed and regenerated by the Holy Spirit. Christ
has made the difference in them.

V. Conclusion (3:10-15)

Paul ends the letter with a series of brief instructions. He tells
Titus to remove divisive people from the assembly after they have

had two warnings. He encourages believers to be diligent in doing good deeds. (In this letter, there are several places where the importance of good deeds is emphasized.) Also, Titus is told that someone will be coming to Crete to replace him and that he, then, is to return to the apostle Paul, who will be at Nicopolis.

23

2 TIMOTHY

INTRODUCTION TO 2 TIMOTHY

A. AUTHORSHIP OF 2 TIMOTHY

The letter was written by the apostle Paul to his co-worker Timothy.

B. PLACE AND DATE OF 2 TIMOTHY

Paul wrote this letter from Rome in A.D. 64. Some place it later at about A.D. 67.

C. PURPOSE OF 2 TIMOTHY

Paul wrote to encourage Timothy in his ministry He exhorted Timothy to be strong and faithful in that ministry. He warned him to be aware of trouble that lay ahead both in the church and in the world. Also, Paul wrote to request Timothy to come to Rome to visit him in prison there.

D. BASIC OUTLINE OF 2 TIMOTHY

    I. Personal Greetings (1:1-7)
   II. The Command to Guard the Gospel (1:8-18)
      A. The Character of the Gospel (1:8-10)
      B. The Responsibility to the Gospel (1:11-18)

E.   THEME OF 2 TIMOTHY

Second Timothy is a very personal letter from the aged apostle to his younger co-worker. The letter emphasizes the necessity to guard the treasure of the gospel (1:14) and to carry on the ministry that had been passed on to him by Paul (2:2).

F.   SPECIAL CONSIDERATIONS ON 2 TIMOTHY

Second Timothy, along with 1 Timothy and Titus, gives clear and forceful instructions on the issue of false teachers and their teachings. The apostle was deeply concerned about the terrible effect of false teaching on the church (In fact, Paul speaks more about this subject than any other throughout his letters.)

Paul tells the church that false teaching originates with Satan though it is proclaimed by men; it is usually very close to the truth; it can affect any area of life or doctrine; and error will progressively become worse as the end time nears. To identify and counter error, the truth must be known and taught. Also, the life of a false teacher will eventually reveal that he is not really of God. Second Timothy reveals that spiritual warfare is continuous and that the Word of God is the major battleground.

SUMMARY OF 2 TIMOTHY

I. Personal Greetings (1:1-7)

The opening reveals something of the closeness of Paul and Timothy. He recalls the excellent spiritual heritage that Timothy had, encouraging him to serve the Lord in light of it.

II. The Command to Guard the Gospel (1:8-18)

A. The Character of the Gospel (1:8-10)

The gospel is God's good news that sinners can be saved from their sin and receive eternal life. It is the power of God unto salvation. In these verses, the steps of that salvation are seen: (1) election, (2) the work of Christ historically, (3) God's call of us— a process leading to our salvation, (4) God's saving of us as individuals—the climax of the process, and (5) immortality—the future and final aspect of our salvation.

B. The Responsibility to the Gospel (1:11-18)

The believer has been given a message that is to be shared with others; a message that he did not originate. Paul discovered that the message cost him his personal freedom, but nevertheless he had faithfully kept what was entrusted to him.

III. The Command to Suffer for the Gospel (2:1-26)

A. The Participants of Suffering (2:1-2)

Paul instructs Timothy in the multiplication aspect of the ministry. The gospel ministry is to be committed to those who have proved faithful in their reception and handling of the Word of God. These are to be trained, and they in turn are to train others.

B. The Illustrations of Suffering (2:3-7)

Paul tells Timothy that a faithful man is like a soldier (willing to suffer, single-minded, and desirous of pleasing his commander), like an athlete (playing by rules and playing for a prize), and like a farmer (working hard and looking ahead with confidence to the harvest). These are the kind of men to look for in entrusting the treasure of the gospel.

C. The Inclusiveness of Suffering (2:8-13)

Paul had a realistic view of the gospel ministry. He understood that the gospel is offensive to people and that it brings persecution. But he was willing to endure those troubles in order that the gospel might reach men.

D. The Evaluation of Suffering (2:14-22)

The job of the "workman" is to teach the truth. The approved workman accurately and plainly handles the Word, and this leads to godliness. The bad workman falsifies the Word, confusing people, which in turn leads people away from God.

In any house, Paul says, there are vessels of honor used for special occasions (like fine china). Other vessels are common (like plastic plates). The church is like a house, and believers are like the vessels in it. Some are more valuable to God than others. Paul then explains how to become a vessel of honor. There must be a cleansing from the contaminents of false teaching, a fleeing of lusts, and an active pursuing of righteousness, faith, love, and peace.

E. The Character of Suffering (2:23-26)

Paul states that those who handle the Word must avoid futile controversies ("word battles"). Controversy because of false doctrine will come and must be dealt with, but it must be dealt with kindly, without quarrelsomeness, and with a knowledge of the Scriptures.

IV. The Command to Endure for the Gospel (3:1-17)

A. Because of Vigorous Opposition (3:1-9)

Timothy was aware of the fact that there was opposition to the gospel, but he needed to realize that this was not a passing situation; it was a permanent condition that would characterize the age. Though Satan stands behind this opposition, men carry it out. The moral conduct of these men reveal that they are not really from God. The key to understanding them is the four expressions that use the word "love." (There are a total of nineteen expressions.) They love themselves, money, and pleasure, but they do not love God.

B. Because of Faithful Teaching (3:10-15)

Timothy is encouraged to keep on faithfully in the gospel ministry in spite of the realization that opposition will always be there.

C. Because of Inspired Scriptures (3:16-17)

In one of the greatest declarations on the source and value of the Scriptures, Paul declares that the Scriptures are sufficient for righteous living.

V. The Command to Preach the Gospel (4:1-22)

As Paul concludes his final letter, he exhorts Timothy to always be preaching sound doctrine. Although there will be hardship in the ministry, it will be worth it all when we are rewarded by the Lord in a future day. Paul himself is ready to depart this life, knowing that he has faithfully served Christ. He concludes by giving greetings from numerous individuals and information about others.

THE GENERAL EPISTLES

THE GENERAL EPISTLES

Letter	Date (A.D.)	Written from
James	45	Jerusalem
Hebrews	65	(unknown)
1 Peter	65	Rome
2 Peter	67	Rome
Jude	70s	(unknown)
1 John	85	Ephesus
2 John	90	Ephesus
3 John	90	Ephesus

24

JAMES

Introduction to James

A. Authorship of James

Several individuals with the name of James appear on the pages of the New Testament. But since the author of this letter simply identifies himself as "James" (with no further identification), it is evident that he was known to all in the early church. Therefore, two individuals could possibly be the author, namely James the brother of John, or James the Lord's brother. Church tradition declares that James the Lord's brother wrote it. Since James the brother of John was put to death very early in the church age, it is best to agree with church tradition. (James the brother of John was probably martyred in A.D. 44.)

B. Place and Date of James

It seems best to date this letter around A.D. 45, making it the first New Testament book written. The letter is distinctly Jewish, which would fit the early days of the church when very few Gentiles were part of it. (If the letter were written after A.D. 50 one would expect references to Gentiles.) The sins condemned in the epistle are those characteristic of early Jewish Christians. Also, the book reflects the era before the Jerusalem Council of Acts 15. If this early date is accurate, then it was most likely penned from Jerusalem.

C. PURPOSE OF JAMES

The letter was written to these believers because their lives apparently did not match their profession of faith in Christ. They were guilty of a number of "acceptable" sins, such as envy and gossip. James felt it necessary to remind them that genuine faith in the Savior is more than mere mental acceptance of historical facts. Genuine faith is seen in a life that is changed.

D. BASIC OUTLINE OF JAMES

I. The Believer's Trials, 1:1-18
II. The Believer's Genuineness, 1:19-27
III. The Believer's Obstacles, 2:1–5:6
IV. The Believer's Challenges, 5:7-20

E. THEME OF JAMES

The theme of this epistle is the necessity of living faith. James deals very little with doctrinal issues; rather he spends time on the outworking of genuine faith, which is righteous living.

F. SPECIAL CONSIDERATIONS ON JAMES

1. The Author of the Letter

James is commonly called the brother of the Lord Jesus, though we understand that to actually be His "half-brother" (Matt. 13:55; Mark 6:3). James was not a believer in Jesus during His earthly ministry (John 7:5). But his reception of his own half brother as the Savior-Messiah of Israel probably took place at a special appearance of the risen Christ to him (1 Cor. 15:7). Along with many others, James was in the Upper Room praying and waiting for the coming of the Holy Spirit on the great Day of Pentecost (Acts 1:14). In the years that followed, James became well known and became the leader of the church in Jerusalem (Gal. 1:19; 2:9; Acts 12:17; 15:13 ff.; 21:18-25; Jude 1:1). His influence and importance to the early church is emphasized by the apostle Paul's statement in Galatians 2:9, where he is called a "pillar" of the church. According to 1 Corinthians 9:5, James was married. Church tradition says that he died as a martyr in A.D. 62 at the hands of the Sanhedrin.

2. The Destination of the Letter

The opening verse of this letter states that this epistle was addressed to believers that had been scattered by persecution. These were Jewish Christians who had been driven out of Jerusalem as a result of the stoning of Stephen (Acts 7-8) and the persecution led by Saul of Tarsus. Therefore, this letter was not sent to just one local church but rather to believers in various places.

SUMMARY OF JAMES

I. The Believer's Trials, 1:1-18

James instructed these persecuted believers that everyone will have trials in his life. There is a wide variety of trials, but they are all for our development. He acknowledged that trials can cause confusion and uncertainty, but he noted that wisdom is available from God to see us successfully through. He observed that God is good and does not try and get us to sin. James encouraged these believers by reminding them that blessing and reward is there for those who respond correctly.

II. The Believer's Genuineness, 1:19-27

We experience our greatest happiness and freedom when we live our lives according to God's standard (the law of liberty). This kind of righteous living comes to us when we hear and apply the truth of God to our lives (hearing it is not enough). Righteousness will be evidenced by such things as a separation from the world, freedom from sins that used to control us, and by acts of compassion.

III. The Believer's Obstacles, 2:1–5:6

The Christian walk is not without its problems. The world system, Satan, and the Christian's own fallen nature (''the flesh'') all place obstacles on the road of righteousness. James discusses some of these major obstacles faced by the average believer and the consequences of either overcoming them or being overcome by them. He deals with the obstacle of favoritism (2:1-13), theoretical faith (2:14-26), the tongue (3:1-12), worldly wisdom

(3:13-18), worldliness (4:1-10), censoring other believers (4:11-12), independence from God (4:13-17), and riches (5:1-6).

IV. The Believer's Challenges, 5:7-20

James exhorted his readers to be patient in the midst of trials and persecutions. He points out that God desires to produce a harvest of righteousness in us and that this takes time and difficult experiences. He notes that believers are important in this process in other believers' lives, especially in prayer.

25

HEBREWS

Introduction to Hebrews

A. AUTHORSHIP OF HEBREWS

The author does not identify himself in the epistle, and the tradition of the church concerning authorship is unclear. The result is that a large number of individuals have been suggested, including Paul, Luke, Barnabas, Silas, Philip, and Apollos.

Of all those suggested, the apostle Paul has received more support than any other single individual—either that he wrote it or that someone else (such as Luke) wrote it but based it on Paul's teachings. But many scholars are absolutely against Pauline authorship, noting that the vocabulary, writing style, and the anonymous nature of the letter stand firmly against Pauline authorship.

When all is said, there simply is no agreement on the human author. We can be certain, however, that the Spirit of God moved the author to write this great epistle for the benefit of the church.[1] It should be be remembered that inspiration is not affected at all. Many Old Testament books are not clear on the matter of authorship, and yet they are fully inspired.

B. PLACE AND DATE OF HEBREWS

The place of writing is uncertain. Some traditions have Hebrews written from Alexandria, Egypt (where there was a large

---

1. B. F. Westcott, *The Epistle to the Hebrews* (Grand Rapids: Eerdmans, 1965), pp. lxii-lxxxiv.

Jewish community). Some have proposed that Rome is the place, based on the phrase "those from Italy greet you" (13:24). However, the better interpretation of that phrase is that the writer is surrounded by a group of believers from Italy who join with him in sending their greetings home. Thus, the original destination of Hebrews was probably Rome.

The date of writing was about A.D. 65. Hebrews was most likely written before A.D. 70 when the Temple (and thus the sacrificial system) was destroyed.

"Since the epistle argues that the death of Christ renders obsolete the Old Testament sacrificial system it seems certain that mention would have been made of the destruction of the Temple if that had already taken place."[2]

Also, the mention of persecution coming on the Christians suggests a time near the beginning of Nero's persecution of the church. Hard times apparently lay ahead (12:4).

C. PURPOSE OF HEBREWS

The author was deeply concerned that his readers were in danger of drifting away from faith in Christ Jesus. He wrote to issue a serious warning about such a defection from the truth. In doing so, he also encouraged them to strive toward spiritual maturity in Christ, noting that Christ is superior in every way to what they had under the old Mosaic law code.

D. BASIC OUTLINE OF HEBREWS

　　I. Christ's Superiority in Revelation (1:1-4)
　　II. Christ's Superiority over Angels (1:5–2:18)
　　　　A. Because of His Sonship (1:5-14)
　　　　B. Because of His Sufferings (2:1-18)
　　III. Christ's Superiority over Moses (3:1–4:13)

2. Charles F. Pfeiffer, *The Epistle to the Hebrews* (Chicago: Moody, 1962), p. 7.

E. THEME OF HEBREWS

The main theme of Hebrews is the superiority of Jesus Christ. Hebrews emphasizes that Christianity (the New Covenant) is better than the old system in every way. Therefore, the New Covenant, and not the old, is to be the basis for the life of the believer. An underlying theme in Hebrews is the danger of apostasy (the willful turning away from the truth of God.)

F. SPECIAL CONSIDERATIONS ON HEBREWS

1. The Recipients of the Letter

The writer of Hebrews was not writing to an anonymous group of people scattered everywhere, but rather to people that he knew well (cf. 5:11-12; 6:10-12; 13:18-19, 23-24). (Note: Hebrews is not really a general epistle since it is addressed to a specific group. However, because the author and the recipients are anonymous to us, it is included in this section of our study.) The author clearly identifies himself with his readers, as is seen by his constant use of "we" and "let us" (e.g. 2:1; 4:1, 14, 16; 10:19-25; 12:1) and his use of "brethren" (e.g. 3:1, 12; 10:19). This points to the fact that the writer viewed his readers as Christians. The ancient title of the epistle, "To Hebrews," suggests that the readers were primarily Jewish Christians. This is supported by church tradition and by the constant reference back to the Old

Testament Scriptures. Also, the elevated place given to Moses, Aaron, and the priesthood would be important to Jewish readers but would not greatly impress Gentiles. It must be concluded, then, that this epistle was directed to those who were Jewish Christians.[3]

2. The Warnings in the Letter

In the book of Hebrews there are five passages that give serious warnings about turning away from the truth of God. The main controversies of Hebrews revolve around these sections. Although these warning passages are not essential to the argument of the book, they are important to an interpretation of the book. These passages are 2:1-4; 3:7 4:13; 5:11 6:20; 10:26-39; and 12:12-29. It is important to interpret each passage in its own context.

These passages generally warn against turning away from God's truth and God's way of salvation through Jesus Christ. Some see these passages as revealing the possibility that a genuine believer can lose his salvation. But the New Testament stands against this idea with many proofs and with lines of argument that support the eternal security of the genuine believer.[4] Others say these portions view those who merely profess to be Christians but are not. However, the force of certain words and phrases seems to point to those who are genuinely saved. And, as has just been seen, the recipients of the letter were viewed as true Christians by the author.

These viewpoints and others have been presented and debated over the years by Bible teachers. Although no final and complete answer can be detailed here, perhaps it is best to view these passages in a practical way from the perspective of the author. As he wrote to a group that he knew professed to be Christians (and he apparently thought that they were), he also knew that some might not be genuinely saved people. As he viewed their lives (not knowing their hearts), he noted tendencies on the part of some to forsake faith in Jesus Christ and to retreat back into law-

---

3. D. Edmond Hiebert, *An Introduction to the Non-Pauline Epistles* (Chicago: Moody, 1969), p. 91.

4. Charles C. Ryrie, *Basic Theology* (Wheaton, Ill.: Victor, 1988), pp. 328-32.

keeping. Some others gave no evidence of growth in Christ. He was deeply concerned that some would leave God's only way of salvation through Christ Jesus. To do this was to leave a person with no way to be saved. However, to go on in the Christian faith toward spiritual maturity revealed the genuineness of one's faith.

SUMMARY OF HEBREWS

I. Christ's Superiority in Revelation (1:1-4)

In order to keep his readers from drifting away from Christ and back into Judaism, the author of Hebrews emphasized the superiority of Jesus Christ. First, he points out that He is the greatest revealer of God. Although God did reveal Himself in the Old Testament through the prophets, it is the revelation through Christ that is primary and complete.

II. Christ's Superiority over Angels (1:5–2:18)

He observes that no angel is called God's Son. Using seven quotes from the Old Testament, the writer notes the obvious superiority of Christ over the angels. He then states that Christ took on humanity and became, for a period of time, lower than the angels in order to secure man's salvation. As a result of His work, He has not only procured man's salvation but has received great glory for Himself.

III. Christ's Superiority over Moses (3:1–4:13)

The Jews would revere Moses, and it was important that they clearly understand that Jesus Christ is superior to Moses. Moses is a creature and a servant; Christ is the Creator and a Son. Moses was faithful in God's house, but Christ is over God's house. He then encourages his readers to believe and obey. Not to believe in Christ and obey Him is to lose out on God's rest (the enjoyment and satisfaction of salvation).

IV. Christ's Superiority over Aaron (4:14–10:18)

This section emphasizes the contrast between the New Covenant and the Old Covenant. Although the Old Covenant with its priesthood, sanctuary, and sacrificial system was good and needful, it was inferior and temporary. However, the New Covenant with its eternal High Priest, Jesus Christ, is superior in every way. One great illustration of this superiority is seen in the sacrifice of Christ as compared with the animal sacrifices of the Old Covenant. Those sacrifices could only cover sin and had to be repeated again and again. However, Christ's sacrifice takes away sin and never needs to be repeated.

V. Christ's Superiority over Self (10:19–12:29)

The author encourages his readers to approach Cod in worship through Jesus Christ, the "new and living way" (10:20). He then reminds them that the great principle of the spiritual life is to live by faith. Trusting God and what God has said pleases Him and has been the characteristic of those who were spiritual successes. We are to live our lives reverencing God, persevering in difficulty, and accepting the disciplines of a loving heavenly Father (12:1-29).

VI. Conclusion (13:1-25)

Since the author knows his readers, he knows some of their needs. He exhorts them to a greater love for one another, to hospitality, to obedience to spiritual leaders, and to sound doctrine. The letter ends with a few personal words to the readers.

26

1 PETER

INTRODUCTION TO 1 PETER

A. AUTHORSHIP OF 1 PETER

The opening verse claims that this letter was written by the apostle Peter, one of Jesus' closest followers. This is supported by church tradition. "The early Church had no doubts concerning the authenticity of 1 Peter. The evidence for the epistle is early and clear, and it is as strong as for any other book in the New Testament. It was universally received as an acknowledged part of the Christian Scriptures."[1]

The letter itself reflects an acquaintance with the life and teachings of Christ. There are also several similarities between Peter's sermons in Acts and his words in this book (e.g. 2:7-8 with 4:10-11).

B. PLACE AND DATE OF 1 PETER

1 Peter 5:13 states that the letter was written in "Babylon." This could mean the Babylon located in Mesopotamia, but there is no tradition that Peter ever went there and there is no record of any church in Babylon. As a result, many scholars view "Babylon" as a symbolic name for Rome.

1. D. Edmond Hiebert, *An Introduction to the Pauline Epistles* (Chicago: Moody, 1971), p. 109.

Rome was a luxurious city given over to the worship of false gods much like Babylon, and perhaps it came to be known as 'Babylon' in Christian circles. It may be observed that the entire sentence in which the expression occurs has a figurative tone, since Mark was not the natural son of Peter (5:13). It is more probable that Mark and Silvanus would join Peter in the capital of the empire rather than some distant outpost (5:12-13).[2]

This has been the tradition of the church from earliest times.

The letter was probably written about A.D. 65. First Peter speaks of persecution, which may refer to the persecution of Christians by Nero. This persecution began in 64. Peter himself is said to have been martyred about 67 by Nero.

C.   PURPOSE OF 1 PETER

The epistle was written to encourage believers in the midst of suffering. They were undergoing persecution for their faith, and Peter gave them hope by reminding them of their future inheritance (1:4-5); that suffering is for a purpose (1:6 7); and that Jesus also suffered (2:21). Peter encouraged them to be faithful to Christ in the midst of their persecutions.

D.   BASIC OUTLINE OF 1 PETER

I. Opening Praise (1:1-12)
II. Exhortations Because of Our Position in the Lord (1:13–2:10)
   A. To Holiness (1:13-21)
   B. To Love (1:22-25)
   C. To Growth (2:1-10)
III. Exhortations Because of Our Position in the World (2:11–4:19)
   A. Regarding Good Works (2:11-12)
   B. Regarding Good Citizenship (2:13-17)
   C. Regarding Household Relationships (2:18-25)

2. Louis A. Barbieri, Jr., *First and Second Peter* (Chicago: Moody, 1977), p. 28.

E.   THEME OF 1 PETER

The letter was written to emphasize the proper attitude and conduct that believers are to have when undergoing persecution. This proper attitude is developed by understanding how Christ suffered and by growing in appreciation for the greatness of Christ's salvation.

F.   SPECIAL CONSIDERATIONS ON 1 PETER

The man Peter is probably the best-known apostle of Jesus Christ. Because of his outgoing personality, he was prominent in many of the incidents recorded in the gospels. (Peter's name is mentioned more than 150 times in the New Testament.) Along with his brother, Andrew, he fished the Sea of Galilee. He left that trade to follow the Lord Jesus during His three-year ministry, probably on a full-time basis for the last half of that time.

After Christ's resurrection and ascension, Peter played an important role in the early days of the church, taking the gospel to the Jews, Samaritans, and Gentiles. Peter was married and apparently took his wife with him as he traveled preaching the gospel (1 Cor. 9:5). Peter figured prominently in the crucial discussion at the Jerusalem Council (Acts 15), but after that event his name is not found in the book of Acts.

Perhaps after the Jerusalem Council Peter ministered in many places outside Palestine, including the five provinces of Asia Minor that are mentioned in 1 Peter 1:1, and probably at Rome. Church tradition strongly supports the idea that Peter ministered in Rome and was later martyred there.

SUMMARY OF 1 PETER

I. Opening Praise (1:1-12)

Peter encouraged these believers (probably primarily Jewish believers who had been scattered because of persecution) by reminding them that they had been born again and that a marvelous inheritance was theirs. The present persecution, although painful, would result in good—their refinement and God's glory.

II. Exhortations Because of Our Position in the Lord (1:13–2:10)

We have not been saved to live as we used to. Peter challenged his readers to pursue a life of personal holiness (1:13-21), since the God that they were now related to was Himself holy. Now that they were Christians, they were to exhibit love for one another (1:22-25) and were to live as uniquely called priests unto God (2:1-10).

III. Exhortations Because of Our Position in the World (2:11–4:19)

The credibility of one's faith and claims is seen by the quality of life that is lived. Peter instructed these Christians who were being persecuted to have proper attitudes in the midst of their persecution. Good conduct in marriage, the family, and in the community all validate one's faith in Christ as genuine. Even in their relationship with human government, which was often hostile, they were to behave wisely.

IV. Exhortations Because of Our Position in the Church (5:1-11)

Elders were addressed first. Peter taught that elders are to care for God's flock and to lead them by example. They are not to act like dictators, and they are to minister with proper motives. People are exhorted to submit to their leaders with a humble attitude. All are told to be on the alert for Satan, the evil enemy of believers.

V. Conclusion (5:12-14)

The epistle concludes with a word of greeting from Silas and Mark.

27

2 PETER

Introduction to 2 Peter

A. Authorship of 2 Peter

The opening verse states that the apostle Peter wrote this epistle.

B. Place and Date of 2 Peter

This epistle was probably written in A.D. 67 from Rome. Peter apparently wrote it very shortly before his death (1:13-15). According to tradition, Peter was martyred in Rome in 67.

C. Purpose of 2 Peter

There were certain truths that Peter felt these believers needed to know. He realized that he would not be with them much longer and, therefore, wanted to remind them of certain important truths. He not only wanted to remind them of certain doctrines, but he also wanted to warn them about false teachers. Peter knew that his fellow believers needed to have true knowledge in order to resist the false teachers.

D. Basic Outline of 2 Peter

I. Knowledge That Is True (1:1-21)
   A. Truth and Christian Growth (1:1-11)
   B. Truth and Historical Reliability (1:12-21)

E.   THEME OF 2 PETER

Peter wrote to emphasize the necessity of being knowledgable in order to mature in Christ and in order to avoid the doctrinal and practical errors of false teachers (3:1, 17-18).

F.   SPECIAL CONSIDERATIONS ON 2 PETER

1. The Recipients of the Letter

There has been a great deal of discussion among scholars concerning the recipients of this epistle. It is probably best to understand that the readers were essentially the same as those mentioned in 1 Peter (cf. 1 Peter 1:1 with 2 Peter 1:1; 3:1). It may be that Peter's opening statement was more general in this letter because he intended this letter to have wider circulation due to the widespread problem of false teachers. False teachers were infiltrating churches everywhere, not only the churches located in Asia Minor.

2. The Authenticity of the Letter

No book in the New Testament has been more strenuously debated as to its authorship and its place in the canon of Scripture than the letter of 2 Peter. There is less external evidence (evidence from the writings of the church Fathers and church councils) for the Petrine authorship of this epistle than there is for the traditional authorship of any other book of the New Testament. However, in spite of these facts, and in spite of the opinions of many scholars, there is good reason to believe that this book was written by Peter and does belong in the body of New Testament Scriptures.

Although there is not an abundance of external evidence for Petrine authorship, there is some. Some church Fathers did quote from it and believed that Peter wrote it.[1] When 2 Peter was accepted as a canonical book by the church councils of the fourth century, it was done with eyes opened to objections raised against it. We may, therefore, be confident that the evidence was clear enough to overcome all reasonable doubt.

Evidence within the book points to Peter as the author. The author claims to be Peter. First Peter says it was written by "Peter," and 2 Peter says it was written by "Simon Peter." A forger would not have included "Simon" in the second letter, but rather would have copied the introduction exactly. Also, there are a number of points of similarity in the Greek words used when compared with 1 Peter. Second Peter agrees closely with 1 Peter in its practical doctrine. Some of the differences that exist between the two letters can be explained by noting that the purposes of the two epistles are different and by observing that Peter used a secretary in writing his first letter (Silvanus, 1 Pet. 5:12) but wrote the second letter himself. The internal evidence points to the fact "that no document in the New Testament is so like 1 Peter as 2 Peter."[2] When all has been said, the best position is that this is a genuine letter of the apostle Peter.[3]

SUMMARY OF 2 PETER

I. Knowledge That Is True (1:1-21)

    A. Truth and Christian Growth (1:1-11)

Peter began his letter by informing his readers that everything believers need to live godly lives and avoid the corrupting influences of this world system has been provided. True knowledge of God and His ways will produce the excellent virtues of the Christian life—"partakers of the divine nature" (1:4).

    B. Truth and Historical Reliability (1:12-21)

In contrast with false teachers, what Peter had taught them was based on first-hand knowledge; he was an eyewitness to the

1. Charles Bigg, *The Epistles of St. Peter and St. Jude* (Edinburgh: T. and T. Clark, 1961), pp. 199-215.

2. Ibid., p. 232.

3. Donald Guthrie, *New Testament Introduction* (Downers Grove, Ill.: InterVarsity, 1970), pp. 814-20.

life and ministry of Christ. The true Scriptures, Peter observed, came about as men were moved along by the Holy Spirit. This guiding work of the Spirit guaranteed that the Scriptures would be what God wanted recorded and that they would be free from error.

II. Knowledge That Is False (2:1-22)

A. The Presence of False Teachers (2:1-3)

Peter realized that there has been and will be a problem with false teachers entering the church, and so warned his readers to be on the alert for them. They would successfully seduce some into following their ways.

B. The Judgment on False Teachers (2:4-10)

Those who are enemies of God's truth will face the judgment of God. Peter illustrated this fact from the experience of the fallen angels, the world of Noah's day, and the evil cities of Sodom and Gomorrah.

C. The Characteristics of False Teachers (2:11-22)

The words of the false teachers may fool people, but their lives cannot (if they are examined closely). False teachers are characterized by pride, immorality, sensuality, and deceptiveness. They promise liberty, but actually bring bondage.

III. Knowledge That Is Needed (3:1-18)

A. Knowledge of Christ's Return (3:1-10)

The apostle Peter and others regularly taught that the Lord Jesus might return at any moment. With the passing of many years there were those who mocked this truth, pointing to the continuity of life for millenniums. The idea that Christ would return in some sort of cataclysmic event was seen as foolishness. But Peter reminded his readers that God in the past brought such a cataclysmic event on man (the Flood of Noah's day), and He will do it again when the Lord returns in judgment.

B. Knowledge of Holy Conduct (3:11-18)

In light of the Lord's return, believers are to live godly lives, which will benefit them now and in the future. The returning Lord will want to find His people living holy lives and not in the grip of sin.

28

JUDE

A. AUTHORSHIP OF JUDE

The name *Jude* (Judas) was a common one in the New Testament. However, the Jude who wrote this epistle is most likely Jude the half-brother of the Lord Jesus. He identifies himself as the brother of James, and this settles the matter for most (cf. Matt. 13:55; Acts 15:13-21; Gal. 1:19).

B. PLACE AND DATE OF JUDE

The epistle of Jude was probably written very shortly after 2 Peter was written.[1] This would put the writing of the letter in the late sixties or possibly in the early seventies.

C. PURPOSE OF JUDE

Jude was going to write a letter on the subject of salvation (vs. 3), but changed his mind when he evidently received some disturbing news about individuals departing from the faith. Jude is much like 2 Peter in content, except that the turning away from the truth (apostasy) that Peter saw as future, Jude sees as beginning. Jude wrote to counter the apostasy that was starting to take place.

---

1. D. Edmond Hiebert, *An Introduction to the Pauline Epistles* (Chicago: Moody, 1971), pp. 175-79.

D.   BASIC OUTLINE OF JUDE

   I. Salutation (vv. 1-2)
  II. The Issue of False Teachers (vv. 3-4)
 III. The History of False Teachers (vv. 5-7)
  IV. The Description of False Teachers (vv. 8-16)
   V. The Resistance to False Teachers (vv. 17-23)
  VI. Doxology (vv. 24-25)

E.   THEME OF JUDE

The theme of the letter is contending for the faith in the last days.

F.   SPECIAL CONSIDERATIONS ON JUDE

When Jude wrote this letter, he obviously had a specific group of believers in mind. However, he gave no ethnic or geographic statement that helps identify them. It is pure speculation to state that he wrote to the same group that his brother James wrote to (James 1:1). Jude's epistle must therefore simply be classified as a general letter.

SUMMARY OF JUDE

When the disturbing news came that false teachers had infiltrated the group(s) that he was in communication with, Jude wrote a forceful letter on the subject. The presence of false teachers in their midst was clear, and action must be taken to resist and remove them.

Jude cites some historic examples of judgment for apostasy, including the fallen angels and Sodom.

He then describes in vivid detail the characteristics of these false teachers. They are proud, deceptive, rebellious, covetous, and selfish. They are capable of bringing severe spiritual damage to the church. God will judge them.

Jude concludes his letter by encouraging believers to hold firmly to the truth, depending on the Lord Jesus Christ, the great Savior.

29

1 JOHN

INTRODUCTION TO 1 JOHN

A. AUTHORSHIP OF 1 JOHN

The letter of 1 John was written by the apostle John. The writing style, words, and phrases used are very similar to those in the gospel of John. Since the beginning of the church age, this epistle has been considered to be the work of the apostle.

B. PLACE AND DATE OF 1 JOHN

Tradition holds that this letter was written late in John's life, when he was at Ephesus. A date of A.D. 85 is given for it.

C. PURPOSE OF 1 JOHN

Several errors were finding acceptance among believers. One encouraged moral laxity, and the other was an error concerning the Person and work of Christ. John wrote to combat these errors. He did so by emphasizing the believer's fellowship with God. He wrote that they would understand that fellowship brings full joy (1:4), frees from sin (2:1), protects from error (2:26), and brings assurance of eternal life (5:13).

D. BASIC OUTLINE OF 1 JOHN

Note: The book of 1 John is difficult to outline. It is not a tightly reasoned theological treatise, but is more like an informal talk that a pastor might give to his congregation. For this reason, good men widely differ about the outline of this epistle.

I. Introduction (1:1-4)
II. The Focus of the Believer's Fellowship: The Father (1:5–2:17)
   A. Its Basis (1:5)
   B. Its Obstacles (1:6-10)
   C. Its Evidences (2:1-17)
III. The Destruction of the Believer's Fellowship: Various Falsehoods (2:18–4:6)
   A. The Rising of the Antichrists (2:18-28)
   B. The Children of the Devil (2:29–3:12)
   C. The Hatred of the World (3:13-24)
   D. The Prophets of the World (4:1-6)
IV. The Essentials of the Believer's Fellowship: Righteous Living 4:7–5:12)
   A. Mutual Love (4:7–5:3)
   B. Overcoming Faith (5:4-12)
V. Conclusion (5:13-21)

E.   THEME OF 1 JOHN

The theme of this book is fellowship. Fellowship with the Father is built upon the truth and, when experienced, keeps a person from doctrinal and moral error.

F.   SPECIAL CONSIDERATIONS ON 1 JOHN

This letter is a general epistle. There are no names given (as in greetings), no personal details, and very little of a personal relationship hinted at. Yet, John obviously knows of the needs of his readers, including the errors that he must address. Since John had such a close relationship in his life with the church at Ephesus (and thus the churches of Asia Minor), it is highly likely that 1 John was written for the benefit of these Christians.

SUMMARY OF 1 JOHN

I. Introduction (1:1-4)

John declared that he was an eyewitness to the life of Christ (the Word). He stated that one must have life before fellowship with God can be experienced.

II. The Focus of the Believer's Fellowship: The Father (1:5–2:17)

In order to enjoy fellowship with God, who is absolutely sinless and who is absolutely holy, a believer must constantly deal with sin, confessing it to God, and thus experience cleansing from God. John observed that the key to fellowship is obedience to God. He also said that if believers love the world they cannot love the Father.

III. The Destruction of the Believer's Fellowship: Various Falsehoods (2:18–4:6)

One of the major obstacles to a healthy fellowship with the Father is that of error. The child of God must constantly be alert to the devil's attempts to divert him into falsehood through the world system and false teachers. However, the child of God has been anointed, so that now he has the capacity to understand truth and detect error (2:20-27).

IV. The Essentials of the Believer's Fellowship: Righteous Living (4:7–5:12)

John placed great stress on the believer's obligation to love other believers. Love and faith are seen as essential for a right relationship with God.

V. Conclusion (5:13-21)

The letter ends with the encouragement that we can know we possess eternal life and the exhortation to keep away from idolatry.

30

2 JOHN

INTRODUCTION TO 2 JOHN

A. AUTHORSHIP OF 2 JOHN

The apostle John wrote this short epistle.

B. PLACE AND DATE OF 2 JOHN

Tradition states that it was written from Ephesus about A.D. 85 or 90.

C. PURPOSE OF 2 JOHN

John wrote to warn believers about false teachers. John encouraged them to obey the truth and to resist any who would teach unsound doctrine.

D. BASIC OUTLINE OF 2 JOHN

    I. Greeting (vv. 1-3)
    II. Exhortation to Obedient Love (vv. 4-7)
    III. Warning Against False Teachers (vv. 8-11)
    IV. Conclusion (vv. 12-13)

E. THEME OF 2 JOHN

The theme of the letter is abiding in the truth. Abiding in the truth is essential for correct living, which includes avoiding error.

(Twelve times in this brief letter John uses the words ''truth,'' ''commandment,'' and ''teaching.'')

F.   SPECIAL CONSIDERATIONS ON 2 JOHN

In the first verse John writes to the ''chosen lady'' and her children. Some believe this refers to some church that was special to John. However, most believe that the letter was addressed to an eminent Christian woman.

SUMMARY OF 2 JOHN

John was impressed with the love that had been exhibited by the lady and her children. He encouraged her to continue in love and obedience. These two factors are crucial in living correctly now and receiving a full reward later on. He warned her that anyone who does not hold to the full deity and humanity of Jesus Christ is to be separated from.

31

3 JOHN

INTRODUCTION TO 3 JOHN

A. AUTHORSHIP OF 3 JOHN

The apostle John wrote this short epistle.

B. PLACE AND DATE OF 3 JOHN

This letter was probably written from Ephesus around A.D. 90.

C. PURPOSE OF 3 JOHN

John wrote to commend, encourage, and instruct his good friend Gaius. (There are several men with the name *Gaius*. It could be one of them or someone not mentioned in any other Scripture, cf. Acts 19:29, 20:4; Rom. 16:23; 1 Cor. 1:14.)

D. BASIC OUTLINE OF 3 JOHN

    I. Commendation for Gaius, vv. 1-8
   II. Condemnation for Diotrephes, vv. 9-11
  III. Commendation for Demetrius, v. 12
  IV. Conclusion, vv. 13-14

E. THEME OF 3 JOHN

The letter emphasizes the demonstration of truth or error in the believer's life.

F.   SPECIAL CONSIDERATIONS ON 3 JOHN

Third John opens (as does 2 John) with the apostle's referring to himself as the "elder." This is probably not a reference to an official position that he held but rather to the idea of his being "aged."

SUMMARY OF 3 JOHN

This personal letter to a friend, Gaius, begins by praising him for his faithfulness to the truth, for his love, and for his hospitality. John wanted Gaius to extend hospitality to Demetrius, who was probably the one who carried this letter. John also threatened to call public attention to Diotrephes' un-Christian behavior. This man was proud and wanted to be first in the church, even to the point of rebuking this aged apostle of Christ. The behavior of Diotrephes is held up as a negative example. John concludes by indicating that he will come to see Gaius soon.

Part 5

The Revelation:
The New Covenant Fulfilled

32

REVELATION

Of all the books in the New Testament, the book of Revelation gives the most detailed and extensive discussion of prophecy. The end times are important for Christians to understand because they are designed to change the way we live and the way we view life in the present. Prophecy gives us hope as we realize that God does have plans and He is going to accomplish them. Prophecy helps us purify our lives as we become aware of the nearness of the Lord's coming and of our accountability to Him. And prophecy assists us in establishing correct priorities in our lives as we realize that we need to be putting our time and resources into that which has eternal value.

A. AUTHORSHIP OF REVELATION

The book claims to have been written by John (1:1, 4, 9; 22:8). And since there is no further identification of the writer, other than ''John,'' it presumes a familiarity on the readers part. It is, therefore, not just anyone named John, but the apostle John. The testimony of the church Fathers, especially Irenaeus, was that the apostle John wrote this book. Also, the book states (1:9) that the author was on the Isle of Patmos and both Eusebius and Clement of Alexandria say that John the apostle was exiled there by the Roman government. Furthermore, the author was quite familiar with the churches of Asia Minor and this would fit well with apostle John who ministered at Ephesus. All of these facts point with great certainty to John the apostle as the author of the Revelation.[1]

B. PLACE AND DATE OF REVELATION

John wrote the Revelation while on the island of Patmos (1:9). He had been exiled to this rocky isle during the reign of the Roman emperor Domitian. The church Father Irenaeus said that John received the truths of Revelation toward the end of Domitian's rule. Domitian died in A.D. 96 and so a date of 95 is given for this book.

C. PURPOSE OF REVELATION

John wrote the Revelation in order to unite and complete the prophetic truth of the Bible. Without the book of Revelation there would be many unanswered questions about the end times. John also wrote to encourage the people of his day as they were enduring Roman persecution. They needed to know that persecution would never destroy God's church or God's purposes. This, of course, has continued to be an encouragement to persecuted believers throughout the ages. He also wrote to motivate Christians to godly and wise living.

D. BASIC OUTLINE OF REVELATION

The basic structure of this book is revealed within the book itself (1:19). Most Bible students see this verse as the "divine outline" of Revelation.

  I. Introduction
 II. "The Things Which Thou Hast Seen": The Person of Christ (1:9-20)
III. "The Things Which Are": The Possessions of Christ (2:1–3:22)
    A. The Church of Ephesus (2:1-7)
    B. The Church of Smyrna (2:8-11)

---

1. John F. Walvoord, *The Revelation of Jesus Christ* (Chicago: Moody, 1966), pp. 11-14.

    C. The Church of Pergamum (2:12-17)

    D. The Church of Thyatira (2:18-29)

    E. The Church of Sardis (3:1-6)

    F. The Church of Philadelphia (3:7-13)

    G. The Church of Laodicia (3:14-22)

IV. "The Things Which Shall Be Hereafter'': The Program of Christ (4:1–22:21)

    A. Heavenly Scene (4:1–5:14)

    B. Seven Seals (6:1–8:1)

    C. Seven Trumpets (8:2–11:19)

    D. Important Persons (12:1–14:20)

    E. Seven Bowls (15:1–16:21)

    F. Two Babylons (17:1–18:24)

    G. Final Visions (19:1–22:5)

V. Conclusion (22:6-2l)

E. THEME OF REVELATION

John writes about the great end-time events that will occur during the Day of the Lord. The focus of this book is on the seven-year Tribulation, but also includes information on the second coming of Christ and on His millennial kingdom, which will be established on this earth. The great prophetic themes of the Bible are dealt with in this book.

F. SPECIAL CONSIDERATIONS ON REVELATION

1. Approaching Revelation

Over the years the book of Revelation has been approached in a variety of ways by those wishing to unlock its truths.[2] Though there are many such approaches, three will be mentioned here. First, there are those who view Revelation as a book of allegories. The *allegorical* approach denies the literal reality of Revelation, and sees it containing messages of spiritual challenge and encouragement couched in figurative and symbolic language.

A second basic approach is the *historical*. This view sees the content of Revelation as factual, but sees most all of it as already

2. Gary Cohen, *Understanding Revelation* (Chicago: Moody, 1978), pp. 23-37.

fulfilled (usually all but chapters 20-22). Within this approach are those who view Revelation as a symbolic presentation of church history, while others see the events of Revelation fulfilled during the terrible days of Emperor Nero.

There are significant problems with both of these approaches. One is that the interpreter must allegorize (spiritualize) most everything in the book, making his interpretation terribly subjective. He then becomes the final authority as there is no real way of checking the validity of his interpretation. This point is verified by the fact that there is no harmony among those who approach Revelation in this way. Another problem is that these approaches simply do not harmonize the great, unfulfilled prophecies of the Old Testament Scriptures. Also, these approaches do not faithfully deal with the stated purpose of Revelation, which is that the book is prophetic (1:1, 19).

The third approach is the *futuristic*. This view (which is the position of this study) takes Revelation 4-22 as yet future. The Tribulation period is dealt with in chapters 6-19, while chapter 20 views Christ's thousand year reign on the earth, and chapters 21-22 focus on eternity. The futuristic is the best approach because it alone systematizes with itself the other prophetic portions of the Bible. "The futuristic approach to the Apocalypse is the only approach that harmonizes Daniel 7:19-27; 8:23-25; 9:24, 26-27; Matthew 24-25, especially 24:15-23, 29-31; 2 Thessalonians 2:1-12; Jeremiah 30:4-10; Romans 11:25-28; John 5:43; Zechariah 12:9-14; 8:23; and Jeremiah 23:5-8 into one unified eschatological program."[3] The futuristic approach is best because it alone accomplishes the purpose of 1:1, which states that the book is prophetic.

> The correct interpretation of any book of the Bible depends chiefly upon a proper understanding of its main theme. The central theme of the Apocalypse is declared by the title which is given to it in the first line of its text. . . If the book was intended to be read to a listening congregation, as the initial beatitude states (1:3), the opening verses must have con-

3. Ibid., p. 49.

tained some directive for thinking to make it intelligible. The audience would have to know the theme in order to follow it as the various details of action are presented in quick succession. Although there may be other approaches to the book of Revelation, this one is the most direct and the most logical.[4]

The futuristic approach is best because it alone interprets Revelation literally, just as the rest of the Bible is interpreted.

In contrast to the other approaches to the book of Revelation, the futuristic position allows a more literal interpretation of the specific prophecies of the book. Though recognizing the frequent symbolism in various prophecies, the events foreshadowed by these symbols and their interpretation are regarded as being fulfilled in a normal way. Hence, the various judgments of God are actually poured out on the earth as contained in the seals, trumpets, and vials.[5]

2. Interpreting Revelation

For many, the book of Revelation is a confusing, unintelligible series of symbols. But much of the confusion can be removed by properly interpreting the book. It must be remembered that this book was given to be an unveiling of truth and therefore can be understood and appreciated (1:1-3; 22:10).

The very first interpretive principle is that Revelation must be approached literally.

The concept of a literal interpretation always raises questions since it seems to preclude anything symbolic, and the book obviously contains symbols. Perhaps saying "normal" or "plain" interpretation would be better than "literal," since futurists do recognize the presence of symbols in the book. The difference between the literalist and the spiritualizer is simply that the former sees the symbols as conveying a plain meaning.[6]

4. Merrill C. Tenney, *Interpreting Revelation* (Grand Rapids: Eerdmans, 1973), p. 28.
5. Walvoord, *The Revelation,* p. 21.
6. Charles C. Ryrie, *Revelation* (Chicago: Moody, 1968), p. 9.

This normal approach sees language as plain language without deep hidden meanings that almost defy discovery.

Second, it must be understood that the Old Testament is a significant key in interpreting Revelation. There are about 350 direct quotes or clear allusions from the Old Testament found in Revelation.[7] This amounts to an average of about fifteen Old Testament references per chapter. Old Testament concepts (such as "the book of life" and "the wine of God's wrath"), Old Testament names (such as Jezebel, Balaam, and Babylon), titles applied to Christ (such as "first and last" and "root of David"), and numerous symbols are found everywhere in Revelation. It becomes obvious that an understanding of the Old Testament Scriptures is essential for a clear understanding of Revelation.

Third, interpretation is greatly simplified when it is discovered that Revelation is basically in a chronological order. The visions are not haphazardly given. There is a progressive pattern to the book as 1:19 suggests.

CHAPTER TOPICS OF REVELATION

Events	Church Age	Tribulation	Millennium	Judgment: Great White Throne	Eternal State
In Heaven	1	4-5	19-20	20	21-22
On Earth	2-3	6-19	20	— — —	

SUMMARY OF REVELATION

I. Introduction (1:1-8)

Although the book of Revelation reveals Jesus Christ, it was also He who gave its contents to John. John then wrote down the truths given to him and sent them to seven churches located in the

7. Tenney, *Interpreting Revelation*, pp. 101-16.

region of Asia Minor (1:4, 11). Those who understood these truths and applied them to their lives would be blessed (1:3). John sent greetings to these churches and included a word about each Person of the Godhead (1:4-7).

II. "The Things Which Thou Hast Seen": The Person of Christ (1:9-20)

The apostle John knew the Lord Jesus as well as anyone when He walked this earth. Yet, when confronted by Him in His glory, John's response was awed worship (1:17). The description of the glorified Christ is an attempt to convey the greatness and attributes of God with the limitations of human language. The descriptions given are rooted in Old Testament imagery. (For example, the white hair emphasizes His eternality and wisdom [Dan. 7:9]; and the voice like many waters suggests power and majesty [Ezek. 43:2].) This glorified Lord is seen as the Lord of the churches and the One who evaluates them (1:11-20). This vision prepares the readers for the next two chapters.

III. "The Things Which Are": The Possessions of Christ (2:1–3:22)

Revelation is specifically addressed to "the seven churches that are in Asia" (1:4). Why are these churches designated as the seven churches since it is known that there were more than these seven churches in Asia (e.g., Colossae)? The answer is that these seven were selected because they represented all churches of all times.

> Two reasons substantiate the representative character of these seven churches. The first is simply the fact that there are seven. Out of all the churches that might have been chosen . . . only these seven are selected. Second, in the promise to each of these churches at the close of each letter is the exhortation to hear what the Spirit says to "the churches." Though each letter is written to a church, the promise is to all the churches.[8]

8. Ryrie, *Revelation*, p. 20.

The spiritual conditions found in these seven churches would be seen again and again in local congregations throughout the church's history. "In the seven churches we have both every kind of church and every kind of member, which not only existed on earth in John's generation but also will exist throughout all ecclesiastical history. In other words, we have in the seven selected local churches a composite picture of all local churches on earth at any particular time."[9]

But not only are the spiritual conditions given, the evaluation of each condition by the Lord of the church is also included. This has great value and significance to every local church. For if that church can discern its true spiritual situation then it also knows how it is viewed by the Lord Jesus. So then, these historic churches of the first century were chosen because in them the basic spiritual conditions of all churches can be found.

Some have attempted to add a prophetic significance to these seven churches, suggesting that they also represent seven successive periods of church history.[10] While such a view is possible, it does bring problems with it. For example, the truth of the any-moment coming of Christ can be called into question if the church had to go through successive periods of time.

Each of the seven churches has a letter written to it. Each letter follows the same basic format: Christ is described in some way relevant to that church's situation, a word of praise is given, a word of condemnation is given, an exhortation is directed to the church, a warning of possible judgment is stated, and then the letter concludes with a promise to the overcomer. (Note that an overcomer is not a "super saint" or a "victorious Christian" but rather is simply a believer [cf. 1 John 5:5]. Believers are overcomers because they are identified with Christ who overcame.) Each letter is addressed to the "angel" of that church. The word *angel* is normally used of angelic beings, but can be used of human beings (as in the case of John the Baptist, where he is seen as God's "messenger" [Matt. 11:10]).

---

9. Alva McClain, *The Greatness of the Kingdom* (Chicago: Moody, 1968), pp. 446-47.
10. Walvoord, *The Revelation*, pp. 51-53.

A. The Church of Ephesus (2:1-7)

The Ephesian church is praised by Christ because they have held fast to the truth of God and have not tolerated doctrinal or moral compromise. But He warns them to repent of a deadly spiritual condition: they had left their first love (probably their love for the Lord Himself). The overcomer is guaranteed possession of eternal life.

B. The Church of Smyrna (2:8-11)

Christ does not condemn this church for anything, but rather praises them for their endurance in the midst of persecution and poverty. They are encouraged not to be fearful, but to be faithful. The believer will not experience the second death.

C. The Church of Pergamum (2:12-17)

Christ praises this group for their loyalty to Him and their faith. This faithfulness is all the more commendable because they were in a very hostile spiritual environment. But they are warned to repent of their moral compromise. The believer will experience no condemnation but will enjoy Christ.

D. The Church of Thyatira (2:18-29)

For this church the Lord takes note of a remarkable series of praiseworthy items: their love, faith, and hard work. But they are also severely condemned for tolerating "Jezebel," a woman who promoted false doctrine and immorality. The believer will receive the "morning star" (refers to Christ, cf. Rev. 22:16).

E. The Church of Sardis (3:1-6)

Very little good can be found in this church. This church had a reputation for spiritual life and vitality, but in reality it is a dead church. Only a few in it serve Christ and reflect His character. They are exhorted to wake up and remember the truth of God that they had received. Believers are given the guarantee that they will never have their names removed from the book of life. Note that this is a promise and not a threat. It is an absolute guarantee of the believer's security. Also, rewards are promised to those who have not "soiled their garments."

F. The Church of Philadelphia (3:7-13)

This church receives praise because they have faithfully identified themselves with Christ and have not departed from the faith.

They are also praised for ministering effectively for the Lord even though they had "little power." They are exhorted to hold fast and not lose any reward. As believers they would have a position of honor with the Lord. This church is a source of delight to the Lord, and He promises them victory over their enemies and freedom from persecution.

G. The Church of Laodicea (3:14-22)

This church was probably in the worst spiritual condition of the seven churches. While there is no condemnation for doctrinal or moral error, there is no praise for anything. The church was indifferent, apathetic, and self-centered and had been deceived by its material wealth. The true believer is guaranteed that he will be with Christ.

IV. "The Things Which Shall Be Hereafter": The Program of Christ (4:1–22:21)

A. Heavenly Scene (4:1–5:14)

The third and final major division of Revelation begins with the apostle John being taken to heaven in a vision. This vision took place "after these things," that is, after the events related to the churches (cf. 4:1 with 1:19). Apparently, we are to understand that the events of chapters 4-22 take place after Christ's dealings with the church. This suggests that the church is removed from the earth before the time of judgment (the Tribulation) begins. Revelation 4 and 5 seem to be a brief interval after the removal of the church (the "rapture"), and before the judgments of the Tribulation. These chapters record what John saw in heaven and basically are showing that Jesus Christ has the right to judge this world, to rule as king and to establish His kingdom. He is the One who is in control of the events yet to happen.

In the vision, John first saw the throne of God. "Throne" is used over thirty times in Revelation and speaks of the place of authority. When referring to God, it is emphasizing His sovereignty and rulership.

Next, John saw twenty-four elders (possibly representing the church in heaven) and four living creatures (probably angels).

As the vision continued, John observed a sealed scroll in the hand of God. The question is asked, "Who has the authority to break the seals on the scroll?'' Of all persons and powers in the universe, only Jesus Christ had the authority. The scroll most likely contained the judgments that would be poured out in the Tribulation. Only Jesus executes judgment (cf. John 5:22, 26-27).

THE TRIBULATION PERIOD

A.   THE PURPOSES OF THE TRIBULATION

God always has reasons for what He does and that includes the Tribulation period. The primary purpose for the Tribulation is to save Israel, preparing her for her Messiah. God has made covenant promises to Abraham and David, many of which have not been fulfilled.[11] The Tribulation will begin the process of fulfilling these covenant commitments, and so it is to be expected that the Tribulation has a definite Jewish character (cf. Jer. 30:7; Dan. 9:24, 12:1; Matt. 24:15-20). The great work of God in the Tribulation is not judgment, but salvation, as He saves Israel bringing them into the New Covenant (cf. Jer. 31:31; Rom. 11:25; Rev. 7:4). But Gentiles also, and not only Israelites, will be saved (Rev. 7:9, 13-14). There is no greater time of salvation in all of human history as multiplied millions come to receive God's gift of salvation in Jesus Christ.

A second purpose of God in the Tribulation is judgment (Jer. 25:30-32; Zech. 12:3; 2 Thess. 2:12; Rev. 6:15). Sinful rebellious mankind will be held accountable for its wickedness. God will certainly judge unbelieving men and nations.

B.   THE JUDGMENTS OF THE TRIBULATION

There are three series of judgments during the Tribulation. They are referred to as the seals (6:1–8:1), the trumpets (8:2–9:21), and the bowls (15:1–16:21). Each series contains seven specific judgments. The judgments follow one another,

---

11. Paul N. Benware, *Survey of the Old Testament* (Chicago: Moody, 1988), pp. 36-41.

JUDGMENT SERIES OF REVELATION

Judgment Series Identified	Judgment Series Interrelated		
The Seven Seals (6:1—8:6)	1. Antichrist 2. War 3. Famine 4. Death 5. Martyrs' prayers 6. Great earthquake	7. Opening of Trumpets	
The Seven Trumpets (8:7—9:21)		1. ⅓ of vegetation burned 2. ⅓ of the sea judged 3. ⅓ of fresh water judged 4. ⅓ of the luminaries darkened 5. Increased demonic activity 6. Invasion of an eastern army	7. Opening of Bowls
The Seven Bowls (15:1—16:21)			1. Malignant sores 2. Sea turned to blood 3. Fresh waters to blood 4. Men scorched with fire 5. Throne of Beast judged 6. Invasion from the east 7. Greatest earthquake

with the trumpets coming out of the seals and the bowls coming out of the trumpets.

The Lord Jesus spoke of these Tribulation judgments as "birthpangs" (Matt. 24:8). This suggests that as the Tribulation progresses, the judgments become more severe and the intervals of time between the judgments become shorter.

B. Seven Seals (6:1–8:1)

These judgments take place during the first half of the Tribulation period (probably covering about 3 1/2 years) and apparently no one is exempt from them. The 144,000 are saved during this time and become God's evangelists in the Tribulation. It should be noted that the 144,000 are Israelites, but they are just a small part of total Israel who will be saved during the Tribulation.

C. Seven Trumpets (8:2–11:19)

These judgments take place during the second half of the Tribulation and are directed at unbelievers, particularly those who have persecuted believers (cf. 6:9-11 with 8:2-5). These judgments are more severe than those of the seals. Note that the "three woes" (8:13) are the same as the final three trumpet judgments.

An important interpretive key to Revelation is found in this section in 10:11 where John is told that he "must prophesy again." Up to this point the book has been proceeding along in chronological sequence. This is an interruption of that order as additional information is given. But in the chapters that follow there are a number of time notations that help establish when certain events will take place.

During the Tribulation, God will raise up two special witnesses to minister for Him in the heart of the Antichrist's empire (11:1-14). They probably minister during the last half of the Tribulation in the city of Jerusalem. Most likely they are two men raised up for this ministry, but are not Old Testament characters who come back to earth for this time period.

D. Important Persons (12:1–14:20)

In this section, it is prophesied that Satan will aggressively persecute Israel during the last half of the Tribulation (12:1-17) and that the Antichrist will lead the final form of Gentile world power. He will operate in the power of Satan and will rise to the place of world dictator in the last half of the Tribulation. He will be assisted by the Satanically empowered "false prophet" who will deceive the world (along with the Antichrist) and cause the world to worship both Satan and the Antichrist (13:1-18).

The ultimate triumph of Christ will take place at the conclusion of the Tribulation as He saves many and judges many (14:1-20). The Tribulation will end with Christ treading the winepress of God's wrath (Armageddon).

E.   Seven Bowls (15:1–16:21)

The judgment of God ends with these terribly severe series of judgments. These judgments come in rapid succession in connection with the second coming of Christ. The special target of these judgments is the Antichrist and those who have aligned themselves with him. But in spite of the severity of these judgments and the fact that they are divine judgments, these men still refuse to repent.

F.   Two Babylons (17:1–18:24)

The term "Babylon" refers to a religious-political system where the true God is excluded. The name Babylon goes back to Genesis 11 where the first organized, idolatrous religious system was established. Religious Babylon (probably centered in Rome) will be destroyed half way through the Tribulation by the Antichrist and his followers, as they seek to establish only one religion in the world—the worship of Satan and the Antichrist (chap. 17). Political Babylon (chap. 18) is probably centered in Jerusalem and refers to the center of the Antichrist's empire. This will be destroyed by Christ at His second coming.

G.   Final Visions (19:1–22:5)

This section opens with rejoicing in heaven as the nearness of Christ's second coming becomes a reality (19:1-6). Before the second coming takes place, the marriage of the Lamb takes place (19:7-10). This event tells us that the church, the Bride of Christ is in heaven and has been rewarded already and this is *before* the second coming. The glorious second coming is then given as He returns as King of kings and Lord of lords (19:11-16). Those who have blasphemed God and refused to repent are crushed in the battle of Armageddon (19:17-21).

Christ then turns His attention to the archenemy Satan, has him bound, and cast into the abyss. Consequently he will not be able to disturb the glorious millennial reign that Christ establishes (20:1-10). For a thousand years Christ will rule the earth and in so doing will completely fulfill all of God's covenant promises to Abraham and to his descendants. The apostle John does not give much information about the millennial kingdom of Christ because the prophets of the Old Testament give an abundance of information about Messiah's rule. The prophets did not know that the kingdom of Messiah would be a thousand years in length, so John gives that information.

Following the millennium, the final judgments will take place (20:10-15). Satan will receive his final punishment, the old heavens and earth will be destroyed, and all unbelieving people will be judged, being cast into the lake of fire—an everlasting punishment.

John then records that God will create a new heaven and earth to replace the old ones. Apparently, the saints will live on the earth for eternity. God's original plan was that man would live on the paradise earth and enjoy fellowship with God there (Gen. 1-2). Evidently God is returning to His original plan for a redeemed mankind.

V. Conclusion (22:6-21)

CHRONOLOGY OF REVELATION 6-19

Topics	Course of the Tribulation		Climax of the Tribulation
	First 3½ Years	Last 3½ Years	
General Topics	Seven Seal Judgments (6)	Seven Trumpet Judgments (8-9) Seven Bowl Judgments (15-16)	Second Coming (19)
Special Topics	Salvation in the Tribulation (7) Religious Babylon (17)	"Prophesy again" (10:11) Two Witnesses (11) Satan persecutes Israel (12) Antichrists' world rule (13) Christ's ultimate triumph (14) Political Babylon (18)	

Notes on Special Topics

Note A:

THE PERSON OF JESUS CHRIST

Certainly one of the most important areas of theology is that which deals with the Person and work of Jesus Christ. The Bible teaches that Christ is truly human and yet is God.

CHRIST'S DEITY

The deity of Jesus Christ is expressly declared in the Scriptures (e.g., John 1:1, 18; 20:28; Titus 2:13; and Heb. 1:8). Jesus Christ possesses the attributes of God (e.g., holiness, Luke 1:35; truth, John 14:6; and immutability, Heb. 13:8). He performs works that only God can do (e.g., creating the world, John 1:3, Col. 1:16; forgiving sins, Luke 5:21, 7:48; and judging the world, John 5:22-27). He receives worship that only God deserves (e.g., John 20:28; Rev. 5:12-14, 19:10). Some titles given to Him demonstrate His equality with the Father (Matt. 16:16; John 8:58, 10:30). Many other Scriptures and lines of evidence can arrayed to demonstrate the deity of Jesus Christ.[1]

CHRIST'S HUMANITY

Jesus Christ became a perfect man while still being undiminished deity. Jesus was a perfect human being. The New Testament clearly reveals that He experienced the same feelings, limitations, and needs as other human beings. He grew and devel-

---

1. John F. Walvoord, *Jesus Christ Our Lord* (Chicago: Moody, 1969), pp. 106-9.

oped normally. Nowhere in the New Testament does anyone doubt that He was a human being (cf. Luke 2:40-52). When Jesus Christ entered the human race through normal birth (''the Word became flesh,'' John 1:14), humanity was added to deity.

CHRIST'S SINLESSNESS

It must be emphasized that true humanity does not include sinfulness. Adam, before the fall of man was ideal and perfect humanity. Jesus Christ was human, but sinless. ''Sinfulness is not a necessary characteristic of humanity, though it happens to be a universal characteristic of the humanity we know. Because this last is so, men are in the habit of regarding sinfulness and humanity as correlative terms.''[2]

Christ was a perfect man who never sinned, nor could He sin. Possessing a fallen nature would have made Jesus Christ less than true man as God created him. Some theologians have taught that temptability implies peccability. This is a correct assumption when dealing with man, even an unfallen one like Adam, but it is incorrect when dealing with the one and only God-man, Jesus Christ.

Christ was *not able* to sin because He was that way by nature. The divine nature empowered the unfallen human nature, thus keeping the Person of Christ from sinning. Infinite power in the God-man assured Him continual victory. ''The idea that temptability implies susceptibility is unsound. While the temptation may be real, there may be infinite power to resist that temptation and if this power is infinite, the person is impeccable.''[3] This area of discussion has been adequately dealt with in numerous works.[4]

---

2. Alva J. McClain, ''The Doctrine of the *Kenosis* in Philippians 2:5-8,'' *Grace Journal* 8, no. 2 (1967), p. 10.
3. Walvoord, *Jesus Christ Our Lord,* p. 147.
4. G. C. Berkouwer, *The Person of Christ* (Grand Rapids: Eerdmans, 1966), pp. 239-67; L. Boettner, *The Person of Christ* (Grand Rapids: Eerdmans, 1943), pp. 123 ff.

CHRIST'S "EMPTYING"

When Jesus Christ became man He did not set aside His attributes of deity. That would be an impossible position to hold, since one Person of the Godhead would cease for a time to be God. Christ without divine attributes is not God. The biblical doctrine of the incarnation views Christ as perfect humanity united forever with undiminished deity.

According to Philippians 2:5-11, when Christ became a man, He "emptied Himself." The passage does not give the details concerning of what the Son emptied Himself. It states that He was in the "form of God" but took the "form of a servant." The word "form" speaks of the external appearance or manifestation of a person, which accurately represents the underlying nature. Christ did not set aside this "form" of God, but rather veiled it by taking on the "form" of a servant and the "likeness" of man.

This veiling limited the manifestations of Christ's deity but in no way did it bring about any loss of deity. He did not lose His glory, but simply laid aside the external manifestation of it while retaining an inner glory. He did not lose His attributes but instead voluntarily did not exercise them independently. The English word *emptying* conveys the thought of pouring something out, but this Christ did not do. Nothing of His deity was poured out, even temporarily. To His deity was added humanity, and for a short season the full expression of His deity was hidden. Dr. Alva McClain says "It is better to say . . . that Christ gave up the independent use of His divine attributes. This leaves room for all those exhibitions of divine Power and knowledge which appear during His earthly ministry, and at the same time modifies in no essential respect the doctrine of a real kenosis."[5]

When Jesus Christ walked this earth He was no less God than when He created this earth. He had simply chosen to veil His natural glory and to restrict the independent use of His attributes of deity. When He returned to the Father at His ascension, His former glory was again manifested and He no longer restricted the use of His attributes.

5. McClain, "The Doctrine of the *Kenosis*," p. 9.

Note B:

THE APOSTLES OF JESUS CHRIST

The Term "Apostles"

The Lord Jesus had hundreds of disciples. (A *disciple* is a "learner.") Out of His many disciples Jesus selected twelve who would be His followers in a special sense. These twelve were called "apostles" (Luke 6:13). These men would be with Him all the time, and go with Him on all His travels. They would be eye witnesses of all that He did and said. This constant contact with Him would prepare them for their role in the future of taking the gospel of the New Covenant to the world.

The word *apostle* literally means "one sent forth." The term carries with it the idea of one who is sent with a special commission and possessing special authority. He is one who speaks and acts with the authority of his sender. The apostles were granted great power with which they authenticated the message that they were delivering (Luke 9:1; 2 Cor. 12:12).

The Twelve Apostles

The twelve apostles were a unique group. They had been with the Lord since the days of John the Baptist, and had seen Christ's works, heard His words, and been witnesses of His resurrection (Acts 1:22-23). The Twelve are listed in four different passages of Scripture (Matt. 10:2; Mark 3:16; Luke 6:14; Acts 1:13).

1. Simon Peter
2. Andrew [Peter's] brother

3. James the son of Zebedee
4. John the brother of James
5. Philip
6. Bartholomew (Nathanael)
7. Thomas (Didymus)
8. Matthew (Levi)
9. James the son of Alphaeus (James "the less")
10. Simon the Zealot (Simon the Cananaean)
11. Judas the son of James (Thaddaeus)
12. Judas Iscariot

These twelve, with the exception of the traitor, Judas Iscariot, would become part of the foundation for the future establishment called the church (Eph. 2:20).

THE OTHER APOSTLES

A.   MATTHIAS AND PAUL

The apostle Paul was not part of the Twelve. When Judas Iscariot died, Matthias was chosen to fill his place (Acts 1:26). Some have felt that Paul, not Matthias, was God's choice. But Paul himself viewed his apostleship as distinct from the Twelve (Gal. 1:11-17, 2:2-9). It is difficult to believe that the apostles would have made such a bold move of replacing Judas on their own initiative. They saw their own action as a fulfillment of Scripture, which would seem to suggest that this was something the Lord Jesus instructed them to do (Acts 1:20). And too, they had just come from many days in prayer.

Furthermore, it must be remembered that Luke wrote the book of Acts (recording the selection of Matthias) after many years of reflection on the incident and after many years of association with the apostle Paul. Why would Luke record such a monumental blunder by the apostles without indicating that they were in error? Also, in Acts 6:2, Luke seems to accept the fact of Matthias being the one who has filled the ranks of the Twelve. (Acts 6 occurred years before the conversion of Paul.) It is best, therefore, to see Matthias as the twelfth apostle.

B. PEOPLE AND GIFTS

It should also be noted that the word *apostle* was applied to individuals beyond the Twelve and Paul. Others were spoken of as apostles (cf. Acts 14:14; Rom. 16:7; 2 Cor. 8:23; Phil. 2:25; 1 Thess. 2:6). The Scriptures also speak of the "gift" of an apostle (Eph. 4:11). This would suggest a larger group than Paul and the Twelve. While we do not know how many could properly be called "apostles," we do know that their ministries were foundational to the church (Eph. 2:20).

Note C:

MIRACLES IN THE GOSPELS AND ACTS

THE TIMES OF MIRACLES

A miracle is an extraordinary event in the physical realm that goes beyond all known human or natural powers or processes. Although we use the word often applying it to many kinds of situations in life, miracles have very infrequently been experienced. God does not indiscriminantly suspend His own natural laws. When He does, it is for specific purposes. The Bible records three periods in history when miracles were particularly evident: (1) the days of Moses, (2) the days of Elijah and Elisha, and (3) the days of Christ and His apostles.

THE PURPOSES OF MIRACLES

A. AUTHENTICATING SIGNS

The primary purpose of miracles was to authenticate God's messenger, as well as the message that he was carrying. It was to the Jews (the people of the Covenant) that the miracles were particularly directed. The Jews needed and looked for these sign miracles (1 Cor. 1:22-24). The Old Covenant that came through Moses was verified by many miracles, signs, and wonders. The Jews rightly required the same kind of evidences if, in fact, God was setting aside the Old Covenant and establishing the New Covenant. God did just that and authenticated the messengers (Christ and His apostles) and the message (the New Covenant).

B. MESSIANIC REVELATIONS

A second purpose in Christ's miracles was to demonstrate the areas in which He had authority. "These were miracles in the realms of nature, demons, sickness and disease, the physical and the emotional, and death. By His miracles Christ demonstrated His authority in the realms in which He will one day rule as King in His kingdom.''[1] The miracles that Christ worked pointed specifically to the fact that He was the Messiah of Israel.

Many of Christ's miracles were designed to give a glimpse of what His earthly kingdom will be like. "Further, the miracles revealed conditions in the kingdom over which Messiah will rule. It will be a kingdom in which nature is subject to His authority and in which there will be no sickness, disease, or death. It will be a kingdom in which Satan is bound . . . a kingdom in which there is no want.''[2]

The healing of the blind particularly pointed to Jesus as the Messiah of Israel.

> He also gave sight to the blind because the Spirit was upon Him (Luke 4:18). In the Old Testament giving sight to the blind was a prerogative of God (Ex. 4:11; Ps. 146:8) and something Messiah would do (Isa. 29:18, 35:5, 42:7). Thus when the Lord restored sight to blind people He was making a clear claim to be Israel's long-awaited Messiah. . . . More miracles of Christ in this category are recorded than in any other.[3]

THE BENEFITS OF MIRACLES

Miracles obviously helped hurting people. However, that was not the primary reason for their use. Miracles were designed to be unusual occurrences that would point clearly to Christ and the apostles as those who were sent from God. This verification was intended to bring people to faith (cf. John 20:30-31).

1. J. Dwight Pentecost, *The Words and Works of Jesus Christ* (Grand Rapids: Zondervan, 1981), p. 118.
2. Ibid., pp. 118-19.
3. Charles C. Ryrie, *Basic Theology* (Wheaton, Ill.: Victor, 1986), pp. 350-51.

Note D:

THE GIFT OF TONGUES

Generally, spiritual gifts have been given to Christians to benefit other people (1 Cor. 12:7; Eph. 4:12). Spiritual gifts are given sovereignly by the Holy Spirit to enable believers to serve God effectively in some particular way (1 Cor. 12:11). Each spiritual gift was given for a particular reason.

THE DEFINITION OF TONGUES

In understanding the gift of tongues, the definition and the purpose of the gift must be seen. The definition (description) of tongues is given in Acts 2:4-11 and in no other place in the Scriptures. There, Luke describes the gift in terms of known human languages. The tongues were unknown to those who were speaking. Therefore a definition for the gift of tongues might be: "the God given ability to speak in a language that is unknown to the speaker." Such an ability is clearly supernatural.

THE PURPOSE OF TONGUES

The purpose of tongues is explained by the apostle Paul in just one place and that is 1 Corinthians 14:20-22. Tongues are said to be a sign. If something is a "sign," then two questions must be asked and answered: (1) a sign to whom? and, (2) a sign of what? Paul states rather clearly that tongues were not a sign to believers. This fact alone would eliminate a large number of ideas, such as that tongues is a sign to believers that they have been baptized by the Holy Spirit. Tongues were, however, a sign to "this people" (14:21). The quote Paul makes is from Isaiah, and the context of Isaiah identifies "this people" as Israelites. But the sign, according to the apostle Paul, is not for believers. Therefore, we are to conclude that tongues were given as a sign to unbelieving Israel. The Jews were always looking for signs (1 Cor. 1:22).

The context of Isaiah 28 and other portions of the Old Testament must be considered to understand the significance of tongues. In the Old Testament God entered into a covenant with Israel down at Mt. Sinai. This "Old" Covenant was a conditional covenant; that is, God's blessings were conditioned on Israel's obedience. God would bless if Israel would obey. If Israel disobeyed then the disciplines of God awaited them. If Israel failed to respond to God's discipline and repent, then God would bring greater discipline on them.

The final level of discipline by God was bringing foreign invaders into Israel, who would take them over. So when Israel heard the language (tongue) of these foreigners they knew God's judgment was upon them (cf. Deut. 28:49). Tongues were a sign to unbelieving Israel of coming (or present) judgment on Israel.

In the New Testament, Jesus pronounced final judgment on that generation of Israelites because they had rejected (and would murder) their own Messiah (cf. Matt. 23:33-38). On the day of Pentecost tongues were heard. Peter warned Israel that their gen-

THE PERIOD OF ACTIVE SIGN-GIFTS

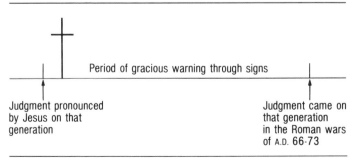

Period of gracious warning through signs

Judgment pronounced
by Jesus on that
generation

Judgment came on
that generation
in the Roman wars
of A.D. 66-73

eration was corrupt and they needed to be separated from their own generation (Acts 2:40). This separation, of course, could be accomplished by obeying God—in this case, believing in Jesus as their Savior-Messiah. God did judge that generation in A.D. 66-73, just as prophesied, by using the foreign army of Rome.

THE USES OF TONGUES

Since the content of tongues was praise to God (1 Cor. 14:2), there could be spiritual benefit to those who heard and understood. But it was a complicated way to edify believers. This, however, was not the major purpose of tongues. Paul encouraged the Corinthian church to seek better gifts to edify the congregation. And since the church was not the place for the gift to be used, Paul did not do so. He probably used this gift as he went from place to place and evangelized the Jews, who were looking for such signs.

SELECTED BIBLIOGRAPHY

Aharoni, Yohanan, and Avi-Yonah, Michael. *The Macmillan Bible Atlas*. New York: Macmillan, 1968.

Beitzel, Barry J. *The Moody Atlas of Bible Lands*. Chicago: Moody, 1985.

Benware, Paul N. *Survey of the Old Testament*. Chicago: Moody, 1988.

Edersheim, Alfred. *Sketches of Jewish Social Life in the Days of Christ*. Grand Rapids: Eerdmans, 1967.

Guthrie, Donald. *New Testament Introduction*. Downers Grove, Ill.: InterVarsity, 1970.

Hiebert, D. Edmond. *An Introduction to the Non-Pauline Epistles*. Chicago: Moody, 1969.

_____. *An Introduction to the Pauline Epistles*. Chicago: Moody, 1971.

Hoehner, Harold. *Chronological Aspects of the Life of Christ*. Grand Rapids: Zondervan, 1977.

House, H. Wayne. *Chronological and Background Charts of the New Testament*. Grand Rapids: Zondervan, 1981.

Jeremias, Joachim. *Jerusalem in the Time of Jesus*. Philadelphia: Fortress, 1969.

McClain, Alva. *The Greatness of the Kingdom*. Chicago: Moody, 1968.

Pentecost, J. Dwight. *The Words and Works of Jesus Christ*. Grand Rapids: Zondervan, 1981.

Pollock, John. *The Man Who Shook the World*. Wheaton, Ill.: Victor, 1972.

Ramsay, William. *The Cities of St. Paul*. Grand Rapids: Baker, 1960.

Scroggie, W. Graham. *A Guide to the Gospels*. Old Tappan, N.J.: Revell, 1962.

Thomas, Robert L. and Gundry, Stanley N. *A Harmony of the Gospels*. Chicago: Moody, 1978.

Moody Press, a ministry of Moody Bible Institute, is designed for education, evangelization, and edification. If we may assist you in knowing more about Christ and the Christian life, please write us without obligation: Moody Press, c/o MLM, Chicago, Illinois 60610.